WITHDRAWAL

The Modern Age

The Modern Age

Turn-of-the-Century American Culture and the Invention of Adolescence

Kent Baxter

THE UNIVERSITY OF ALABAMA PRESS

Tuscaloosa

Copyright © 2008
The University of Alabama Press
Tuscaloosa, Alabama 35487-0380
All rights reserved
Manufactured in the United States of America

Typeface: Caslon

∞

The paper on which this book is printed meets the minimum requirements of
American National Standard for Information Sciences-Permanence of Paper for
Printed Library Materials, ANSI Z39.48-1984.

Library of Congress Cataloging-in-Publication Data

Baxter, Kent.
    The modern age : turn-of-the-century American culture and the invention of
adolescence / Kent Baxter.
        p.   cm.
    Includes bibliographical references and index.
    ISBN 978-0-8173-1626-6 (cloth : alk. paper) — ISBN 978-0-8173-8074-8
(electronic) 1. Adolescence—United States—History—19th century. 2. Adolescence—
United States—History—20th century. 3. Teenagers—United States—History—
19th century. 4. Teenagers—United States—History—20th century. 5. Teenagers—
United States—Societies and clubs—History—19th century. 6. Teenagers—United
States—Societies and clubs—History—20th century. 7. Alger, Horatio, 1832–1899—
Fictional works. 8. Stratemeyer, Edward, 1862-1930—Fictional works. I. Title.
    HQ796.B3434 2008
    305.2350973—dc22

                                                                    2008010013

November 21, 2008

For Angela and Graeme

Contents

Acknowledgments

Completing this book would never have been possible without the support and encouragement of Jim Kincaid, whose brilliant insights into age categories and enthusiasm about this topic have both inspired and enlightened my work in innumerable ways. Joseph Boone has been an incredible mentor over the years; his thoughtful and patient guidance has helped me grow as both a writer and a scholar. Peggy Kamuf contributed greatly to this project in its early stages and, as a teacher, introduced me to ideas that continue to resonate in much of my work.

I have the privilege of working with some wonderful colleagues in children's and young adult literature at California State University, Northridge—Charles Hatfield, Dorothy Clark, and Jackie Stallcup—whose knowledge and creativity always extend my learning and challenge my ideas in new and interesting ways. Joseph Thomas has also been a great colleague and offered a good deal of intellectual and moral support with the research and publishing process. Scott Andrews generously provided assistance with my research on Indian boarding schools. Carol Nackenoff shared her extensive knowledge of Horatio Alger with me, providing suggestions for my analysis and advice on editions. Kimberly Embleton kindly helped out with the research of some of the more obscure texts. And my good friend Kevin Volkan gave some invaluable advice on the publishing process.

Special thanks to the staff members at The University of Alabama Press, who have been incredibly responsive and professional in bringing this book to print.

Part of the work for this project was completed under the auspices of a Research, Scholarship, and Creative Activity award and a College of Humanities Faculty Fellowship award at California State University, Northridge. I would like to thank my department chair, George Uba, for his support.

A portion of chapter 4 was published as an article entitled "Taming Little Savages: Adolescent Crime and the Woodcraft Indian Movement," *American Studies Journal*, 47 (Summer 2001); and a portion of chapter 6 was published as an article entitled "Desire and the Literary Machine: Capitalism, Male Sexuality, and Stratemeyer Series Books for Boys," *Men and Masculinities* 3, no. 2 (2000). I am grateful to these publications for allowing me permission to reprint.

Most important, I would like to thank my family and friends for their support of this and other scholarly projects, especially my wife, Angela, and son, Graeme, who have given so much to help me realize this dream and to whom this book is lovingly dedicated.

The Modern Age

Introduction

What Adolescents Are Really Like

Featured prominently at newsstands across the country and a free gift for renewing subscribers, a special 2005 issue of *U.S. News & World Report* is devoted to exposing one of the most widespread and sinister cover-ups of contemporary American society. Surprisingly, the scandal has nothing to do with Enron or Iraq's fictitious weapons of mass destruction. "Mysteries of the Teen Years: An Essential Guide for Parents" features the latest data from statisticians and out-of-the-box insights from psychologists that attest to the fact that there has been something of a misunderstanding about America's teens: it turns out they're not so bad after all. "[M]any of the common complaints about generation Y, also known as the 'millennial' generation, are quite simply wrong," the magazine announces on its inside front cover. "Adolescents now are less likely than their parents were to smoke, do hard drugs, get pregnant, commit violent crimes, drop out of school, and drive drunk . . . the current generation is doing well by doing good."[1]

Although its enticing cover, catchy headlines, and wide distribution garnered the attention of many readers, it turns out that *U.S. News & World Report* cannot be fully credited with the scoop on the widespread misunderstanding of the country's least favorite age demographic. Over the past decade, scholars in a variety of disciplines have reached similar conclusions about America's attitude toward its young people. An extensive two-year study completed by the FrameWorks Institute and the UCLA Center on Communications and Community in 2001, for example, revealed not only a marked dislike and distrust of teens but also a pronounced discrepancy between this view and all of the current data relating to the age group. A summary of public opinion polls in the study revealed that "[o]nly 16% of Americans say that 'young people under the age of 30 share most of their moral and ethical values,'" putting teens only slightly above homosexuals, welfare recipients, and rich people. Furthermore, when a 1989 Gallup Poll asked 1,249 adults to compare contemporary youth to those twenty years ago, topping the list were the words "Selfish" (81 percent), "Materialistic" (79 percent), and "Reckless" (73 percent). These descriptors and the other data cited in the study are diametrically opposed to how teens actually view themselves. A survey of 1,015 high school students cited in the study found that the values teens hold most dear are "being honest" (8.6 on a 10-point scale), "working hard" (8.4), "being a good student" (7.9), and "giving time to helping others" (7.6). Furthermore, 75 percent of teens surveyed said that they felt happy most of the time. But perhaps even more striking than this discrepancy was the study's findings regarding the persistency of adult misconceptions. When six different focus groups from three separate cities were given a news story that outlined positive trends for teens, an overwhelming majority of the adults rejected it as false. "I questioned almost the whole story," one father vehemently asserted.[2]

In his 1999 book *Framing Youth*, Mike Males meticulously exposes the falsity of negative myths about contemporary teens. From mistaken reports of excessive violence to hysteria about rising pregnancy and substance abuse, Males demonstrates that data has consistently been disfigured by government agencies, interest groups, and the media to perpetuate fear about the next generation. Consistently, as studies continue to reflect more positively on teens, unfavorable stories persist with increased vigor. "Whether the issue is violence, crime, suicide and self destruction, drugs, smoking, drinking, risk, or attitude, the sequence is the same," Males concludes. "Teenagers are universally denigrated when, in reality, they are behaving well amid severe stresses."[3]

Indeed, there is no shortage of data indicating that American society relentlessly clings to negative misconceptions of adolescents. But even though the veil has begun to be lifted from this misunderstanding, very little has yet been proffered to explain why such myths exist. If there are consistently negative beliefs about teens being recirculated in American society, whom do they benefit and why does our culture sustain them? I believe the answers to these questions lie in the earliest constructions of the developmental stage of adolescence, the precursor to the contemporary teen.

The Modern Age: Turn-of-the-Century American Culture and the Invention of Adolescence examines both theoretical and fictional discourses that circulate around the developmental stage of adolescence in order to argue that the common construction of the impulsive, conflicted, and rebellious adolescent found its origin and most vigorous articulation in America at the turn of the twentieth century and was inspired by broader cultural anxieties that characterized American society at that time. Adolescence, as a concept, came into being because it fulfilled specific cultural needs. This "invention of adolescence" was largely motivated by the need to define a new and quickly expanding segment of the population, but also, it became a vehicle for expressing many concerns associated with the movement into a new era. Adolescence is a "modern age" not only because it was a result of changes in American society that are synonymous with modernity, but also because, at the turn of the century, this new age category came to represent all that was threatening about "modern life." Such an examination of how adolescence was constructed at the beginning of the century illuminates the current status of the concept and exposes how much our current problem owes to our recent past. We cannot understand the nature of contemporary misconceptions of teens or treat realistically today's misunderstood adolescents until we begin to unravel the cultural history of this stage of development itself.

The Century of Adolescence

The notion that adolescence is a twentieth-century invention is supported by the fact that the term had little currency before 1900 and made a sudden and pronounced appearance in a wide variety of discourses at the century's beginning. Chapter 1 provides an examination of the appearance of this unique developmental stage in the second half of nineteenth-century American society. In his hallmark study of the evolution of the child and the family, *Centuries of Childhood: A Social History of Family Life,* Philippe Ariès argues that there was little distinction between adolescents and children in European society before 1900. A similar case might be made about American society. Increasing urbanization and industrialization in late nineteenth-century America had many long-lasting effects on the population, and in particular, those individuals in their teens. New jobs in the cities, for example, led to a significant restructuring of the education system because the new economy preferred workers with high school and college degrees. As rural labor traditions disintegrated, enrollment in high schools doubled in the 1890s, and in that same period, there was a 38.4 percent increase in college enrollment.[4] From the very beginning, the new demographic created by these changes was viewed as a growing problem. Indeed, the majority of references to individuals in their teens in the newspapers and popular literature at the turn of the century describe not how more of them were going to school, but how more of them were committing crime. Articles on "wayward youth," "hoodlums," "street girls," and "gangs" pepper the many books about urban life that were published at the end of the nineteenth century. This hysteria over juvenile delinquency gave rise to the first official juvenile court in Illinois in 1899. By 1917 juvenile court legislation had been passed in all but three states, and by 1932 there were over six hundred independent juvenile courts throughout the United States.

The development of the public high school and the juvenile court system are material effects of a new space opening between childhood and adulthood, and these changes made teens a more conspicuous presence in American society. But also, such rehabilitative measures were predicated upon largely negative assumptions about this new demographic. These attitudes were articulated and justified in the earliest full-length theoretical treatments of what would become popularly known as "adolescence": G. Stanley Hall's two-volume work, *Adolescence: Its Psychology and Its Relations to Physiology, Anthropology, Sociology, Sex, Crime, Religion, and Education,* published in 1904, and Margaret Mead's three studies of adolescence in primitive cultures: *Coming of Age in Samoa* (1928), *Growing Up in New Guinea* (1931), and *Sex and Temperament in Three Primitive Societies* (1935). In chapter 2, I delineate what exactly these authors meant by the term *adolescence* and discuss how their "invention" functioned in a broader theoretical and cultural context. Attempting to reinstitute biology as the base of psychology, Hall envisioned adolescence as a tension between the recapitulation of primitive qualities inherited from ancestors and the possibility of inheriting new, "higher" human traits. In direct reaction to Hall, Mead's observation of "primitive" cultures led her to the conclusion that adolescence was largely a socially constructed conflict created by the intense demands Western society placed upon those in their teen years. Although they provide diametrically opposed approaches to the "problem" of adolescence, Hall and Mead were both responding to a cultural need to define a (seemingly) new and growing segment of population, a new theory of human development spawned by the works of Sigmund Freud, and a host of other anxieties related to the movement into the "modern world." Hall and Mead were also united in the rehabilitative nature of their work, which claimed to provide objective observations of adolescents, but really outlined methods to deal with members of this demographic if they got out of control. As such, their works gave rise to some markedly negative connotations that are still with us today.

The extremely evocative yet quite evasive notion of the "storm and stress" of adolescence, perpetuated by Hall and Mead, was an immensely popular way of depicting this age group, and the anxiety of what might happen if this tempest got out of control was shared by many Americans. Although Hall and Mead put a name to this fear, the invention of adolescence was a process that involved many changes in American society, all occurring roughly around the turn of the century. New initiatives, new social movements, and new mythologies built the foundation for an understanding of adolescence that would remain in public consciousness for more than a century. Although the rise of racialized educational establishments such as Indian boarding schools is rarely mentioned in the same context as the changes in American education at the turn of the century that made teens more conspicuous, these two movements had a great deal in common, and the texts surrounding uniquely American establishments such as the Carlisle Indian Industrial School can tell us a great deal about the late nineteenth-century American culture that inspired the invention of adolescence. Beginning with the founding of Carlisle in 1879, a remarkable number of educational institutions appeared on the American landscape with the intent of moving Native Americans away from their tribal homes and mainstreaming them for success in "civilized" society. Chapter 3 examines these schools, arguing that their policies were often predicated upon a social evolutionary approach to age that aligned the Native American youth with the adolescent in their propensity for delinquency but also in their potential for assimilation, if directed down the "right" path. Such rehabilitative programs were far from seamless or successful, however. Autobiographical accounts of this imposed adolescence—such as the 1891 book *Stiya: A Carlisle Indian Girl at Home* and Zitkala-Ša's autobiographical essays—reveal the many problems such assimilationist programs created. The "crisis of identity" described by these authors was symbolic of fundamental tensions and anxieties in American society itself and the way this society conceived the movement from adolescence to adulthood.

Amazingly, at the same time attempts to obliterate Native American culture through assimilationist programs such as Indian boarding schools were most prevalent, the image and (mostly fabricated) mythology of the "Red Man" were reaching their height of popularity as part of a miracle treatment for the troubled years of adolescence in the form of youth movements. Organizations such as the Woodcraft Indians and the Camp Fire Girls reached their peak of popularity at the turn of the century. How could American society sustain two such differing views of Native American culture as was reflected in the romanticizing taking place in youth movements and the demonizing taking place in Indian reform? In his history of the image of the Indian in American society, Philip Deloria explains this seemingly paradoxical attitude in terms of a broader cultural crisis brought on by modernity: "[By the twentieth century] the noble savage—still offering cultural criticism and justifying imperial conquest—could be found most comfortably residing inside American national boundaries," he argues. "The absorbed Indians wearing white man's clothes represented the ambivalent success of American imperialism. Becoming one with the empire, they justified the noble rhetoric of the white man's burden, which bespoke concern for converted savages. At the same time, however, some twentieth-century critics used the same figures to illustrate the new savagery of the modern. Coded as drinking, tramping, and laziness, Americanized Indians were powerful examples of the corrosive evil of modern society."[5] I would add to this list of "corrosive evil" the impending threat of juvenile delinquency and add to Deloria's adroit analysis that the space in which this conflict between interior and exterior was played out was adolescence. Turn-of-the-century youth movements and attempts to assimilate American Indians both fed off of fears of juvenile crime and used a social evolutionary understanding of age to justify a space where both Indians and youth playing Indian could be transformed into upstanding adults. This space, for all intents and purposes, is adolescence. Chapter 4 examines how this space was institutionalized in the Woodcraft Indian youth movement—the American precursor to the Boy Scouts—and its sister movement, the Camp Fire Girls. Hall's notions of recapitulation and the storm and stress of adolescence would serve as a theoretical justification for something that the founders of these movements already knew: which was that if left to their own devices, adolescents would regress to their "primitive" ancestry, with wicked acts of juvenile delinquency surely following. The notion of getting boys and girls out of the stifling environment of the modern city and into nature reflects a broader cultural anxiety over the urbanization and industrialization of American society at the end of the nineteenth century. The need to let adolescents "develop naturally"—which, ironically, involved an endless series of organized games and lists for memorization—fit seamlessly with Hall's notions of storm and stress. These commonplace beliefs about the developmental stage construct adolescence as a significant threat unless the energies and desires associated with it are correctly funneled into a productive, and morally acceptable, activity. Additionally, as with the work of Hall, the literature surrounding these youth movements became a way to both articulate and contain anxieties over "modern sexuality."

Attempts to contain and control this new demographic went far beyond boarding schools and youth movements, however. Chapters 5 and 6 examine teen reading at the turn of the century, focusing specifically on two of the most popular writers of the "juvenile": Horatio Alger and Edward Stratemeyer. Immensely prolific writers, both Alger and Stratemeyer have come to be seen as the first to capitalize on the growing teen reading market at the turn of the century. As such, they have been both celebrated and denigrated as literary "producers" rather than authors. Such a characterization, I argue, reveals a great deal about the status of juvenile literature and teens themselves at the turn of the century and provides an interesting approach to the work of both authors, who present the "problem" of adolescence in terms of value—both economic and moral. Alger's most popular series, *Ragged Dick,* was literally an attempt to reform homeless "street Arabs," who were commonly thought to be overtaking the streets of New York, but on a broader level, the series was a tool to rehabilitate the implied reader, who was asked to emulate Alger's model hero. Alger took a popular worldview that combined evolutionary theory, economics, and morality and turned it into a fictional universe, which provided a way to control and contain the seeming threat of adolescence. In Alger, "storm and stress" is translated into capital, which is the ultimate indication of moral evolution.

Taking literary production to a new level, Edward Stratemeyer founded his own "Literary Syndicate," which consisted of ghostwriters who would flesh out his outlines into two-hundred-page hardbound books that sold for an affordable fifty cents. As writer/producer, Stratemeyer is reportedly responsible for over thirteen hundred books, including such classic series as the Bobbsey Twins, the Hardy Boys, the Rover Boys, Tom Swift, and Nancy Drew. Although each series has its distinctive "hook," the underlying story-structure is basically the same. Focusing on episodes from the Tom Swift, Hardy Boys, Nancy Drew, and X Bar X Boys series, chapter 6 concludes that these early twentieth-century series books for adolescents code gender and desire as capitalist production and, at the same time, serve as scripts that reinforce and perpetuate this type of sublimation in their characters and implied readers. In this case, sexual desire is regulated (and masked) less by a centralized morality—as it was with the work of Hall and the youth movements examined above—and more by a capitalist work ethic. In their attempt to manage the storm and stress of adolescence, the Stratemeyer series books reflect a broader relocation of the topography of gender from nature to the theater of capitalist production.

Much more than just a term defined and popularized by G. Stanley Hall and others, adolescence was a cultural invention that involved and influenced many aspects of American society, and its roots can be traced back to at least the middle of the nineteenth century. Furthermore, adolescence, from its inception, was a rehabilitative tool developed as a way to contain an increasingly more conspicuous and troubling teen demographic that represented a host of fears associated with the movement into the "modern age." From the middle of the nineteenth century, when changes in American society made teens more conspicuous, the "problem" of adolescence has been seen as an economic one. So it is perhaps no surprise that the proposed solutions that came in the form of this juvenile literature were economic as well. The anxiety about teens that gave rise to juvenile courts and changes in education was largely an anxiety about unemployed youth on the streets of the cities; it was a problem fueled by urbanization and industrialization that disrupted the traditional social orders of the family and the community. By the time of the Stratemeyer series books, adolescents, I will argue, were largely turned into adults, and the threat was sublimated by a capitalist script that contained them through both production and consumption. Such a sublimation is not seamless, however, and fears and anxieties continue to shape the way we discuss adolescents or teens to this day.

The Wild Child, the Teenager, and Other Siblings

Although adolescence was not part of the popular lexicon until the turn of the century, its roots go back well into the early nineteenth century, most recognizably in popular recapitulation-based notions of childhood. As Kenneth Kidd has so effectively demonstrated, the genre of the bad-boy book, theories of recapitulation that equated childhood with savagery, and the concept of the feral child all influenced the many works on "boyology" that surfaced at the turn of the century. Works such as William Byron Forbush's *The Boy Problem* (1901) and Henry William Gibson's *Boyology* (1916) were the articulation of an attitude toward the preadolescent male that had been brewing since the early nineteenth century. "By the century's turn," Kidd argues, "the boy had become an important social as well as literary subject, appearing at the expense of the 'vanished' native. According to its champions, who subscribed to the doctrines of recapitulation and progressive diversification, boy culture was analogous both to earlier stages of civilization and to contemporaneous primitive societies."[6]

The invention of adolescence was greatly informed by such works and in particular their use of recapitulation as a way of explaining the "savage" behavior of the child and, perhaps more important, as a way of essentializing this behavior as not only biological but also evolutionary. But if "boyology" essentialized such savage behavior as natural, adolescence provided a way to repress it for the common good. In many ways, the invention of adolescence can be seen as a reaction to nineteenth-century notions of the savage child; adolescence, as a concept and methodology, served as a path by which such children could become adults.

One of the ways that such a transformation took place was through the many youth movements that appeared on the American landscape at the turn of the century. David Macleod has demonstrated the manner in which nineteenth-century recapitulation notions of childhood and turn-of-the-century theories of adolescence informed such movements. Theories of the savage child with his or her gang instinct provided a theoretical justification for the mythology of youth movements and supported the notion that boys and girls needed to get outside to stave off the stifling influences of city life. Thus, many youth movements worked to extend childhood into the teen years. Like the bad-boy books of the same era, these movements demonstrated a kind of nostalgia for and romanticization of childhood, which was usually thought of as a natural, primal state of being. On the other hand, new notions of the storm and stress of adolescence provided justification for controlling the free time of youth, lest they get out of control. Macleod explains:

American Boy Scout leaders sought to foster adolescent idealism by inculcating patriotism, making the Boy Scout oath and law the centerpiece of Scouting, and tentatively urging Scoutmasters to draw upon adolescent hero-worship. In practice, however, the busy-

ness which Boy Scouting fostered amounted to an effort to prolong boyhood and dilute or circumvent adolescence. Men who mis-
trusted emotionalism, sexuality, and independence wanted to lead
teenagers like frightened horses past the fire. . . . Since the activities
were those favored by smaller boys—woodsy ramblings rather than
team sports—and since the gang age which Boy Scouting mimicked
through its patrol system was basically preadolescent, plainly the
BSA's [Boy Scouts of America] strategy was to prolong energetic,
asexual boyhood while delaying and distracting boys from adolescent problems.[7]

Although they attempted to circumvent this new stage, these youth movements themselves actually became a type of adolescence, in that they served
as pathway into adulthood, a way to turn the savage boy into a member of
society. Though the mythologies of these movements were built upon notions of savagery and the gang, the activities often took the form of taming
such impulses and preparing the boy for adulthood. Such a pattern relied
upon adolescence in another way as well, in that it was predicated upon the
specter of the rebellious teen or the juvenile delinquent: in other words,
what would happen if the savage boy was not controlled and went down
the "wrong path." These youth movements and the texts that surrounded
them for all intents and purposes created the adolescent they were attempting to circumvent. Thus the theories of boyology and adolescence
worked in tandem with one another. The wild child needed adolescence to
keep him or her from getting out of control; adolescence needed the wild
child to provide the energy to propel him or her into adulthood.

In her recent examination of the nineteenth-century boy book genre,
Marcia Jacobson makes the argument that changes in American culture
at the turn of the century "demanded a new paradigm to explain human
experience. What emerged to meet this need and to become a governing
idea in autobiography was the concept of adolescence." According to Jacobson, boy books, such as Thomas Bailey Aldrich's *The Story of a Bad Boy*,
William Dean Howells's *A Boy's Town*, and Booth Tarkington's Penrod
books, largely focused on protagonists below the age of twelve or fourteen,
and although they presented a series of adventures over time, these novels
were not concerned with how the boy ultimately developed into a man.
"Focusing on a limited period of time and deemphasizing the passage of
time," she argues, "the boy book is not about growing up, but is instead
about the meaning of boyhood for the adult author." In the case of the

various authors she cites, this encounter with boyhood became a way to confront a crisis of male adulthood. According to Jacobson, this paradigm was supplanted by theories of adolescence proffered by Hall and Freud, which focused on the latter teen years and described this time period as a passage to adulthood. This new paradigm spawned what Jacobson calls the "coming-of-age book," which arose in the 1920s and included such titles as Sherwood Anderson's *Winesburg, Ohio*, Ernest Hemingway's Nick Adams stories, and Katherine Anne Porter's Miranda stories. Jacobson concludes: "The book that emerged to take the place of the boy book— the coming-of-age book—is necessarily quite different from its predecessors. In embodying the Freudian paradigm, whether explicitly or implicitly, it treats childhood as part of the passage to adulthood. It focuses more often on adolescence than on childhood with the protagonist's developing sexuality a major theme and the parents less central in the fuller world the protagonist inhabits."[8]

Jacobson's observation about adolescence being characterized as a process, in contrast to the static concept of the "boy" or "girl" of an earlier century, is a point well taken. At the turn of the century and to this day, the adolescent stage of development is often seen as the path by which the child becomes an adult. Adolescence, as a concept, became a way of understanding and defining this process of becoming. But "understanding," "defining," and "depicting" this path, I would argue, has also become a way to control it. Whether the path has taken the form of "storm and stress," the Woodcraft Indian, or Nancy Drew, the depiction has been a way both to define a seeming threat and to provide a possible solution to this threat. As such, the adolescent has always been defined by the adult that he or she will become—or, rather, the adult we want him or her to become. As a process, adolescence is certainly less stagnant than the narratives of boyhood analyzed by Jacobson, but it's no less reductive. Jacobson argues that this notion of a distinct passage between childhood and adulthood was articulated in the "coming-of-age" books of the 1920s, but I believe a detailed examination of adolescence will reveal that it can be seen much earlier. There clearly were changes in American society in the mid- to late nineteenth century that made individuals in their teens a more conspicuous presence, and many texts, such as the tracts surrounding Indian boarding schools and the fiction of Horatio Alger, were not only written partially for this demographic but also became ways to describe it and in some ways to control it.[9]

From its inception, adolescence has been a developmental scheme imposed on teens in order to prevent a return to savage childhood or a degeneration into an equally wild "modern" adult. The "invention" of adolescence that took place at the turn of the century gave rise to two distinct and interrelated conceptions of this age category: the squeaky-clean "ideal" adolescent, who is controlled, controllable, and will enable the human race to attain a type of moral perfection; and what I will call the "real" adolescent (as much a construction as the ideal), who represents a kind of cultural anxiety of the physical and sexual threat the adolescent can become if left to his or her own devices. Such a bifurcation between the real and ideal bears a resemblance to the process of differentiation Peter Stallybrass and Allon White discovered in their analysis of low/high-value hierarchies in literary and cultural history. In *The Politics and Poetics of Transgression*—which includes an examination of urban crime in the nineteenth century—they conclude:

> The bourgeois subject continuously defined and re-defined itself through the exclusion of what it marked out as "low"—as dirty, repulsive, noisy, contaminating. Yet the very act of exclusion was constitutive of its identity. The low was internalized under the sign of negation and disgust. But disgust always bears the imprint of desire. These low domains apparently expelled as "Other," return as the object of nostalgia, longing and fascination. . . . These contents, or domains are subject to misrecognition and distortion precisely because idealization and phobic avoidance have systematically informed their discursive history.[10]

As with the low and high domains identified by Stallybrass and White, the ideal and the real conceptions of adolescence work in tandem, one conception often serving as the inspiration and theoretical premise for the other. For example, G. Stanley Hall's idealized description of the adolescent's love for nature and the gang, which became the theoretical basis of so many youth movements, is predicated upon a kind of violence and savagery that was a threat to a society that did not follow the prescription provided in his work. Similarly, the squeaky-clean portrayal of the "millennial generation"—which sounds suspiciously like those characters that inhabit the works of the Stratemeyer Syndicate—is predicated upon a predatory monster that, as various polls attest, is taken to be "real" by so many contemporary Americans, but has turned out to be a fabricated myth. Such a bifurcation has also served to mask a common double discourse about gender, race, and class in many of the early depictions of adolescence. Even though adolescence is often configured as a "universal experience," the specific form it takes reveals very subjective and value-laden attitudes. *The Modern Age* poses the possibility that the history of the discursive category of adolescence has been a self-perpetuating and never-ending dance between the "real" and "ideal" adolescent, where the constructed image of one has served as cultural repression of the other, all under the guise of seeing, finally, what adolescence is really like.[11]

In his recent history of American childhood, Steven Mintz makes the point—which is repeated in the *U.S. News & World Report* article—that the word "teenager" did not really enter the popular lexicon until it was used in a 1941 article in *Popular Science Monthly;* emerging from this decade, according to Mintz, was "the bored, restless, volatile teenager who combined a child's emotions with an adult's passions and was estranged from parents and other authority figures."[12] Although Mintz accurately argues that the term became more prevalent in the middle of the century, "teenager" as a theoretical construct, with these markedly negative connotations, I would argue, has been with us at least since the second half of the nineteenth century, when it was used as theoretical justification for the restructuring of the public school system and the invention of the juvenile court. Furthermore, the "teenager" can be seen in texts throughout the twentieth century as the "real" adolescent—the specter of our worst fears of what this ever-present demographic population could become if left uncontrolled and unsupervised and the dark side of that "ideal" adolescent upon whom we pin all our hopes for the future. In his new book *Teenage: The Creation of Youth Culture,* which he describes as a "prehistory of the Teenager," Jon Savage makes a similar case for the earlier appearance of this category. Savage identifies the symbolic beginning of the teenager in 1945 when the *New York Times* magazine published "A Teen-Age Bill of Rights," but argues that the site that this term represented had been a part of Western society for many decades. "From the last quarter of the nineteenth century," he observes, "there were many conflicting attempts to envisage and define the status of youth—whether they were concerted efforts to regiment adolescents using national policies, or through artistic, prophetic visions that reflected the wish of the young to live by their own rules." Tracing the material manifestations of this site in cultural texts as diverse as the British public school system and the German *Wandervogel* groups and its symbolic manifestation in texts such as L. Frank Baum's *The Wonderful Wizard of Oz* and J. M. Barrie's *Peter Pan,* Savage also identifies a bifurcated conception of youth, noting that "youth became on the one hand a source of hope and a symbol of the future, and on the other hand an unstable and dangerous cohort."[13]

Consistent with the commonplace association of the teenager with the middle of the twentieth century, which Savage's work begins to dismantle, a common conclusion reached by many scholars in the field of children's and young adult literature (YAL) is that the genre of adolescent literature (or young adult literature, as it has become officially known) did not appear until the 1960s. For example, in their popular book *From Hinton to Hamlet: Building Bridges between Young Adult Literature and the Classics,* Sarah Herz and Donald Gallo have this to say about the history of the genre:

> Years ago, before the advent of YAL in the late 1960s, Nancy Drew, the Hardy Boys, Tom Swift, and the adventures of Frank Merriwell were considered teen literature. These novels avoided controversial topics such as sexuality, substance abuse, divorce, and death. . . . They were considered superficial by many literary critics because they lacked credibility in portraying the true nature of adolescents' lives. . . . The turning point for YAL came in 1967 with the publication of *The Outsiders* by S. E. Hinton, which describes the problems of alienated youth. . . . Other authors began to change the focus of YAL as more novels addressed the realities of teenage life and offered readers an honest view of the main characters' hopes, fears, and dilemmas.[14]

Such an association between the genre of young adult literature and the "realism" of novels published about teens in the 1960s is at the core of Marc Aronson's meditation on the history of young adult publishing in his oft-cited 2001 book *Exploding the Myths: The Truth about Teenagers and Reading.* Also privileging the 1960s as the watershed moment, Aronson makes the argument that during this decade, the children of the World War II generation, "that baby boom born in the hope of new life and new opportunity after so much economic pain in the Depression and human suffering in the Holocaust and the war," did not recognize themselves in any of the books of the time, "which were very tame novels of dating at seventeen or becoming a nurse or boys who lived long ago and far away." This led to two major changes: "First, as the teenagers whose lives mandated the creation of the sections got older, or into more trouble, they started to publish books about their own experiences. . . . Soon an entire and flourishing wing of young adult publishing was created around what is called the problem novel. . . . [Second,] it was not until the 1970s that a publisher at Bantam Doubleday Dell named George Nicholson (who is still active in the field as an agent) realized that books for teenagers would be ideal paperbacks."[15]

The dismissal by these and other critics of anything written by and for teens before this watershed decade commonly hinges on the assumption that such works, many of which were of course printed in paperback form, were not "realistic." But what is the standard of "reality" here? Whose reality? A cultural history of the developmental stage of adolescence indicates that the characterizations that appeared at the turn of the century are considerably less "tame" than is popularly believed. Indeed, in many ways the notion of the adolescent arose in direct contrast to earlier beliefs about the angelic and innocent child. Similarly, since it was so closely tied to fears about juvenile delinquency, which ultimately mask fear about "modern life," adolescence from the beginning took on very distinct connotations of savagery and barbarity. As a rehabilitative concept, adolescence at the turn of the century was portrayed as a sort of ideal, but inherent in these portrayals is the fear of a growing threat, and this threat has very specific, negative qualities. Adolescence has always defied history; it is spontaneous, spur of the moment, cutting edge, "taboo breaking." This is what makes it such a threat, but also what makes it function so well as a scapegoat for other fears and anxieties. Its volatility is essentialized as its most characteristic trait. In many ways, the focus on "realism" in the genre of young adult literature has served to eclipse this history, thereby essentializing contemporary portrayals of adolescence—and even portrayals dating back as far as the 1960s—as being more "real" in comparison to the "artificial," "inaccurate," "tame" portrayals of the past. In terms of young adult literature, essentializing adolescence as volatile and eclipsing its history has allowed the perpetuation of certain myths about the developmental stage and creates a naturalized connection between such myths and the age demographic associated with the genre, thus constituting it as "real." The adolescent and teen are stages of development that are often approached as if they have no history; freeing them of history has only served to perpetuate some of the myths that have remained relentlessly tied to these categories to this day.

Although the invention of adolescence I am tracing here is a unique turn-of-the-century phenomenon, it looks both back to recapitulation notions of the child and forward to the concept of the teenager, back to the nineteenth century and forward to the twentieth. Such a correlation between the transition of the individual as depicted in portrayals of the adolescent and the transition of the nation as it entered a new millennium was not lost on many writers at the time. In *Adolescence*, G. Stanley Hall often makes the connection between America as a nation and the unique teen demographic that populated it. He ends the preface to his work, for example, with a resounding sense of hope in the fact that America is in a transition stage, a stage that is defined by the evolved adult it can become:

> In vigor, enthusiasm, and courage we [the United States] are still young, and our faults are those of youth. Because they have been great our suffering has been also great, and pain is the world's best teacher whose lessons are surest to be laid to heart. The very fact that we think we are young will make the faith in our future curative, and we shall one day not only attract the youth of the world by our unequaled liberty and opportunity, but develop a mental, moral, and emotional nurture that will be the best preparation for making the most and the best of them and for helping humanity on to a higher stage.[16]

This theoretical intersection between theories of individual development and conceptions of the developing nation meant that these two seemingly diverse entities often reflected and informed one another. As such, this intersection provides a particularly rich glimpse into the cultural value system of American society at the turn of the century. I have therefore focused this cultural history of adolescence on the second half of the nineteenth century and the early decades of the twentieth. This book is divided into roughly three sections, of two chapters each, that focus on three different aspects of turn-of-the-century American society and the invention of adolescence: theoretical treatments of adolescence; the motif of the Indian in boarding schools and youth movements; and teen reading. With a topic as complex and widespread as the concept of adolescence in American society, it would have been very easy to look at a number of different aspects of turn-of-the-century American society and/or push this study forward into the middle of the twentieth century. Such an overarching perspective of the evolution of the concept of adolescence, while interesting and important, I believe, risked a lack of depth. In order to examine these various literary and cultural texts in sufficient depth, I chose to approach them as representative "case studies" of broader phenomena in American society at the time. I chose three areas that were central to this invention and resonated broadly. So, for example, even though there clearly have been other theoretical explanations of adolescence—some published in the early years of the twentieth century—the works by Hall and Mead are representative of two approaches (psychobiological and sociological) that have been extremely influential. Along the same lines, the conclusions I draw regarding the treatment of Native Americans as adolescents at the end of the nineteenth century might serve as a model for further inquiry into the treatment of other ethnic minority populations. These three sections show a certain evolution of thought, but more accurately I have conceived of them as three glimpses into a very rich and complex cultural moment. While there were situations in which texts "set the stage" for subsequent movements or concepts—such as the relationship between G. Stanley Hall and the Woodcraft Indian/Camp Fire Girls youth movements I cover in chapter 4—analyzing the invention of adolescence in a chronological manner proposes an evolutionary relationship between these various texts that, I believe, are reactions to the same "crisis."

The Age of Adolescence

A detailed study of the earliest attempts to define adolescence not only reveals a great deal about American cultural history in the early decades of the twentieth century but also can provide many insights into how culture uses age as a mode of difference. Like race and gender, age is a discursive category that often frames our discourse and the ways in which we understand the world around us. Also like race and gender, because it is often associated with the body, age is "naturalized" in the sense that its social constructedness becomes illusive, often ignored. But unlike race and gender, age has been a largely undertheorized and unchallenged category. Although a fair amount of scholarship has been devoted to "old age"—in particular, the study of gerontology—little has been done to demonstrate how the forms of ageism that affect our conceptions of the elderly impact and (mis)inform other age categories as well, and what these constructed categories themselves have in common.

If we can very broadly describe ageism as "discrimination based on age" then current attitudes toward teens, as revealed in the many sources cited above, would unequivocally stand guilty as charged. When an overwhelming majority of people persistently characterizes a group as "selfish" and "reckless" in the face of data that indicate otherwise, and when such characterizations become so commonplace as to be accepted without question, clearly there is a problem. But it's not enough only to prove that discrimination exists. The only way to dismantle the ageism displayed toward teens is to understand what we have to gain by perpetuating it. The first step toward answering this lies in the history of the developmental stage of adolescence. Ageism toward teens is not something unique to this historical moment, but has existed for over a century and is, arguably, synonymous with the term *adolescence* itself.

A cultural history of the developmental stage of adolescence may also serve to inform the development of a theory of age in general. In *Declining to Decline: Cultural Combat and the Politics of Midlife,* Margaret Morganroth Gullette describes what might be the initial steps toward a comprehensive understanding of age: "If 'ideology' can be defined, most simply, as any dominant system that produces and maintains consciousness through discourses, institutions, and practices, so completely that its effects then become invisible to this extent, then twentieth-century North America certainly has its own age ideology. The first task of an age-oriented criticism is to make the textual effects visible."[17] The earliest constructions of adolescence and the manner in which these constructions have recirculated in American society throughout the twentieth century reveal a telling example of age ideology. The storm and stress of adolescence has become so naturalized that the exposure of its illegitimacy makes national headlines, but still the reasons why this particular characterization was favored over all others remains invisible. One question we have to ask is: Why has society maintained this invisibility?

Furthermore, a discussion of adolescence as a construct might shed some light on other age categories as well. As the many life-span theories of aging will exemplify, age often functions as a comprehensive system of stages that work in a symbiotic relationship with one another.[18] A focused, singular discussion of one category is almost impossible, because in the study of age, attitudes toward one category affect or are effects of attitudes toward another. This is most certainly the case with adolescence. If, for example, as James Kincaid has demonstrated in his work on the cultural construction of children, the child has been constructed as "empty innocence," then possibly the adolescent has been constructed as this child's evil older sibling, bursting at the seams with unbridled sexuality and an innate disrespect for the rules and regulations that maintain adult society.[19] The construction of the adolescent as such has served to solidify and naturalize ageist notions about the child. If the beginning of adolescence is marked by the onset of secondary sexual characteristics, then the child is by definition not sexual. If adolescence is characterized by an often-contentious independence from parental authority, then the (normal) child should demonstrate an untroubled dependence on the parent. The child, simply put, is everything the adolescent is not.

But the same could be said for the adult. The more dramatic the storm and stress experienced by the adolescent, the more stable the grown-up stage the individual ultimately achieves. The more ways in which youth becomes associated with beauty and sexuality in our society, the more closely adulthood is associated with physical and sexual decline. Adolescence always already implies the existence of the other age categories with which it forms a system, and the way in which it is constructed shapes these categories indefinitely and often invisibly.

Inventing the Modern

What characterizes the various articulations of adolescence in the early decades of the twentieth century is an anxiety about a (seemingly) new and growing demographic and a need to control and contain it. For many of these authors, adolescence represented the new "modern" generation that was coming of age and, with its progressive behavior, was threatening to swamp old verities. For example, in the preface to his psychological examination of this stage, G. Stanley Hall has this to say about the threats that the new millennium posed: "The momentum of heredity often seems insufficient to enable the child to achieve this great revolution and come to complete maturity, so that every step of the upward way is strewn with wreckage of body, mind, and morals. There is not only arrest, but perversion, at every stage, and hoodlumism, juvenile crime, and secret vice seem not only increasing, but develop in earlier years in every civilized land. Modern life is hard, and in many respects increasingly so, on youth." Adolescence, for Hall and others during this time period, is intimately related to "modern life" because, as an ideal, it became a way to resist the degeneration that "seemed" like such a widespread threat, but also, in reality—or at least in the "reality" constructed by Hall and others—it was the time during development when the individual was most susceptible to this threat.[20]

Adolescence as a distinct stage of life became a way of articulating a number of prejudices that characterized American culture at the turn of the century, prejudices that reflect the largely middle-class Protestant values of self-restraint and self-denial. Shaped by anxieties about topics as far reaching as modern urbanization and industrialization, juvenile delinquency, Freud's new theories of human development, religion, and the disintegration of traditional gender roles, the process of inventing adolescence was a process of taming a threat, and thus these definitions often reveal more about those who create them than the actual parameters of adolescence itself. This strange preponderance of interlocking texts that I am calling "the modern age" created a cohesive if inchoate image of adolescence that has remained remarkably influential throughout the past century. We continue to invent adolescence because it satisfies a cultural need to define ourselves in relation to this liminal space that is close enough to share our hard-won values and distant enough to accommodate our deepest fears. The invention of adolescence is the invention of ourselves.

I

New Kids on the Block

School Reform, the Juvenile Court, and Demographic Change at the Turn of the Century

The Hero of the Twentieth Century

Given the commanding presence of the adolescent in all aspects of contemporary Western culture, it is hard to imagine a time when such a concept and its representative demographic did not exist, but most scholars are in agreement that one need glance back only a hundred years or so to find evidence of such a reality. In his frequently cited 1960 study of the evolution of childhood and the family, *Centuries of Childhood: A Social History of Family Life,* Philippe Ariès surveys a wide scope of Western literary and cultural texts and doesn't see anything that resembles our contemporary concept of adolescence until the late nineteenth century. Historically, in Western culture, Ariès tells us, the adolescent has been subsumed by the much more common category of the child. For example, "[i]n school Latin the word *puer* and the word *adolescens* were used indiscriminately. Preserved in the Bibliothèque Nationale are the catalogues of the Jesuit College at Caen, a list of the pupils' names accompanied by comments. A boy of fifteen is described in these catalogues as *bonus puer,* while his young schoolmate of thirteen is called *optimus adolescens.*"[1]

According to Ariès, the lack of distinction between the *puer* and the *adolescens* is indicative of a society that made no distinction between the two as demographic entities and a culture in which individuals passed from childhood to adulthood with no pronounced and extended transition period. In a detailed study of the European school system, for example, Ariès concludes that "[i]n the twelfth and thirteenth centuries, children of ten and boys of fifteen were mixed up with adults; in the fourteenth and fifteenth centuries, children and adolescents continued to study together but were separated from adults." And even though there was a "recognition of adolescence" in the seventeenth century with the appearance of the academy, the physical separation of children and adolescents did not begin until the latter part of the eighteenth century, when an "increasingly close correspondence between age and class" and a new interest in the officer and the soldier began to carve out a space between the child and the adult: "The medieval school made no distinction between the child and the adult. The college at the beginning of modern times had merged adolescence and childhood in the same scholastic system. In the eighteenth century, the officer and the soldier were to introduce into sensibility the new notion of adolescence." This new notion became more commonplace, according to Ariès, throughout the nineteenth century, as age segregation in the schools became more pronounced. With as much fanfare as is deserved by what Ariès deems the "privileged age" of the twentieth century, the adolescent had arrived: "The first typical adolescent of modern times was Wagner's *Siegfried:* the music of *Siegfried* expressed for the first time that combination of (provisional) purity, physical strength, naturism, spontaneity and joie de vivre which was to make the adolescent the hero of our twentieth century, the century of adolescence."[2]

Ariès's conclusions are not without controversy, however. Often in direct rebuttal to his work, scholars have identified "adolescentlike" spaces in the "chusing time" of colonial New England, London apprentices during the seventeenth century, apprentices in Bristol during the sixteenth century, sixteenth-century youth abbeys in France, and confraternities in Florence during the fifteenth century, among other places.[3] The problem, of course, is one of definition. If adolescence is defined as an identifiable stage between—and distinctly different from—childhood and adulthood, then it is not difficult to find evidence of its existence in texts from a wide variety of cultures and time periods. But, as John Gillis has demonstrated, the parameters of such a stage, which was commonly known as "youth" in preindustrial society, were much less precise than is the case with our contemporary conception of adolescence. "What they commonly called 'youth,'" he tells us, "was a very long transition period, lasting from the point that the very young child first became somewhat independent of its family, usually about seven or eight, to the point of complete independence at marriage, ordinarily in the mid- or late twenties."[4] Gillis goes on to argue that the term *adolescence*—and the more precise age group and stage of development it represents—did not enter the popular lexicon until the end of the nineteenth century, largely as a result of industrialization, urbanization, the growth of the middle class, and changes in education.

A number of critics have expanded upon Gillis's conclusions, arguing that although "adolescentlike" spaces have existed in other cultures and historical periods, Western society did not use the term with any frequency or precision and thus did not recognize the stage of development, as we know it, until the end of the nineteenth century. For example, in his book *Adolescence and Culture,* Aaron Esman concludes: "Puberty has, of course, always been with us, and some process of adaptation to it, of assimilation into the body image of the newly acquired sexual capacities and the concurrent growth spurt, is certainly universal. Similarly, some process of socialization, of direction and channeling of sexual impulse, of inculcation of cultural values, is an essential component of all human societies. But the form with which we are familiar—protracted, indeterminate, conflict-laden, marked by gross dyssinchrony between sexual and social maturity—is our own cultural property." Similarly, in *The Fin-de-Siècle Culture of Adolescence,* John Neubauer proposes that "adolescence 'came of age' in the decades around 1900, not only because the term itself had little currency earlier, but . . . because interlocking discourses about adolescence emerged in psychoanalysis, psychology, criminal justice, pedagogy, sociology, as well as in literature. Adolescence may have been used sporadically earlier, but the appearance of the interlocking discourses testifies that human life was perceived in terms of a new category by the end of the nineteenth century."[5]

A number of critics have identified a similar "coming of age" in America during this same time period.[6] Most notably, Joseph Kett, in his 1977 book *Rites of Passage: Adolescence in America, 1790 to the Present,* has explicated the complex ways in which urbanization, changes in the family, and new educational practices culminated in the invention of adolescence at the turn of the century. "The key contribution of the 1900–1920 period was not the discovery of adolescence," he points out, "for in one form or another a recognition of changes at puberty, even drastic changes, had been present long before 1900. Rather, it was the invention of the adolescent, the youth whose social definition—and indeed, whose whole being—was determined by a biological process of maturation."[7]

Kett's distinction as to the "invention" of adolescence is a point well taken, for, arguably, the most convincing evidence to support the notion that adolescence is a uniquely turn-of-the-century concept is, first, the widespread recognition of the concept in literary, theoretical, and cultural texts from a wide range of disciplines and readerships and, second, the immense influence this concept has had on twentieth-century American society and its image of the teen demographic. Additionally, Kett makes the excellent point in his explication of this invention that although adolescence was often posited as a scientific concept, something observed and recorded, it was largely a theoretical construct imposed upon youth. "To speak of the 'invention of the adolescent' rather than the discovery of adolescence," he argues, "underscores a related point: adolescence was essentially a conception of behavior imposed on youth, rather than an empirical assessment of the way in which young people actually behaved. The architects of adolescence used biology and psychology (specifically, the 'storm and stress' thought to be inherent in youth), to justify the promotion among young people of norms of behavior that were freighted with middle-class values."[8]

Kett has made a convincing case that material and cultural changes in American society during the nineteenth century gave rise to a unique developmental stage known as adolescence and, perhaps more important, that this stage was as much a reflection of the society that created it as the new teen demographic it was describing. Adolescence was largely a reactionary concept that was "invented" for rehabilitative purposes. This invention can be seen in a wide variety of disciplines and discourses in American society, and the concept that these discourses promoted spoke so well to that society and was so influential that not only does it remain with us today, but we accept it almost verbatim as "truth." Arguably, the two most profound changes in American culture at the turn of the century in regard to individuals in their teen years were educational reform and the development of the juvenile court system. These social programs were systematic approaches to both education and crime that served to segregate teens from the child and adult populations and thus made them a more conspicuous and unique demographic. The new segment of the population these changes created was greeted with a great deal of reprehension and anxiety and, interestingly, the social practices and modes of understanding developed in reaction to this new segment can most accurately be seen as ways to contain a new and dangerous threat. People resist change, and adolescence, even before it was named as such, represented the future to late nineteenth-century American society, a modern future full of difference and the shock of the new.[9]

Reading, 'Riting, and (Age) Reform

As has been recounted in many histories of turn-of-the-century American society, increasing industrialization in the United States in the second half of the nineteenth century inspired a mass migration from the country to the city. According to U.S. Census statistics, in 1860, of a total population of 31,443,321, slightly over 6,000,000 lived in urban communities— defined as those with populations over 2,500. In 1890 the population, now numbering 62,947,714, included over 22,000,000 urban dwellers. In 1860 there were only 392 communities in the United States with populations over 2,500; by 1890 the number had increased to 1,348.[10]

This urbanization had profound and wide-reaching effects on young Americans. The new economy meant the opening up of a wide range of occupational opportunities for those who were just beginning to venture into the working world. Industries, banks, warehouses, and insurance companies needed labor to satisfy a suddenly international market that was growing by leaps and bounds. According to U.S. Census statistics, in 1860, of the 10,533,000 "gainful workers" in the country, 6,208,000 were on farms and 4,325,000 were in nonfarming occupations. In 1890, of the 23,318,000 who made up the total labor force, 9,938,000 worked on farms and 13,380,000 at other tasks.[11] Many of these workers were young men, turning their backs on their fathers' profession and migrating to the city for a taste of the "modern life." Such a phenomenon was apparently widespread enough to warrant a number of articles in major publications, such as an 1858 piece in the *Atlantic Monthly* in which the author posits the following explanation for the deterioration of the farmer's life: "Let the son of such a home as we have pictured get a taste of a better life than this, or, through sensibilities which he did not inherit, apprehend a worthier style of existence, and what inducements save those which necessity imposes, can retain him? . . . It is not strange that the country grows thin and the city plethoric. It is not strange that mercantile and mechanical employments are thronged by young men, running all risks for success, when the alternative is a life in which they find no meaning, and no inspiring and ennobling influence."[12]

But the effects of urbanization went much deeper than just opening new mercantile and mechanical employment opportunities for Americans in their teens. These opportunities had a significant impact on the manner in which the middle class prepared their children for the workplace. Kett has observed that, although industrialization created an increasing demand for cheap boy laborers at the turn of the century, a resistance to "dead-end" jobs and a proliferation of white-collar positions made the prolongation of education an increasingly attractive alternative to the parents of children in their teens:

> Only in the latter part of the 19th century did the sheer length of time passed in the setting of formal education become a major determinant of one's economic prospects. . . . Even at the end of the 19th century the correlation of prolonged schooling and enticing job opportunities was far from perfect, but a truncated education was likely to lead to a poor job. The more attractive crafts did not want anyone under 16. Advertisements for bookkeepers or accountants were usually addressed to those around 16 or 17, if not older. The colleges did not want anyone who had not attended secondary schools, and employers were increasingly prone . . . to look to the colleges as sources of managerial recruits.[13]

The attractiveness of such professional careers, according to Kett, is largely responsible for the dramatic increase in enrollments in the schools commonly populated by students in their teen years. High school enrollments doubled in the 1890s, for example. Similarly, there was a 38.4 percent increase in college enrollment, and the number of professional schools established between 1876 and 1900 in law, medicine, pharmacy, dentistry, and veterinary science was more than double the number established from 1851 to 1875.[14]

The rise in enrollment to meet the new demands of the workplace was both inspired and shaped in very specific ways by a mass overhaul of the country's schools. Most of the northern and western states passed compulsory education laws in the second half of the nineteenth century, beginning with Massachusetts, which, in 1852, required that "[e]very child between eight and fourteen was to attend some public school for at least twelve weeks each year, six weeks to be consecutive."[15] These laws, along with closely related child labor laws, affected more and more teens as the upper end of the statutes were raised to fifteen, sixteen, and even eighteen as the century progressed. As a result of these laws, teens were required to be in school for a significant part of the year, which, along with the fact that labor laws decreased the length of their workday, made them much less attractive to many employers. But on a broader level, such laws represented a new attitude toward the value of education and a widespread belief that educational institutions and the students who attended them should be controlled and regulated by the state. As mentioned earlier, part of the reason for the massive increase in high school enrollment at the end of the nineteenth century was the need to train teens for new employment opportunities, but it was also a result of the proliferation of public high schools, which, in many states, were becoming mandatory by law.[16]

Changes in the nation's schools made a significant impact on the classroom environment as well. During the nineteenth century, loosely structured academies containing young people between the ages of five and twenty-five gave way to educational institutions that exclusively served teenagers. According to Kett, the blueprints for school reform were largely based upon European models, which lengthened the school year, disseminated graded textbooks, and carefully monitored environment and personnel, all in the name of making "school as coextensive with the life of the child as conditions would allow." This school reform movement inevitably led to an age-grading practice in public schools that both segregated children and put an end to the wide range of ages in the more open classrooms of earlier decades. It also had the effect of concentrating the age range of students enrolled in school; more specifically, many of the older students were eliminated from the high schools, which became populated mainly with students in the teen years. A similar phenomenon occurred in both private schools and colleges: "In place of the mixture of boys, youth, and men in the original academies, academies in the decades between 1850 and 1870 generally tended toward concentration in the teen years," Kett explains. "In colleges the entire period from 1850 to 1900 saw a gradual concentration of students in the 18–22 range. Neither the median nor average age at graduation from college actually changed much in the period from 1830 to 1900, but the age spread contracted."[17]

At the end of the nineteenth century, teens became a more pronounced and distinct demographic in a number of ways. New job positions in the cities were populated by young Americans, who became the new working class. Furthermore, a restructuring of the school system and changes in the relationship between schools and an increasingly urban job market delayed the point at which individuals achieved "adult" status; educational institutions segregated teens and isolated them from both children and adults. These changes, it might be argued, not only made teens more conspicuous but also shaped society's attitudes toward this new population in many different (largely negative) ways. First, extending the education of many teens meant that they left home at a much later age. Teens who in earlier eras would have been providing a new source of income for their families as they left school or attended school only intermittently were now attending school full time—and later into their teen years. Such teens were not only an economic burden to their families, they were also significantly changing the traditional family structures of an earlier century. As David Macleod has argued in his work on the rise of youth movements in America at the turn of the century, keeping teens in school until they were older and putting off the age when they could enter the workplace meant that they actually had more free time on their hands. Turn-of-the-century youth organizations such as the Boy Scouts and Girl Scouts were a reaction to this: "While work had brought a measure of independence to nonfarm boys, full-time jobs (except street trades) generally meant adult surveillance and long hours. Ironically, prolonged schooling gave many school boys far more free time. A favorite computation was to take the hours in a week, deduct those spent in school, asleep, and eating meals, and then announce some staggering remainder as free for play. [Boy Scout founder] Baden-Powell came up with fifty hours a week, while the BSA's James West claimed 'school provides leadership for only about one thousand of the five thousand hours a year a boy has for activity.'"[18] As I'll explain later in this chapter, much of the hysteria about juvenile crime at the turn of the century was directed simply at the presence of youth—hanging out on street corners and "passing time." Such a sentiment must have been greatly informed by the fact that fewer teens went directly into the workplace and thus were an "unnatural" presence in the home and an unwelcome strain on family income.

Second, new systematic approaches to education were often predicated upon the need to control this new population. Ostensibly, age segregation and the creation of the high school for older students was an attractive alternative because it let primary schoolteachers focus on a more cohesive, young demographic. For example, in an 1857 article in the *American Journal of Education* outlining the social benefits of this new entity called the high school, the author argues that "[e]very thing which is now done in the several district schools, and schools of lower grade, can be better done, and in shorter time, because the teachers will be relieved from the necessity of devoting the time and attention now required by few of the older and more advanced pupils, and can bestow all their time and attention upon the preparatory studies and younger children."[19] But such a removal of the "older and more advanced pupils" and the "relief" it provided was also an attractive alternative from a disciplinary standpoint. As Kett has argued, age grading was initially inspired by a desire to protect a largely female teaching force from adult male students: "As long as schools were ungraded," he explains, "it was difficult to justify the widespread use of female teachers, mainly because of doubts that tender ladies of 16 could manage plowboys of 18 in a classroom. Gradation, on the other hand, would permit the year-round employment of women, with older boys placed in high schools under male tutelage."[20]

Such problems of discipline were of concern to Americans during the second half of the nineteenth century, and they must have had an effect not only on the changes made to the classroom but also on the rationale of these changes. For example, in an 1864 article on "the proper school age" in the *Pennsylvania School Journal,* the author provides the following argument for narrowing the age of admission for common schools, from the spread of five to twenty-one to a more practical spread of six to sixteen: "Our present arrangement takes in a class hard to govern,—boys from sixteen to twenty. To this period of life belong generally our fast boys, young rowdies and lazy country boys that go to school just to shirk labor at home. Some few I admit go to learn and behave. What teacher has not experienced this to his annoyance? It is out of this class that most of our school troubles rise; and on account of this class many a teacher is employed more on account of his muscular power than his apt scholarship. It is the boys of this age that give many schools a hard name."[21] Whether they were "older and more advanced pupils" or "fast boys, young rowdies and lazy country boys," or both, students in their teen years were seemingly a problem that needed to be controlled, and the answer was to place them in their own (highly regulated) space.

In one sense, adolescence was invented at the end of the nineteenth century because changes in the nature of the workforce and in education at that time served to make the teen years a more conspicuous presence in society. Additionally, these changes shaped people's attitudes toward this new demographic because they disrupted some traditional structures in society, such as the family, and because such changes were predicated upon a fear that teens would challenge new progressive approaches to education. As Kett sums it up: "The growth of cities, increase in population mobility, and rise of egalitarianism, combined with evidence of social disorder, all contributed to the conviction that moral development of the young should no longer be shaped by casual contacts with adults in unstructured situations but had to be regulated at every turn."[22] And regulated young people were.

Rats, Weasels, and Other Wanderers of the Streets

Although various changes in the American educational system at the end of the nineteenth century accommodated (and controlled) this new segment of the population, the number of teens enrolled in these new public high schools, colleges, and professional schools was relatively low. For example, the percentage of individuals between the ages of fourteen and seventeen enrolled in secondary schools in 1900 was 11.4 percent; even though that is a remarkable increase from 7 percent in 1890, it is still a relatively small part of the overall population.[23] Many American youth at the turn of the century simply did not go to school—even when faced with compulsory education laws. And perhaps even louder than the cry to better educate the teens who populated America's schools was the cry to save those who did not. In the United States at the turn of the century an entire legal system was created to reform this population. The first juvenile court was established in Illinois in 1899. The Illinois juvenile court act was well received throughout the nation, and juvenile courts were quickly established in Wisconsin (1901), New York (1901), Ohio (1902), Maryland (1902), Indiana (1903), and Colorado (1903). By 1917 juvenile court legislation had been passed in all but three states, and by 1932 there were over six hundred independent juvenile courts throughout the United States.

The title of the country's first juvenile court law is succinct and simple: "An act to regulate the treatment and control of dependent, neglected and delinquent children." "Dependent" and "neglected" children are rather broadly defined in the legislation to include any child under the age of sixteen

> who for any reason is destitute or homeless or abandoned; or dependent upon the public for support; or has not proper parental care or guardianship; or who habitually begs or receives alms; or who is found living in any house of ill fame or with any vicious or disreputable person; or whose home, by reason of neglect, cruelty or depravity on the part of its parents, guardian or other person in whose care it may be, is an unfit place for such a child; and any child under the age of 8 years who is found peddling or selling any article or singing or playing any musical instrument upon the street or giving any public entertainment.

Obversely, the act's definition of delinquent children is rather concise: "[T]he words delinquent child shall include any child under the age of 16 years who violates any law of this State or any city or village ordinance."[24] But this definition was soon expanded to include every type of negative behavior imaginable. In the very next session, the legislature broadened "delinquent" to include the "incorrigible" and children "jeopardized by their associates," and in 1905 the definition was expanded to include

> any male child under the age of seventeen years or any female child under the age of eighteen years who violates any law of this State or any city or village ordinance; or who is incorrigible; or who knowingly associates with thieves, vicious or immoral persons; or who, without just cause and without the consent of its parents or custodian, absents itself from its home or place of abode, or who is growing up in idleness or crime; or who knowingly frequents a house of ill-repute; or who knowingly frequents any policy shop or place where any gaming device is operated; or who frequents any saloon or dram shop where intoxicating liquors are sold; or who patronizes or visits any public pool room or bucket shop; or who wanders about the streets in the night time without being on any lawful business or occupation; or who habitually wanders about any railroad yards or tracks or jumps or attempts to jump onto any moving train; or enters any car or engine without lawful authority; or who habitually uses vile, obscene, vulgar, profane or indecent language; or who is guilty of immoral conduct in any public place or about any school house.[25]

Sections of the act call for private, informal hearings; protection of court records from publicity; detention of children apart from adults; and the appointment of a probation staff. Children heard in juvenile court were not actually charged with crimes but put under the protection of the court as a wise parent (*parens patriae*). The juvenile delinquent, if found as such, was not given a criminal record but rather subjected to a process of reform.

I'll have more to say about the strangely broad definition of juvenile delinquency in a moment, but first it's important to make note of the various changes in public opinion about incorrigible and wayward youth at the time that inspired the creation of the juvenile court. Throughout the nineteenth century, reform schools, industrial schools, and even private military schools served as ways to house juvenile delinquents, and almshouses, county homes, and state institutions cared for dependent children. One of the more well known and influential was the New York City House of Refuge, which was opened in 1823 by the Society for the Reformation of Juvenile Delinquents. The first state reform school for delinquents was established in Westboro, Massachusetts, in 1847. But these were, at least in the minds of the experts and legislators, too far and few between to accommodate the stream of juvenile delinquents that appeared to be rising uncontrollably as the end of the century approached. Furthermore, incidences of corruption and mistreatment in these institutions soured the opinion of the public and the legal community as to their ability to safely house wayward or delinquent youth, making them appear not much different from prisons.

As Robert Mennel has pointed out in his history of juvenile delinquency, the disenchantment with these institutions is reflected in changes in state laws that filled the books in the latter decades of the nineteenth century. In Illinois, for example, an 1870 Supreme Court decision, reversing the earlier sentencing of a youth to the Chicago Reform School, made it impossible for many reform schools to receive any children other than those who had been convicted of felonies. Similarly, an 1888 Supreme Court decision denied Catholic charities access to delinquent children, thus blocking one of the main paths through which many privately organized industrial schools filled their beds. Such changes can be seen throughout the second half of the nineteenth century, in many states and counties, leading Mennel to conclude that "[b]y the late nineteenth century, little remained of the enthusiasm and hope which had produced the asylum, the penitentiary, and the reform school. Internal as well as external attacks upon reform schools were indicative of a larger collapse of faith in the healing powers of the edificial world."[26]

Ironically, it was this very collapse of faith that inspired various philanthropists and government officials to erect a new edifice in the reform school's place—the juvenile court. In addition to the growing dissatisfaction with existing institutions for delinquent and wayward youth was a belief among welfare experts and private child-saving organizations that juveniles should not be processed through the criminal courts or incarcerated with older offenders. Before the juvenile court was established in Illinois, the prosecution of juvenile criminals was generally still based upon English common law, which defined the age of maturity as fourteen. Children under the age of seven were considered incapable of committing a crime, and those who were fourteen or older were largely tried as adults, with special circumstances taken into consideration at sentencing. Interestingly, children between seven and fourteen were considered incapable of committing a crime as well, but were to be judged "in terms of such factors as apparent physical maturity based on inspection, severity of punishment for the crime, evidence of capacity to understand the difference between right and wrong, and evidence of malice or cunning."[27] All offenders were processed through the adult court system and, more often than not, housed with adults in the jail.

Such mixing of juvenile offenders with adults caused a great deal of public outcry. For example, in a trenchant critique of the legal system entitled *Our Penal Machinery and Its Victims* (1886), John Peter Altgeld, governor of Illinois from 1893 to 1897, describes the cruel fate of over ten thousand young persons arrested for crimes in the city of Chicago: "But what was the treatment they received? Why precisely the same as if they had been criminals. They were arrested, some of them clubbed, some of them handcuffed, marched through the streets in charge of officers, treated gruffly, jostled around. At the police station the name and a complete description of the person of each was written on the prison records, there to remain. Some of them were bailed out, while the remainder were shoved into cells and forced to spend a night and sometimes a week there, forced to stand around with criminals, before they were discharged."[28] Such brutal treatment, according to Altgeld and many others, would not deter the young but only harden their hearts, making them abhor the system and further motivate them into lifelong criminality.

Running counter to this sympathy for youth housed with adults and for children sentenced to prisonlike reform schools was a widespread fear about the increase in juvenile crime. Many documents from this time testify to what was believed to be a growing epidemic of "child crime." In his widely read exposé of the New York underworld, *The Dangerous Classes of New York and Twenty Years' Work among Them* (1872), for example, urban reformer and founder of the Children's Aid Society Charles Loring Brace shines a particularly focused light on the growing presence of corrupt street children in New York. "There seemed to be a very considerable class of lads in New York who bore to the busy, wealthy world about them something of the same relation which Indians bear to the civilized Western settlers," Brace warns. "They had no settled home, and lived on the outskirts of society, their hand against every man's pocket, and every man looking on them as natural enemies. . . . Sometimes they seemed to me, like what the police call them, 'street rats,' who gnawed at the foundations of society, and scampered away when the light was brought near them."[29] Perhaps even more pervasive were the images of the big city espoused by Jacob Riis in his immensely controversial and commonly cited study of slum life, *How the Other Half Lives: Studies among the Tenements of New York* (1890). In a well-known chapter, "The Street Arab," Riis regrets that

> [n]ot all the barriers erected by society against its nether life, not the labor of unnumbered societies for the rescue and relief of its outcast waifs, can dam the stream of homelessness that issues from a source where the very name of home is a mockery. The Street Arab is as much of an institution in New York as Newspaper Row, to which he gravitates naturally, following his Bohemian instinct. . . . The Street Arab has all the faults and all the virtues of the lawless life he leads. Vagabond that he is, acknowledging no authority and owning no allegiance to anybody or anything, with his grimy fist raised against society whenever it tries to coerce him, he is as bright and sharp as a weasel, which, among all the predatory beasts, he most resembles.[30]

Although this hysteria about the rise of juvenile crime was and is commonplace, actual data supporting this "epidemic" are characteristically unreliable and hard to come by. Analyzing data on juvenile delinquency is notoriously difficult and was particularly so at the turn of the century, when the definition of "delinquency" was still quite open to interpretation, and the Federal Children's Bureau—the source of juvenile court statistics—did not yet exist. Such complications are what led a 1932 White House Conference on Child Health and Protection to conclude that "[t]here exists no accurate statement as to the amount of delinquency in this country, nor whether it is increasing or decreasing."[31] But this often was of little importance to "experts" who were much more interested in contemplating the causes of this epidemic—and implementing solutions—than proving that the epidemic existed in the first place. The "considerable class" or "stream" of juvenile delinquents graphically depicted by Brace, Riis, and others was a threat all the same. For example, in a well-known and often-quoted treatise on juvenile crime, W. Douglas Morrison's 1897 work *Juvenile Offenders*, the author announces in the opening pages: "Whether . . . we look at the Old World or at the New, we find that juvenile crime is a problem which is not decreasing in magnitude with the march of civilization. Every civilized community is confronted with it in a more or less menacing form." Morrison's evidence for such a "menace" is an 1895 publication by special census agent Frederick Wines—*Report on Crime, Pauperism, and Benevolence in the United States at the Eleventh Census, 1890*—which Morrison admits "only affords a partial view of the full extent of crime in the United States," but "as far as it is possible to see," "it is highly probable" that crime is on the rise.[32] Even as excessively qualified as it is, such a conclusion is actually at odds with Wines's own summary of the data, which states, "The relative increase of inmates of juvenile reformatories has been very slight. . . . The ratio in 1880 was 229 to the million of the population, in 1890 it was 237, a gain of 8 to the million." Wines goes on to demonstrate that there was actually a decline in crime in the North Atlantic division—a much less spectacular summary than that given by Morrison. Regardless of how they were interpreted, the figures of the 1890 census were all theoreticians of juvenile delinquency in the United States had to go on at the turn of the century, but as Morrison sheepishly admits, they were not much help, mainly because they listed only the number of individuals who were housed in prison or one of the fifty-eight reformatories and, therefore, did not include those juvenile delinquents who were fined, put on probation, released with a warning, or not caught. They also weren't very effective in proving an increase in crime, since there was nothing to compare them to. As Wines states in his report: "The differences in conditions and methods of enumeration prior to 1880 prevent comparisons of accurate value."[33]

Whether juvenile delinquency was on the rise or not is open to interpretation, but what is apparent is that people perceived that it was on the rise. Furthermore, what is clear from the many descriptions of rising juvenile delinquency at the end of the nineteenth century is the tacit association made between the (seemingly) soaring crime rate and urbanization. In *How the Other Half Lives,* for example, Riis attributes the steady stream of "Street Arabs" to the corrupting influence of the city: "[T]he young are naturally neither vicious nor hardened," Riis observes, "simply weak and undeveloped, except by the bad influences of the streets." Similarly, Brace's solution to the proliferation of "street rats" is simply to get them to the countryside—"Emigration as a cure for Pauperism."[34]

However, it is important to note that that in these texts the negative influence of these conditions is not portrayed as a threat solely to teens. Indeed, in most theoretical treatments of juvenile delinquency, city life is most often explained in how it vitiates all ages. For example, in Morrison's *Juvenile Offenders,* the author has this to say about the negative influence of the city: "[A] dense population heightens the proportion of offenders to the population, inasmuch as it intensifies the struggle for existence. . . . In a large city the old disposition to regard the stranger with suspicion, if not as an enemy, is to a large extent revived, and as each citizen is a stranger to the other the whole of the inhabitants live in an atmosphere of suspicion and distrust. These conditions of existence are destructive of social cohesion in its highest forms, and have a tendency to develop the selfish instincts till they overstep the borderland which separates selfishness from crime."[35] As is the case with all of the other passages about the negative influence of the city, the victim of this influence is not a determined age— the city corrupts one and all, bringing everyone's, young and old, selfish instinct to the surface. It might be argued, therefore, that, to a certain extent, the negative connotations of city life that were common in a wide variety of texts in the latter half of the nineteenth century were grafted onto new notions of adolescence. As the city grew, the teen population became more conspicuous. Children in their teens became almost synonymous with urban growth and therefore symbolic of all of the evils this growth represented.

Additionally, the hysteria about the rise in juvenile crime at the end of the nineteenth century seems to be less about specific crimes committed by teens and more about their conspicuous presence in society—loitering in alleys and on street corners. This is reflected in the absurdly broad definitions of delinquency included in the laws behind the juvenile courts; in the case of the Illinois law cited above, a teen may be classified as a delinquent for using indecent language, associating with an immoral person, attempting to jump onto a moving train, or simply wandering around the streets in the nighttime. In one 1872 publication, *The Nether Side of New York; or, The Vice, Crime and Poverty of the Great Metropolis,* for example, New York journalist Edward Crapsey presents "without extenuation or exaggeration" the facts he has collected in a four-year study concerning the number of vagrants and delinquents in the city, only to conclude that "it is impossible to give the exact numbers of juvenile thieves of all classes to be found at all times in New York. All outcast children are so liable at any moment to pass the line between vagrancy and crime, that the two classes are practically only one."[36] The fine line that was drawn (or erased) between vagrancy and crime might indicate that it was simply the commanding presence of teens in society that is at the root of the hysteria about juvenile delinquency. The social changes that made teens more conspicuous were sudden and dramatic at the turn of the century, and the effect of the appearance of this previously undetected category of the population—not quite children and not yet adults—must have caused some concern and even fear.[37]

But, on a broader level, the gray area between those just loitering and those committing more serious offenses also facilitated a new understanding of the reformative nature of teens and how much further away from adulthood they were than everyone originally thought. In his exposé of the child-saving movement in Illinois that gave rise to the first juvenile court, Anthony Platt makes the excellent point that the main theoretical thrust of the child savers was to stop juveniles from entering a life of crime, not necessarily to punish them once they had already gotten there; it was a preventative movement. This attitude was inspired by new progressive attitudes toward crime, which posited that criminals were made by environmental factors rather than born to a life of crime. Such theories, according to Platt, were particularly suited to youth, who could be shaped before it was too late: "The 'rehabilitative ideal' presupposed that crime was a symptom of 'pathology' and that criminals should be treated like irresponsible, sick patients," notes Platt. "The older a criminal, the more chronic was his sickness; similarly, his chances of recovery were less than those of a young person. Adult criminals, particularly recidivists, were often characterized as nonhuman. Children, however, were less likely to be thought of as nonhuman since universalist ethics, especially the ethic of Christianity, made it almost impossible to think of children as being entirely devoid of moral significance."[38] Such a "rehabilitative ideal" is reflected in the broad definitions of what constitutes juvenile delinquency. These acts were not so much about containing criminals—many of whom would be sent to adult prisons anyway—but about defining, systematizing, and containing all of those threatening characteristics that would become associated with the adolescent. This is evidenced by the 1886 Illinois Board of Public Charities' report on private and public facilities for delinquent children, which concluded that institutional care should be given to "those children and others who swarm in the streets, gather about docks and wharves, and are almost sure to take up crime as a trade."[39] "Almost sure," indeed.

But, also, the preventative thrust of the new juvenile court represents a significant change in the way people understood this segment of the population. The juvenile court not only made teenagers more conspicuous but also signified a belief that they were still in a pliable developmental phase and therefore could be shaped and (re)formed. The invention of the juvenile court is the effect of a shift in the popular understanding of age. Such a shift is reflected in the changing of the age of responsibility from fourteen to sixteen and beyond. Although the Illinois Juvenile Court was unique in that it ensured children who broke the law were treated not as criminals but as wards of the state, legal precedent for raising the age of adult legal responsibility from fourteen to sixteen existed before the court, but these changes are largely a phenomenon of the late nineteenth century. Various laws were enacted throughout the country to separate children from adults in the legal system, indirectly raising the upper age limit. Under an 1869 Massachusetts statute, for example, an agent of the state board of charity was to attend juvenile trials, investigate the children's cases, protect their interests, and make suitable recommendations to the judge; later laws in 1870, 1872, and 1877 provided for the separate trial of children's cases. Sponsored by the Society for the Prevention of Cruelty to Children in New York City, a law passed by the New York legislature in 1877 provided: "Any child under restraint or conviction, actually or apparently under the age of sixteen years, shall not be placed in any prison or place of confinement, or in any court-room, or in any vehicle for transportation, in company with adults charged or convicted of crime, except in the presence of proper officials." And in 1892 a new section was added to the penal code in New York, providing: "All cases involving the commitment or trial of children for any violation of the penal code, in any police court or court of special sessions, may be heard and determined by such court, at suitable times to be designated therefore by it, separate and apart from the trial of other criminal cases, of which session a separate docket and record shall be kept."[40]

Laws passed in the late nineteenth century providing alternatives to prison sentences for juveniles had a similar effect on raising the legal age when a child became an adult. In 1880 Massachusetts established the first probation system without restriction as to age in any county. Similarly, an 1884 state law in New York provided: "When a person under the age of sixteen years is convicted of a crime, he may, in the discretion of the court, instead of being sentenced to fine or imprisonment, be placed in charge of any suitable person or institution willing to receive him." Illinois and Indiana followed the examples of Massachusetts and New York in establishing their own forms of juvenile probation systems.[41]

Interestingly, in all of these laws, in the legislation for the first juvenile court, and in the compulsory education laws, no justification is given as to why the cutoff point where an individual should be defined legally as an adult was raised from fourteen to sixteen and above. But given the legal precedent for such a designation one might surmise that the legislatures must have agreed with a broader late nineteenth-century belief in the rehabilitative possibilities for the older teen. The window of opportunity was widened to give juveniles a second chance, but the widening had the effect of lengthening childhood and was predicated on the idea that children—even those in their late teens—were reformable and therefore still not fully developed. In Morrison's 1897 book *Juvenile Offenders,* the author has the following to say about crime and age:

> England has no place of detention for juveniles over sixteen except a prison, and even in prisons all juveniles over the age of sixteen are treated as if they were men. A very different method of dealing with young offenders exists in the United States. . . . Maturity of character is largely dependent on physical maturity, and, according to the evidence of Dr. Roberts before the Secondary Education Commission, the children of the poorer classes do not attain physical maturity till they have reached their twenty-fifth or twenty-sixth year. . . . If the investigations of Dr. Roberts are correct (they are accepted by other investigators of equal eminence) as to the age when bodily and mental maturity is attained among the poorer classes, our existing penal laws and our present methods of administration, in so far as they relate to juveniles over sixteen, are at once cruel and absurd. American legislation is, on the whole, based upon much more defensible principles, and it is along the lines laid down by the American people that European legislation will sooner or later have to move.[42]

Changes in legislation that raised the age at which individuals officially became adults must have been symptomatic of a new understanding of the relationship between physical and mental maturity and acknowledgment that such maturity was happening much later in teens than the current legal system allowed for. These changes were partly indicative of a new attitude toward age, not just a fear of rise in crime. As Morrison sums it up: "If it is necessary in the interests of public security that juveniles over the age of fourteen should be liable to imprisonment, it is equally essential that prison treatment should not be the same for them as for adults. Adults have reached a period of life when bodily and mental maturity is complete, but this cannot be said of juveniles between the ages of fourteen and eighteen."[43]

With the development of the juvenile court, Illinois raised the age of separation between child and adult from fourteen to sixteen and then a few years later to seventeen (for boys) and eighteen (for girls). These ages are consistent with the juvenile court acts that followed throughout the rest of the country. But, interestingly, many courts and legislatures made accommodations for individuals a few years past these ages, some even affecting those in their early twenties. For example, in 1914 a "boys' court" branch was established by rule of court in Chicago for the specialized treatment of boys from seventeen to twenty years of age. In 1923 the New York legislature passed a law that outlines procedures for dealing with girls between sixteen and twenty-one who could be considered "wayward minors"; boys were added to the law two years later. The Pennsylvania law relating to wayward minors, as amended in 1917, provides that the municipal court of Philadelphia shall have exclusive jurisdiction in "all proceedings concerning, or trials of charges brought against all minors between 16 and 21 years who shall disobey their parents' commands, or be found idle in the streets, and against all disorderly children."[44] Such amendments and qualifications are the beginnings of a long tradition that continues to this day of accommodating individuals who are technically not juvenile delinquents but also not adult criminals. Such legal maneuverings open up one of the most problematic aspects of adolescence: where does it end?

Even though the development of juvenile court systems throughout the United States at the turn of the century was motivated by a wide variety of reasons, each unique to its geographic location, three generalizations could safely be made about its effect on the notion of adolescence. First, there was a new awareness of a group of "criminals" who were not quite young enough to be considered children (and thus considered subjects of "neglect") but also not old enough to be mixed with adults. Second, the general consensus on when one became an adult was getting older— at least a few years above the age of fourteen, which was the definition of an earlier era. Third, because of an increase in the presence of this group, a systematic method needed to be developed to take care of its members, and this systematic method was predicated upon—and directly promoted and disseminated—notions that teens were a threat but still developing and therefore redeemable. Like educational reforms at the turn of the century, the juvenile justice system isolated and segregated the teen population, making it more defined and conspicuous. Additionally, like the educational reforms, this systemization was a way to control a threat.

The cultural forces at work in the development of the juvenile court, in particular the fear of the teen demographic, become particularly apparent when delinquency is analyzed in terms of gender. In his history of juvenile delinquency in America, Joseph Hawes notes that, by and large, while the offenses that were cited for the boys arrested in the early years of the courts were as diverse as the many acts cited in the laws, the girls were most commonly arrested for crimes relating to sexuality. "The most common offenses of girls were 'incorrigibility,' 'immorality,' and 'disorderly conduct,'" he notes in terms of the cases heard in the first year of the juvenile court in Chicago. "For girls incorrigibility and disorderly conduct usually meant staying out late, going to dances, or associating with 'vicious persons.' Immorality meant some sort of sex offense, but in order to 'protect the good name' of many of the girls who appeared before the juvenile court they were listed as being incorrigible or disorderly. Often 'immorality' was reserved for girls found in houses of prostitution. Nevertheless, 80 per cent of the delinquent girls who appeared before the court were there because their virtue was 'in peril' if it had not already been lost."[45]

In his history of the child welfare system in Boston, Peter Holloran has made the point that throughout the nineteenth century attitudes toward female delinquents—which of course included the homeless and destitute as well those who committed crimes—were greatly informed by an antebellum "cult of true womanhood" that emphasized piety, purity, submissiveness, and domesticity. Thus any hint of sexual impropriety—or often any expression of sexuality whatsoever—in teen girls was seen as the first step down an irreversible path of moral destruction. Holloran states: "Boys were considered more redeemable than girls because a vagabond boy might, in the popular imagination, be strengthened by the school of hard knocks and mature into a successful man like the impoverished bootblack, Ragged Dick, in Horatio Alger's novels. The loss of sexual innocence was irreversible for the female, and her sin was believed to doom her to a life of total corruption or at least to place her outside the bounds of normal society, like Hawthorne's Hester Prynne."[46] The threat of the loss of "sexual innocence," then, became a way to contain and control adolescent girls. The irreversible nature of the offense and also its broad definition meant that it could be applied to a wide variety of "offenses," and often the same laws were used to incarcerate prostitutes, girls who had engaged in premarital sex, chronic masturbators, and even girls whose "wantonness" was a sign of bad things to come.

Such an antebellum "cult of true womanhood" can be seen well into the twentieth century in the double standard of the juvenile court, which made clear distinctions between what was considered delinquency for boys and girls. In regard to juvenile crime, then, the construction of the adolescent, who was old enough to pose a serious threat to society if not managed correctly but also malleable enough to be reformed if institutionalized before he was eighteen, becomes more complex in the case of the female, who, like her male counterpart, could be a (sexual) threat, but was seen either as an asexual, virginal child or as an irredeemable and corrupted adult. Once again, according to recapitulation-based theories of childhood, both the male and female adolescent had the propensity for primitive behavior, but the specific type of behavior and the path of redemption was very gender specific.

There Goes the Neighborhood

The material changes that most affected youth at the turn of the century and were most responsible for making them more conspicuous were created to help this segment of the population take advantage of the opportunities provided by industrialization and urbanization, yet they were also a method of control. The systemization of both education and delinquency were material effects of specific changes in demographics, but also they were reactions to the fear of this new demographic. This fear was and remains an extremely complex phenomenon, but clearly adolescence as a concept became a lightening rod for anxieties that were projected onto this new, enticingly blank space.

Some of these fears were inherited from the past. Many of the studies of "adolescentlike" spaces in pre-nineteenth-century Western societies mentioned at the beginning of this chapter discuss the anxieties these populations engendered in the adult population. Gerald F. Moran and Maris A. Vinovskis, for example, identify manifestations of what they call "troubled youths" in early modern England and colonial American society. Moran and Vinovskis rightly argue that tensions between youth and adult society are not "universal" but the result of specific cultural forces, such as demographic and economic changes in early modern England and religious ideology in colonial New England. One wonders, though, to what extent, by the middle of the nineteenth century, "youth" and later "adolescence" simply inherited a connotation of conflict that had been brewing for centuries.

More significantly, of course, these fears were unique to this historical moment. As discussed earlier, economic changes meant teens became an economic burden and the symbol of a changing family structure. Adolescents also became symbolic of mass urbanization. Inheriting a long tradition that equated urban life with lack of morality, disintegration of the family, the dissolution of distinct class and ethnic divisions, and poor health, Americans to a certain extent may have grafted these fears onto adolescents, who were a major part of this new urban population. The following chapters will examine a number of forms of this fear, including fears of "modern" sexuality, a loss of national/individual virility, the dissolution of traditional gender and race categories, and the perils of "cheap reading." On the verge of adulthood, the next generation in the making, adolescents represent the future. The future holds the promise for change, but not everyone is interested in change, especially if the direction is uncertain.

G. Stanley Hall, Margaret Mead, and the Invention of Adolescence

Adolescence Invented, Not Described

Urbanization, industrialization, and the various social reforms that accompanied these changes in America in the latter half of the nineteenth century had the effect of making teens a more conspicuous presence. These changes in society, to a certain extent, also engendered a markedly negative attitude toward this suddenly more pronounced population. Such a sentiment blossomed and reached its full form in the earliest theoretical treatments of this new developmental stage, soon to be commonly known as adolescence.

As Aaron Esman has maintained in his history of adolescence, most theoretical treatments of the developmental stage fall into two distinct groups. One group emphasizes "the central role of biological factors in the adolescent process," while the other focuses on the "determining influence of changing social role expectation in the transition from child to adult status in society."[1] Esman's observation is an apt summary of the theoretical history of adolescence and, indeed, his distinction between biological and social approaches applies to the earliest full-length treatments of the developmental stage. In his 1904 two-volume work, *Adolescence: Its Psychology and Its Relations to Physiology, Anthropology, Sociology, Sex, Crime, Religion, and Education*, G. Stanley Hall—commonly regarded as the father of adolescence—attempts to reinstitute biology as the base of psychology by arguing that individual development recapitulates the history of the species, wherein the child moves from a savage love of nature through adolescence to a humanistic learning of culture. In reaction to Hall's psychobiological approach, Margaret Mead's three studies of adolescents in primitive cultures—*Coming of Age in Samoa* (1928), *Growing Up in New Guinea* (1931), and *Sex and Temperament in Three Primitive Societies* (1935)—argue that the various characteristics of adolescence result not from biology but from culture, specifically the unique pressures placed on this age group in Western society. The distinction that, according to Esman, characterizes the theoretical history of adolescence flows from the conflict that lies at its "invention": Are the qualities that distinguish adolescence biological or social in nature? Although the work of Hall and Mead was separated by two decades, these "inventors" of adolescence were the two most influential voices about adolescence in the first half of the twentieth century, and their works neatly encapsulate the two common approaches to the developmental stage, approaches that largely have stayed with us to this day.

But whereas various critics such as Esman have noted the contrast between these early treatments of adolescence, little has been said about what they have in common. First, the tightly knit historical context of this early theorizing of adolescence implies a significant interchange of intellectual concepts among Hall, Mead, and, as I will argue here, Sigmund Freud. From 1888 to 1920, G. Stanley Hall was the president of Clark University. He is heralded as being the person who "introduced Freud to America," as he sponsored Freud's trip to the States to lecture at a conference at Clark in 1909. Hall also hired Franz Boas to work at Clark, and it was Boas, mentor of Margaret Mead and ardent critic of the social evolutionary school of thought, who convinced her to write *Coming of Age in Samoa* to prove that the various qualities of adolescence characterized as biological by Hall were actually a uniquely cultural phenomenon.

More important, however, than the historical connections between the inventors of adolescence are the theoretical continuities in their work. Both Hall and Mead articulate certain characteristics of adolescence that were commonly associated with the developmental stage in the early decades of the twentieth century and, to a large degree, have remained part of the definition to the present day. For example, the developmental stage begins with puberty and ends with the individual's assimilation into the adult world. In terms of age, adolescence runs roughly through the teen years, thus making it distinct from the category of "youth" from an earlier era. The "storm and stress" of the developmental stage and the adolescent's ability to "acquire new traits"—both phrases popularized by Hall—

are reflective of the turmoil commonly associated with adolescence and also the common narrative in which the youth searches for his or her place in the world.

On a broader level, both Hall and Mead offer not only descriptions of this new segment of the population but also prescriptions that help deal with adolescents when they get out of control—and, most assuredly, they will get out of control. The psychobiological description of adolescence offered by Hall and the sociological description offered by Mead are presented as solutions to various problems. One of these is the rising tide of juvenile delinquency, which was discussed in the last chapter, and subsequent fears of adolescents out of control. The other is a sexual permissiveness that was associated with the modern theories of human development proposed by Freud. The works of Hall and Mead were extremely popular because they provided the theoretical justification for new social programs aimed at this (seemingly) new population of individuals in their teens, programs such as the juvenile court and the secondary school system discussed earlier, and a host of youth movements and institutions I will discuss later. But as rehabilitative approaches, the works of Hall and Mead are predicated upon the notion that adolescence is a "problem" and, as such, they have had the effect of demonizing this population in ways that are very much still with us today.

The Storm and Stress of Modern Life

Although the impulsive, irrational nature of the unconscious and the conflict with authority inherent in the Oedipus complex are topoi often aligned with adolescence, the term *adolescence* is almost entirely absent from the writings of Sigmund Freud. In "On the Psychical Mechanism of Hysterical Phenomena: Preliminary Communication" (1893), Freud speaks of adolescence (*Adoleszenten*) when discussing the possibility that puberty creates the disposition to hysteria. Later, in "On the Grounds for Detaching a Particular Syndrome from Neurasthenia under the Description 'Anxiety Neurosis'" (1895), Freud uses the term again when discussing the anxiety produced in girls by their first encounter with sex.[2] In both cases, adolescence is not only associated with hysteria, an association Anna Freud develops later, but used almost synonymously with puberty, and, as an entirely distinct developmental stage, could therefore be considered of little significance in Freud's work. Although Freud of course speaks of a period of "latency" following the dissolution of infantile sexuality and has a great deal to say about the instigation of the sexual drive during puberty, he chooses to focus on infantile sexuality and how experiences during infancy shape adult behavior. But the fact that Freud does not make much of adolescence per se does not mean that his work is not crucial to the meaning of the concept. In addition to establishing much of the terminology used by twentieth-century theoreticians of human development, Freud proves central to the theoretical treatments of adolescence because this stage of development was invented, to a certain degree, in reaction to his work.

G. Stanley Hall supported Freud's views throughout his career and indeed in *Life and Confessions of a Psychologist* (1923), the work in which he has the most to say about Freud and Freudianism, he claims that "Freudianism marked the greatest epoch in the history of science." But while he was willing to praise Freud for bringing "the element of feeling . . . into the very foreground of attention"—and I think it is safe to assume he means sexual feeling here—he was not willing to grant this feeling as central a role in his theory as Freud. In his most elaborate critique of Freudianism he concludes:

> I cannot believe that normal children show to any marked extent the infantile aberrations which are postulated. . . . I am convinced from years of study of my own dreams and those of my pupils that while there is a class of them which pretty strictly conforms to Freud's rubrics there are others that cannot possibly be explained by them; that I hold that the Oedipus complex is unhappily named because Oedipus did not know his father or mother and that the phenomena it designates are somewhat less common than this theory assumes, and also that the incest notion in general has been still more overworked since Rank . . . ; that I deprecate from the assumption of Freudian physicians that the key to all the symptoms of their patients is to be found in sex, so that analysis is prone to leave them unduly sexually-minded.[3]

Hall disagreed with Freud on a number of issues, but there are two that are most important for our study here. First, although Hall would agree with Freud that there was such a thing as an unconscious, Freud saw this unconscious as the product of repressed infantile desire, whereas Hall saw it as the inherited past of the progenitors. In order to get away from the "mysticism" that he thought characterized the work of Freud and his followers, Hall saw his work as a way of rebasing psychology on biology. According to Hall, any true study of psychology must focus on the physical aspects of the individual because, simply put, "character might be in a sense defined as a plexus of motor habits."[4] And thus a major portion of Hall's fourteen-hundred-page work on adolescence is devoted to documenting the physical changes in the individual as he or she develops from infant to adult.

In terms of the early development of the individual, Hall deduces that the individual recapitulates the history of the species. He states: "Thus we rehearse the activities of our ancestors, back we know not how far, and repeat their life work in summative and adumbrated ways. It is reminiscent, albeit unconsciously, of our line of descent, and each is the key to the other. The psycho-motive impulses that prompt it are the forms in which our forebears have transmitted to us their habitual activities. Thus stage by stage we reenact their lives."[5] Hence, according to Hall, the child's acquisition of vertical posturing is a recapitulation of the same development in the species, just as the preponderance of theft in childhood recapitulates a more primitive attitude toward property.[6] All in all, from embryo through the early years of adolescence, the past development of the species determines how the individual develops. This "history of the species," as Hall points out in the passage quoted above, is a type of "unconscious."

Although Hall was unique in developing specific characteristics for the stage of adolescence, his recapitulation approach to age had precedence in the social evolutionary theory of the time and much popular literature as well. Herbert Spencer's work, for example, is informed by age categories and notions of aging as a "natural" linear progression. In his 1876 work *The Principles of Sociology*, he has this to say about the evolution of humankind:

> Infancy shows us an absorption in sensations and perceptions akin to that which characterizes the savage. In pulling to pieces its toys, in making mud-pies, in gazing at each new thing or person, the child exhibits great tendency to observe with little tendency to reflect. . . . Want of power to discriminate between useless and useful facts, characterizes the juvenile mind, as it does the mind of the primitive man. . . . Again, we see in the young of our own race a similar inability to concentrate the attention on anything complex or abstract. The mind of the child, as well as that of the savage, soon wanders

from sheer exhaustion when generalities and involved propositions have to be dealt with.[7]

Similar age metaphors can be seen in Lewis Henry Morgan's 1877 work *Ancient Society*, in which Morgan attempts to outline the course of cultural development. Period I, which he entitles "Lower Status of Savagery" and equates with Australia and Polynesia, is described as the "infancy of the human race."[8] Hall cites both of these authors a number of times in *Adolescence*, and he borrowed from them a theoretical connection between the individual and the race, but perhaps more important a contextualizing of this connection in terms of age, which essentialized his theory as a natural and linear process and globalized it as something we all experience.

Evolutionary approaches to age were not the mainstay of sociologists and philosophers only, however. In her book *Being a Boy Again*, Marcia Jacobson has demonstrated the ways in which theories of recapitulation appeared in education tracts and other popular writing in nineteenth-century America, including the unique genre of the boy book, popularized by Thomas Bailey Aldrich, Mark Twain, William Dean Howells, Booth Tarkington, and others. Theories of recapitulation, she argues, "struck an immediately responsive chord. They seemed to account for the wildness of boy behavior in a time when boys were not yet part of the male world of work but were no longer a part of the family world at home. . . . They are explicitly cited in nearly all of the boy books and are the literal subject of two of them."[9]

Hall's theory of adolescence, then, is partially informed by a popular concept of recapitulation that provided a "scientific" explanation of the savagery of childhood. But while early development follows a set evolutionary pattern, Hall assures us that "[t]he soul is thus still in the making" and the individual can still acquire new characteristics.[10] This assertion leads to Hall's second main disagreement with Freud. Whereas Freud focuses on infantile sexuality and how experiences during infancy shape adult behavior, Hall shifts the focus away from infancy to adolescence, which he configures as a stage where the individual can acquire new character traits that, in a sense, override those established during infancy. This could be at the root of Hall's criticism in *Life and Confessions of a Psychologist* that "Freud's rubrics," in particular the Oedipal paradigm, could not account for "all" psychological conflicts.

According to Hall, adolescence is a time of unusually rapid growth, and thus puberty signals a "new birth" in the individual: one develops so rapidly and changes so dramatically that one can move beyond the recapitulation of the species and develop new qualities. Hall states:

> So puberty is not unlike a new birth, when the lines of development take new directions. The trace of individuality in nearly all respects—size, strength, motion, mental ability, etc.—is greatly increased, extremes are wider apart, and average variations ampler, as seen in wider distributions among the percentile grades. This means increased plasticity and docility, so that powers of acquisition are increased and deepened. . . . Changes of ethnic development best occur now, and the point of departure for higher and more evolved forms is adolescence and not adulthood, just as upward steps in the development of the phylon have not been from the terminal types of earlier periods, but have started from stages farther back.[11]

Growth is so rapid during this "new birth" that the individual can actually surpass the history of the species and acquire new genetic qualities: the adolescent becomes the genetic pioneer. Thus a great deal of Hall's work is devoted to documenting the rapid growth of the individual during this period. There are long sections called "Growth in Height and Weight" and the "Changes in the Senses and the Voice," filled with elaborate graphs and the latest medical statistics.

This notion of adolescence as a "point of departure" also marks Hall's differentiation from—or, perhaps more accurately, extension of—recapitulation theories of childhood that were so popular in nineteenth-century American thought. Whether it was referenced in the theoretical works of Spencer and Morgan or the novels of Aldrich and Tarkington, recapitulation made savagery an inescapable "trait" of childhood. Hall, for all intents and purposes, posits adolescence as an extension of this trait but also as a path to "evolve" beyond it. As such, Hall was taking issue with what he saw as the determinism of theories of recapitulation and of Freud's psychoanalytic theories as well; Freud, in Hall's eyes, not only restricted human behavior to a product of childhood experience but also often couched his theories in the rhetoric of recapitulation as well.

According to Hall, these qualities of adolescence are not strictly physical in nature. A large portion of *Adolescence* discusses how new "powers and faculties" are developed during adolescence, such as the ability to love and pronounced interests in religion, nature, and art. These powers and faculties are representative symptoms of the "higher and more evolved"

form of the species for which adolescence serves as a path. Although Hall
tries to base his psychology on biology and his discussion of adolescence
on physical data, there is a pronounced philosophical subtext in his work,
and, indeed, a clear division is made between the base, primitive qualities
of the "race," as he calls it, and the higher, more advanced qualities that
mark the rebirth of the individual during adolescence. The child learns
how to walk, but the adolescent learns how to love. Ultimately, in a markedly moral fashion, Hall categorizes this distinction between childhood
and adolescence, between the lower and higher qualities, between recapitulation and development, as a movement from selfishness to altruism: "In adolescence," he tells us, "individuation is suddenly augmented
and begins to sense its limits and its gradual subordination to the race
which the Fates prescribe." In a word: "Before youth must be served; now,
it must serve."[12]

Hall is very specific in his assertion that the only true path of development the species can follow through adolescence is an altruistic one, one
in which the individual looks away from him- or herself, looks beyond the
primitive qualities of selfishness, and engages in activities and emotions
that promote the "higher" species. One either moves forward through
these altruistic qualities, or one doesn't move at all. According to Hall,
there are certain societal changes that must take place in order to allow the
space for these new altruistic qualities to emerge in adolescence and to
flourish thereafter. Hall is somewhat indecisive and vague, however, in his
description of what these societal changes should be. On the one hand, he
asserts that the best way to allow the adolescent to take full advantage of
this intense period of growth and acquisition of new genetic qualities is
simply to leave him or her alone: "We are conquering nature, achieving a
magnificent material civilization," he states, "but we are progressively for-
getting that for the complete apprenticeship of life, youth needs repose,
leisure, art, legends, romance, idealization, and in a word humanism, if
it is to enter the kingdom of man well equipped for man's highest work
in the world."[13] Thus while the regimens and rules of adult society have
been useful in "conquering nature," what adolescents need are freedom
and space—"repose" and "leisure"—to acquire new genetic qualities that
will ultimately benefit the species. On the other hand, Hall is careful to
point out that this repose and leisure should not get out of hand—and, indeed, work and education will make certain that the adolescent develops
tendencies that will move the species forward rather than backward. As a
cure for the "secret vice"—which Hall would definitely see as symptomatic

of too much repose and leisure—he somberly suggests: "Regimen rather than special treatment must, however, be chiefly relied on. Work reduces temptation and so does early rising, while excessive mental or physical effort easily fatigues before the power of resistance, caused by rapid growth is acquired."[14]

It quickly becomes apparent to the reader of Hall's work that his theory of human development is based upon a contradiction. Hall's description of the individual's ability to acquire new traits is tempered—and indeed, countered—by his discussion of which traits are proper and which are not. As with many turn-of-the-century theorists and authors of narratives of adolescence, Hall finds a certain empowerment in the adolescent's ability to acquire new traits, because this ability offers a way out of what he sees as the problems with society, problems recapitulation theory equates with savagery. But he is also very uncomfortable with this facility and thus, with a pronounced pomposity, he undertakes to prescribe a strict moral code to be followed by the adolescent: "While adolescence is the great revealer of the past of the race," Hall explains, "its earlier stages must be ever surer and safer and the later possibilities ever greater and more prolonged, for it, and not maturity as now defined, is the only point of departure for the superanthropoid that man is to become. This can be only by an ever higher adolescence lifting him to a plane related to his present maturity as that is to the well-adjusted stage of boyhood where our puberty now begins its regenerating metamorphoses."[15] As the "point of departure," adolescence provides the only path out of the present predicament; it is the only space of true freedom.

Hall is fairly specific about the physical attributes he assigns to adolescence. The beginning of adolescence is marked by puberty, and puberty, he determines with much assuredness, is marked by hair: "Hair first develops in the pubic region at about fourteen in boys and thirteen in girls, generally before menstruation, later under the arm-pits just before the period of most rapid development of the breasts, and last comes the beard at the age of eighteen and nineteen." The appearance of pubic hair, menstruation, rapid growth, and the development of sexual and reproductive capacity are the physical signposts that mark the beginning of adolescence around the age of fourteen in boys and thirteen in girls.[16] This rapid period of growth tapers off between the years of eighteen to twenty, when the individual has reached his or her full size. These characteristics of rapid growth and heightened sexual feeling are summarized for Hall in the expression *Sturm und Drang,* or "storm and stress," a phrase he borrows from Goethe's *Sor-*

rows of Young Werther. More than any other characterization of adolescence, the notion of storm and stress will resurface in descriptions of this developmental stage throughout the twentieth century.

Perhaps more important than the unique physical characteristics of the adolescent is his or her ability to acquire new traits for the species. As he concludes in his preface to his two-volume treatise: "Adolescence is a new birth, for the higher and more completely human traits are now born. The qualities of body and soul that now emerge are far newer. The child comes from and harks back to a remoter past; the adolescent is neo-atavistic, and in him the later acquisitions of the race slowly become prepotent. Development is less gradual and more saltatory, suggestive of some ancient period of storm and stress when old moorings were broken and a higher level attained."[17] Although Hall distinguishes this path of adolescence from the period of savagery associated with the child, this path is still an uneven one, and the motif of storm and stress is a characteristic that has remained relentlessly tied to this developmental stage to this day.

The Stresslessness of Primitive Life

Although some critics complained about the length of Hall's magnum opus—which inspired him to publish a condensed version entitled *Youth: Its Education, Regimen, and Hygiene* three years later—by and large his work was heralded as the first theoretical treatment to capture the nature of this new and perplexing segment of modern society. In a review in the *New York Times* entitled "Stanley Hall on Youth's Problems, President of Clark University Discusses Adolescence—The 'Cave-Man' Period of Life," the reviewer—slightly misrepresenting Hall's theory but clearly understanding how his work would appeal to the reading public—promises, "Many a puzzled and despairing parent will be glad to learn from this volume that the reason why 'that boy is so bad' is not necessarily because he has started upon a downward road of wickedness and sin. Probably it is only because he has reached the age when it is necessary for him to live through the cave-man epoch of the race. . . . A little badness now, inconvenient for his elders, it is true, but not necessarily harmful, will make the child immune to worse things in after years."[18]

But this is not to say that *Adolescence* did not have its ardent critics. Many have noted the fact that Margaret Mead's three studies of adolescence in primitive cultures (*Coming of Age in Samoa, Growing Up in New Guinea,* and *Sex and Temperament in Three Primitive Societies*), which she composed in the 1920s and 1930s, were a direct reaction to G. Stanley

Hall's work and in particular the social evolutionary school of thought that informed it. And indeed, within the first few pages of *From the South Seas* (a compilation of these works, published in 1939), Mead takes direct aim at Hall: "In those days [when these works were written] it was important to show that the physiological changes of adolescence were not of themselves sufficient to account for the period of storm and stress through which our children passed, but that the ease or difficulty of this transition should be laid at the door of a different cultural setting."[19] In direct rebuttal to Hall's assertion that the storm and stress that characterizes adolescence has a biological origin, Mead turns to other cultures to show that these qualities are specific to American adolescents and thus can be attributed to social pressures that characterize American society. A comprehensive look at the three books Mead wrote about adolescence shows that although she often alludes to the same physical parameters as Hall when discussing adolescence, the social/cultural rituals that mark this space are as varied as the many tribes she visits throughout her exotic journeys.

Mead's first book on adolescence, *Coming of Age in Samoa*, puts her in a somewhat precarious position in terms of offering a definition of adolescence. On the one hand, she distinctly places adolescence between puberty and marriage, but on the other hand, she wants to emphasize that many of the aspects that are attributed to adolescence in modern American society are absent in the Samoan tribe. Thus while there are certain physical and cultural parameters that mark adolescence, these parameters always vary somewhat and are insignificant in the context of the broader development of the individual. In a word, adolescence, as Mead portrays it in this first study, exists but is "no big deal" in Samoa.

Although the Samoan community "ignores both boys and girls from birth until they are fifteen or sixteen years of age," the bodily changes that result from puberty, which Mead sets at around the age of thirteen or fourteen in the young girls, are also accompanied by an interest in the opposite sex. There is no social ceremony that marks the first menstruation in the Samoan girl but, according to Mead, there are some physical changes that mark the beginning of adolescence and a development of sexual and reproductive functions that is accompanied by a different attitude toward the opposite sex. A few years later, at age fifteen or sixteen, "both boys and girls are grouped into a rough approximation of the adult groupings, given a name for their organization, and are invested with definite obligations and privileges in the community life"; this movement into preconceived roles in the adult community marks a kind of end to the adolescent period.[20]

Thus, even though, in direct reaction to Hall, Mead uses her analysis of the Samoan girls to show that adolescence is a much less definable space in Samoa than in the West, we can nonetheless see some rough parameters emerging from her discussion. Adolescence begins with puberty and the accompanying changes in the physical body, and it ends with the taking on of "obligations" and "privileges" of the adult community; it is characterized by the development of sexual and reproductive capacities and marked by sexual desire; it takes place roughly between the ages of thirteen and sixteen.

Contrarily, in the Manus tribe—the focus of her second study of adolescence, *Growing Up in New Guinea*—the parameters of adolescence are much more concisely defined. There is an elaborate ceremony when the girl reaches puberty (and first menstruates); she then is delivered to the home of her betrothed, where she will spend a period of five to seven years with his family before marriage. Her adolescence is a period of waiting and learning the adult tasks of running a household. Mead states: "[T]hree or four years are spent as a rather bored, very much inhibited spectator to life, years during which she gets the culture by heart. . . . these years are not years of storm and stress, nor are they years of placid unfolding of the personality. They are years of waiting, years which are an uninteresting and not too exacting bridge between the free play of childhood and the obligations of marriage."[21]

The boy, on the other hand, at sometime between the ages of twelve and sixteen, gets his ears pierced (at the command of his mother and father), symbolizing his movement into adolescence. He then spends five to seven years working. Mead states: "War, war dances, heartless revels with one unwilling mistress, occupied the energy of the young men before marriage in the old days. . . . Today this picture is entirely altered. . . . Now all Manus boys go away to work—two years, five years, sometimes seven years—for the white man."[22] Male adolescence is characterized by sexual experimentation and learning the ways of an alien culture. Upon the boy's return, he and his intended bride must "submit" to marriage—they have little choice in a matter mostly arranged by their families—and after their marriage they are considered adults in the society, their days of childhood "play" over. The parameters of adolescence in the Manus tribe are thus fairly distinct for both sexes.

The parameters of the space of adolescence in the lives of the youth in the three tribes on which Mead focuses in her third book on adolescence, *Sex and Temperament in Three Primitive Societies,* once again, are as wide-ranging as the cultures of the tribes themselves. Toward the end of the book, Mead concludes: "As the Arapesh made growing food and children the greatest adventure of their lives, and the Mundugumor found greatest satisfaction in fighting and competitive acquisition of women, the Tchambuli may be said to live principally for art."[23] And indeed, her discussion of the Arapesh, Mundugumor, and Tchambuli tribes serves to illustrate her point that while there are some basic parameters to adolescence, many of its qualities are socially determined.

In the Arapesh tribe, the boy must observe various taboos once he reaches puberty, which is determined often by the first appearance of his pubic hair. These taboos can last up to a year for the boy. The mark of the initiation into the adult community is taking part in the *tamberan* ceremony. Each year the tamberan, a monstrous deity, visits the village and stays in the tamberan house. The men are allowed to go into the tamberan house, which is off limits to women and children. Every six or seven years, young boys of varying ages are separated from the women for a period of two to three months, subjected to various eating taboos, circumcised, and shown marvelous things (masks, carvings, representations, etc.), but most important they are told that there really is no tamberan at all—all the noise and commotion of the tamberan is created by the men. At the end of the initiation, the boy returns to the tribe and to his relatives, from whom he receives presents. Mead states: "His childhood is ended. From one who has been grown by the daily carefulness and hard work of others, he now passes into the class to those whose care is for others' growth. During his pubescence his care was for his own growth, for the observances of the taboo would ensure to him muscle and bone, height and breadth, and strength to beget and rear children. . . . Now this care is shifted and he has instead new responsibilities towards those who after years devoted to his growth are now growing old themselves, and towards his younger brothers and sisters, and his young betrothed wife."[24] As a symbol of this shifting of power, the father formally retires when his son enters the tamberan cult or when his daughter reaches puberty.

An Arapesh girl is betrothed when she is seven or eight to a boy roughly six years her senior, and she goes to live in his home. At the girl's first menstruation, the men in her new family build a menstrual hut, where she will fast for the next five days. Her body is rubbed with nettles and her uncle carves decorative marks on her body. Her new husband makes a ceremonial meal, and she is decorated and presented to her husband. Later the couple will put on a feast for everyone involved in the initiation. Mead summarizes the end of the girl's childhood: "This ceremony which officially ends a girl's childhood is of another order from a boy's initiation, although it has many elements in common with it. . . . the boy passes from one way of life into another; before, he was a boy, now he is a man with a man's responsibilities and therefore he may share in the secrets of men. For the girl there is no such emphasis. . . . Her puberty ceremony is no ritual admission to an order of life, but merely a ritual bridging of a physiological crisis that is important to her health and to her growth." Whereas in the boy's case adulthood is marked by entrance into the tamberan cult, in the case of the Arapesh girl, adulthood is marked by the marriage ceremony, for the period between the beginning of puberty and marriage (sometimes up to a year), as in New Guinea culture, is really one of waiting. Mead states: "No one is fairer or gayer in the whole of Arapesh than these young girls waiting, in lovely attire, for life at last to catch up with them. . . . The girl is fully mature now. The boy is tall and well developed. Some day the two, who are now allowed to go about alone together in the bush, will consummate their marriage, without haste, without a due date to hurry them with its inevitableness, with no one to know or to comment, in response to a situation in which they have lived comfortably for years in the knowledge that they belong to each other."[25]

The diversity and hostility of the second tribe Mead discusses in *Sex and Temperament in Three Primitive Societies*, the Mundugumor, make for difficulties in isolating a common progression of stages, of which adolescence is one. As Mead points out, "It is characteristic of Mundugumor conditions that it is not possible to discuss the development of children as an orderly process in which all young people of a certain age have similar experiences." Sometime before he is an adolescent, the Mundugumor boy possibly has been sent as a hostage to a neighboring tribe or "dispatched" as a captive for a cannibal feast. As a result of all this Spartan training, "pre-adolescent Mundugumor children have an appearance of harsh maturity and, aside from sex-experience, are virtually assimilated to the individualistic patterns of their society by the time they are twelve to thirteen."[26]

Both Mundugumor boys and girls participate in a tamberan ritual, but this ritual seems more for the benefit of the feast givers, who get a chance to torture and abuse the youngsters, than a way of marking a sense of age, identity, or community responsibility: "[T]he adolescent boys," Mead tells us, "are rounded up with blows and curses and scarified with crocodile-skulls, a sadistic exercise that obviously pleases their tormentors. Initiation does not come at any stated period, but is a matter of the time when a big man gives an initiation ceremony, so that it occurs several times in the life of a boy or a girl from twelve to past twenty or so. These are not *rites de passage*, rituals that tide the individual over changes in his life; they are merely something to which one's society subjects one, if one is a boy, permits one, if one is a girl, at a time when one is still young and immature."[27]

Marriage, as a marker of development, is equally random and meaningless among the Mundugumor. Most marriages are based on individual preference, but there are a series of laws regarding the family's ownership of its daughter that often leads to violent conflicts when a marriage is consummated. All in all, there is very little space for a stage such as adolescence in the Mundugumor tribe, as the individuals mature very early and are not controlled by tribal myths and beliefs that they must learn and apply to themselves.

And finally, according to Mead, the life of the third tribe she discusses in *Sex and Temperament in Three Primitive Societies*, the Tchambuli, revolves almost solely around art and ceremony, which means that often the ceremonies and rituals that accompany a movement through a stage of development (such as puberty or adolescence) are done for the sake of the ceremony rather than for the sake of the individual child. At some point between the ages of eight and twelve, "a period that is not determined by his age so much as by his father's ceremonial ambitions," the young Tchambuli boy is taken outside and held down while designs are carved into his back.[28] He then must stay in seclusion for an indeterminate period of time, until his father feels it is the right time to throw a ceremonial feast. At the feast, the boy is given presents and he then begins to court the woman who will become his wife, one of the daughters of his mother's half brothers or cousins. He often pays for the bride with some of the presents he earned during the ceremony. Mead makes no mention of rituals that mark the development of the Tchambuli girl.

Thus, from the circumcision of the Samoan boy to the first menstruation ceremony of the young girl in New Guinea, from the elaborate tamberan ceremony of the Arapesh boy to the significant lack of ritual for either the girl or boy in the Mundugumor tribe, the rites that mark adolescence are as varied as the cultures in which they are practiced. And even though Mead sometimes alludes to the same physical parameters as Hall when discussing adolescence, her works serve to make the point that many of the qualities that characterize this space are cultural constructions.

But while Mead was most certainly working against Hall's "return to biology," she also, as a fellow inventor of adolescence, was working, like him, to come to terms with Freudian psychoanalysis. In a blanket summation of the effect her trips to the South Seas had on her understanding of the Oedipus complex, in *Male and Female: A Study of the Sexes in a Changing World* (1949), Mead outlines what she calls "solutions" to the Oedipus conflict provided by each of the primitive cultures she observed, which, in one way or another, lessen the significance of the rivalry between father and son, leading her to conclude: "The term 'Oedipus conflict' has assumed an aura of unacceptability because it has taken its name from failure—from the unfortunate Oedipus who failed to solve the conflict— and not from the successful, though often compromised, solutions that each civilization has worked out." Mead goes on to show how in the Samoan civilization, the adult-child relationship is dispersed over the whole tribe, which is like a large family, and thus does not exist only between the child and his or her biological parents; this dispersal places less emphasis on the father-son relationship, and thus the father is less likely to fear that the son is vying for his position in relation to his wife. Similarly, the Samoan mother and father place no unrealistic demands upon their spouses and thus don't fear that the son will fulfill the mother in a way that the father never could. All in all, Mead concludes, "Perhaps more sharply than in any known society, Samoan culture demonstrates how much the tragic or easy solution to the Oedipus situation depends upon the interrelationship between parents and children, and is not created out of whole cloth by the young child's biological impulses."[29]

In the case of the Mundugumor tribe, the intense triangle formed between the father and son and daughter eclipses any Oedipal struggle. The daughter in the Mundugumor tribe can be exchanged with another family for a second wife for the father or a first wife for the son. The mother and son often try to save the sister until the son has reached the proper age where he can trade her for a wife; but this attempt is always threatened by the father, who may try to trade the daughter for his own benefit while the son is still young. In this case, "[t]he issues are clearly drawn, the Oedipus situation is solved in a way that sets every man's hand against every man."[30]

With the Arapesh tribe, the emphasis is on obtaining food, and the almost identical function each parent plays for the child in satisfying this desire makes an identification with one parent over another (for example, the son's alliance with the mother against the father) out of the question. All in all, "[i]n this society where the nexus between males is not their competition for women, but their common enterprise of feeding people of all ages and both sexes, attention is shifted from the specificity of the Oedipus struggle to the internal battle that each individual must fight with his own impulses if he or she is to be in turn fertile and able to grow human beings. The parents remain allies in the child's battle, laying no heavy prohibitions, not fighting back, not simulating the child by providing him with a strong and dangerous opponent."[31]

According to Mead, then, various societies posit solutions to the Oedipus complex by restructuring social relationships in order to collapse the triangle Freud posits as the root of the infantile conflict and all subsequent maturation. Mead uses adolescence as a case study to demonstrate the cultural relativity of the Oedipal conflict, a relativity that she did not think Freud, for whatever reasons, emphasized sufficiently. According to Mead, modern society creates the Oedipus complex in a number of specific ways. The close relationship between parent and child makes submission to, or defiance of, the parent the "dominating pattern of a lifetime."[32] The focus on materialism means that parents are seen not as wiser but rather richer and therefore "in the saddle." The characteristic absence of the working father in the son's life means that sons will develop a close relationship with their mother and see their father only as a threat, as his shadow "falls just far enough across their young activities to spoil them."[33]

The specific structure of adolescence in culture is what causes the storm and stress that characterizes this developmental stage. Like Hall, Mead provides a path of rehabilitation, but unlike Hall's, her path does not consist of a series of morally correct patterns of behavior. The way to avoid storm and stress is simply for society to curb its demands. Mead argues that Americans ought to make this time of adolescence more like it is for the primitive societies she has studied. In the final pages of *Coming of Age in Samoa*, Mead concludes:

> The principal causes of [Western] adolescents' difficulty are the presence of conflicting standards and the belief that every individual should make his or her own choices, coupled with a feeling that choice is an important matter. Given these cultural attitudes, adolescence, regarded now not as a period of physiological change,

for we know that physiological puberty need not produce conflict, but as the beginning of mental and emotional maturity, is bound to be filled with conflicts and difficulties. A society which is clamoring for choice, which is filled with many articulate groups, each urging its own brand of salvation, its own variety of economic philosophy, will give each new generation no peace until all have chosen or gone under, unable to bear the conditions of choice. The stress is in our civilization, not in the physical changes through which our children pass, but is none the less real nor the less inevitable in twentieth century America.[34]

Mead argues that modern American culture wants to move its individuals too quickly from childhood to adulthood. Society provides the individual with a number of options and then demands that a choice be made quickly. American culture is too comfortable with the possibility that the child's desire could be at odds with the choices made. What is needed is for society to open up more space between childhood and adulthood, giving the individual more freedom to contemplate choice and thus find happiness.

Prescriptions for the New Century

In the texts that mark the invention of adolescence, we can see a definition of this space forming that will reverberate throughout twentieth-century American culture in a variety of ways. Although the specifics vary—particularly in Mead's studies of primitive tribes—both Hall and Mead rely upon some very basic physical parameters of adolescence: the developmental stage is rooted in the onset of puberty and ends with the individual's assimilation into the adult world; this assimilation is usually marked by some cultural event, such as a marriage or the assumption of an adult role. In terms of age, adolescence runs roughly through the period of the teens. This period is marked by a tremendous amount of growth and the beginnings of active sexual desire.

While, for the most part, Hall focuses on adolescent boys in his work and Mead focuses on girls, they both make a point of claiming that their observations are equally applicable to both sexes. Thus the lengthy discussions of the massive amount of physical growth during adolescence in Hall's work focus both on boys and girls, and in the chapter "Adolescent Girls and Their Education," he concludes that "[m]any of the above features [of the ideal education and curriculum of the adolescent girl] would be as helpful for boys and girls."[35] Similarly, although Mead chooses to focus *Coming of Age in Samoa* on female adolescence, she concludes that "[b]ecause the discussion is principally concerned with girls, I shall discuss the problem from the girl's point of view, but in many respects the plight of the adolescent boy is very similar."[36] And indeed, there is, despite Mead's disclaimers, arguably as much data about the boys' behavior in the primitive tribes in her three books on adolescence as there is about the girls.'

This attempt to make adolescence gender neutral might be seen as a way of ignoring the problem of gender and thus avoiding the fact that, socially, female adolescents did not have access to many of the same opportunities as did their male counterparts at the turn of the century. Also, this attempt to downplay the issue of gender in Hall's and Mead's discussions of adolescence might be interpreted as a reaction to the largely male-centered focus of Freud's work, especially since, as we have seen, both Hall and Mead voiced their dissatisfaction with the Oedipal paradigm. On a broader level, keeping adolescence genderless helped these theorists emphasize the universality of the developmental stage. To the degree that the characteristics of adolescence are applicable to both genders, traditional gender distinctions and gender roles appear less significant and more fluid.

This is, of course, not to overlook the many traditional—and in the case of Hall, the many sexist—generalizations made about gender in these early treatments of adolescence: for example, Hall's quite controversial assertion that "woman's body and soul are made for maternity" and his criticisms of all educational practices that do not address this fundamental fact.[37] Once again, this slippery attitude toward gender is evidence of the contradictory stance regarding adolescence developing in the early decades of the twentieth century. The anxiety created by positing a space where gender is more fluid results in the enforcement of the most traditional gender roles. As with juvenile delinquency, these early constructions of adolescence partake of a double discourse: notions of recapitulation were used to posit adolescence as a universal experience, but the rehabilitative path that adolescence offered was gender specific and often misogynistic.

In any case, Hall and Mead are aligned regarding many of the basic parameters of adolescence, and their articulations of these were immensely influential and continue to reverberate to this day. But on a broader level, it's important to note that they are also closely aligned in the rehabilitative promise of their work. Although both of their definitions of adolescence pretend to be objective observations of this new demographic population, they ultimately turn out to be more theoretical suggestions as to what adolescents could become if a correct path of development is pursued. Hall suggests that if adolescents pursue the "higher traits" of altruism and self-denial, then they will develop in the correct direction of the race. Adolescence, ultimately, is altruism and self-denial. Mead argues that if society would only change its social structures, which place too many demands on the adolescent, then the conflict between generations and the pressure to find one's path would disappear. Adolescence, ultimately, should be "no big deal," as exemplified by primitive cultures.

Arguably, it is this rehabilitative quality of their work that made them so immensely popular in American society, because their prescriptions for adolescence and the squeaky-clean ideal they envision became the theoretical justification for youth groups, advice manuals, and social movements that provided a plan to deal with this seemingly new demographic group. But, also, as rehabilitative texts, the works of Hall and Mead are predicated upon the notion that there is a problem to be solved, and this negative image of adolescence has greatly informed twentieth-century American attitudes as well. Enticingly vague in its details, this problem that looms in the early definitions of adolescence is the fear of what harm this population might inflict if left undefined and uncontrolled. The details of this problem remain powerfully fuzzy in the vague, yet evocative, terms Hall and Mead use to describe it. None of these terms is more powerful than the figurative phrase *storm and stress*. Hall cuts right to the chase in the preface to his two-volume work, letting the phrase, which would have been quite familiar to his literate audience, stand on its own: "Adolescence is a new birth, for the higher and more completely human traits are now born. . . . Development is less gradual and more saltatory, suggestive of some ancient period of storm and stress when old moorings were broken and a higher level attained."[38] According to Hall's recapitulation approach, the fact that this storm and stress is "ancient" implies that it does not necessarily require any explanation; it is a "trait," like vertical posture or opposable thumbs.

In Mead's first work on adolescence, she lets Hall's infamous phrase speak for itself and, ironically, even though she will go on to question his approach, she will never question his tacit assumption that there is a problem in the first place: "If it is proved that adolescence is not necessarily a specially difficult period in a girl's life—and proved it is if we can find any society in which that is so—then what accounts for the presence of storm and stress in American adolescents? . . . What is there in Samoa which is absent in America, what is there in America which is absent in Samoa, which will account for the difference?"[39] Deciphering what accounts for the storm and stress assumes it is already there. Mead's work on South Seas' culture has come in for considerable criticism, especially her findings in *Coming of Age in Samoa*. Most famously, Derek Freeman has taken Mead to task for, among other things, the inaccuracy of her data and her choice of disproving the biological basis of storm and stress by citing a "negative instance" in which this biologically determined problem does not exist. In his critique, Freeman also ponders why Mead's theories were so wholeheartedly accepted, even though their science was suspect, reaching the conclusion that this acceptance was in part due to the desperate need on the part of many scientists of the time to find some "factual" data to support their theoretical arguments as to the prevalence of nurture over nature in the development of human behavior. One wonders, though, to what extent her book and its notions of adolescence storm and stress were accepted by scientists and the reading public alike because they fulfilled a need to verify certain popular notions of American adolescents out of control. Although she argues that storm and stress is social in nature, she still takes as her supposition that it exists. In this case, we get not only the depiction of the American adolescent out of control but also the ideal Samoan adolescent, the doppelgänger that all the more enforces the severity of the "problem" here at home. Such a scientific affirmation of a popular belief must have been extremely attractive to an American reading public, which, as we have seen, projected many fears of modern society upon this new and unknown population. This is strangely revealed in a review of *Coming of Age in Samoa* that appeared in the *Nation*—a review that Freeman cites in his study—in which the writer contemplates the benefits of the "fantasy" adolescence of the South Seas but opts for the storm and stress that has become so familiar with the adolescents at home: "[The Samoan girl's] life as well as her environment apparently fits the fantasy that has become a symbol of relaxation and release to the harried child of the machine-made West. Would we then exchange our unsatisfied desires and complicated choices for her more even progress in the world? Probably not. . . . In the first place personality and individual differences, the objects of such tender consideration in most western lands, are ignored. . . . The whole basis for emotional intensity is lacking."[40] In this case, storm and stress is a critical component of individuality, one of the most cherished qualities of our democracy. American society needed adolescent conflict: whether it was biological, sociological, or both was of little concern.

Part of the appeal of this expression, which has remained relentlessly tethered to this developmental stage to this day, must simply be its vagueness, the fact that storm and stress could mean practically anything; and since both Hall and Mead refrain from defining it in any specific way—but nonetheless proffer elaborate prescriptions for its solution—it can be taken at face value and applied to almost any behavior. The "problem" that these definitions of adolescence solve is whatever fears and anxieties the reader takes to the page.

But furthermore, even though they rely on terms such as storm and stress to blur the edges of the problem they are solving in their work, Hall and Mead also return to various motifs that most assuredly reverberated with early twentieth-century American readers. One of these was the rising threat of juvenile delinquency discussed in the last chapter. "Hoodlumism" was of great concern to Hall, so much so that he devoted one of the longest chapters of his two-volume work to the problem. He opens this chapter with a warning, which must have rung true to his early twentieth-century American readers: "In all civilized lands, criminal statistics show two sad and significant facts: First, that there is a marked increase of crime at the age of twelve to fourteen, not in crimes of one, but of all kinds, and that this increase continues for a number of years. . . . The second fact is that the proportion of juvenile delinquents seems to be everywhere increasing and crime is more and more precocious."[41] As was discussed in chapter 1, even though there was a pronounced hysteria about the rise in juvenile delinquency at the turn of the century, statistics verifying such a rise were largely nonexistent. Hall's work is no different. Remarkably, even though he asserts that the proportion of juvenile delinquents "seems to be" increasing, he provides no statistical evidence to support this. All of the data he cites serve to enforce his point that crime increases with age—quite a different conjecture. And even the evidence to support this point is questionable. Most of the statistics that swell Hall's chapter on delinquency are from studies in European countries because, of course, no reliable statistics existed for the United States. As with many theorists of juvenile delinquency at the time, Hall relies on figures from the 1890 census to support his observations but, as we have seen, these figures were incomplete. These figures also, of course, do not testify to any increase in crime, since they reflect only one year. Hall is aware of this, however, so he uses these statistics to bolster his argument that the number of individuals put in reform school "naturally" increases from age seven to fifteen; such a conclusion is problematic in itself, since this might just mean that judges were more apt to put the older children in reform school or simply that more older kids got caught.

In any case, juvenile delinquents "seemed" to be everywhere increasing in Hall's eyes and, given his attempt to rebase psychology on biology, it is perhaps no surprise that he provides a recapitulation approach to these "sad and significant facts." According to Hall, these criminal tendencies are just echoes of earlier stages in the evolution of the race. So, for example, the antisocial life of crime is a reversion to the "nomadic life" of an earlier civilization, theft is just an echo of a more primitive attitude toward property, and pyromania an expression of primitive fire worship.[42] As was touched upon in the last chapter, such an approach to juvenile delinquency would have been quite familiar to Hall's readers. In his popular 1897 book *Juvenile Offenders*—which Hall cites at length in this chapter— W. Douglas Morrison has this to say about the causes of crime during the teen years: "It will thus be seen that the evolution of criminal characteristics follows in the main the evolution of the organism, and is largely dependent upon its growth and development. In the early stages of life the first anti-social impulse which comes into collision with the criminal law is the vagrant instinct; next comes the instinct which manifests itself in offences against property; finally comes the instinct which shows itself in offences against the person."[43] Such explanations of juvenile delinquency fit well with the prevailing bioevolutionary approaches to crime popularized by Cesare Lombroso and others at the turn of the century—which argued that criminals were set apart from other human beings by perceptible biological differences—but recapitulation also had the added benefit of essentializing criminal tendencies as "instincts" and "impulses" and thus made these qualities seem as natural in the developing boy or girl as pubic hair and breasts. Whether juvenile delinquency was on the rise or not is irrelevant because the "vagrant instinct" and the "instinct" for "offences against the person" are inherent traits in the adolescent that can be corrected only through enforced patterns of behavior. As everyone knows, the problem exists; what we need is a feasible solution. Or else.[44]

Although Mead also raises the specter of juvenile delinquency in her works on adolescence, her description of the "problem" of the American adolescent is much closer to home.[45] As we have seen earlier, part of the American adolescent's "neurosis," as Mead characterizes it, arises from conflicting standards of behavior and the fact that teens are faced with a dizzying array of choices. Also, the structure of the American family leads to an inevitable conflict that gives the adolescent no choice but to rebel. In contrasting the American and Samoan family structures in *Coming of Age in Samoa,* for example, Mead concludes that "[t]he close relationship between parent and child, which has such a decisive influence upon so many in our civilization, that submission to the parent or defiance of the parent may become the dominating pattern of a lifetime, is not found in Samoa." The teen is given very little choice in the equation: whether it's submission or defiance, both lead to neurosis. Such an unavoidable conflict between parent and child and the inevitable form of teen rebellion can take many forms, but one of the more pronounced is purely economical. Mead states:

> Because of the essentially pecuniary nature of our society, the relationship of limitation in terms of allowance to limitation of behaviour are more far-reaching than in earlier times. Parental disapproval of extreme styles of clothing would formerly have expressed itself in a mother's making her daughter's dresses high in the neck and long in the sleeve. Now it expresses itself in control through money. . . . The daughters come to see all censoring of their behaviour, moral, religious or social, the ethical code and the slightest sumptuary provisions in terms of an economic threat. And then at sixteen or seventeen the daughter gets a job. . . . Her parents' chief instrument of discipline is shattered at one blow, but not their desire to direct their daughters' lives. They have not pictured their exercise of control as the right of those who provide, to control those for whom they provide. They have pictured it in far more traditional terms, the right of parents to control their children, an attitude reinforced by years of practicing such control.[46]

The inevitable struggle for control with these individuals who were not quite children and not yet adults must have reverberated with an early twentieth-century reading audience, especially since, as we saw in chapter 1, Americans were coming to terms with the sudden and pronounced presence of this teen population and adjusting to the various ways in which this presence disrupted traditional family structures. The economic problem of a sixteen-year-old child living at home and not providing additional income was a common fact at the turn of the century. How to exert control over this child/adult must have been a common anxiety.[47]

In addition to these anxieties about adolescence out of control, Hall and Mead are aligned in how they envision part of the "problem" of adolescence as related to the onset of sexual desire. This, as we have seen, came out in their criticisms of Freud's work. It might be argued, though, that their disagreements with Freud were less about whether the Oedipus complex was properly named and more about a type of sexual permissiveness that was associated with his work. Hall and Mead can be seen in some sense as being part of the larger American reaction to Freud in the early decades of the twentieth century, which equated Freudianism with "modern sexuality." As Nathan Hale has argued in his historical analysis of the American reception of psychoanalysis, criticisms of Freud often centered around some common "legends": "Then enemies of psychoanalysis constructed their counter-legends. These began, perhaps, with the neurologist Francis X. Dercum, the humanist Paul Elmer More, and reached their apogee in Oscar Cargill, the literary historian, and the sociologist Richard La Pierre. 'Freudian doctrine,' they held, prescribed primitivism, sexual liberation, pessimistic determinism, permissiveness, and decadence."[48] According to Hale, two common criticisms of Freud's work were that the direct correlation he drew between infantile experiences and adult behavior was overly "deterministic," and his discussions of infantile sexuality were "obscene." These criticisms can most certainly be seen in Hall's work, which, as we have seen, criticizes Freud for being "unduly sexually-minded" and posits adolescence as a time when the individual acquires new character traits that are not explained by the Oedipus complex. Similarly, these criticisms parallel Mead's discussion of Oedipal "solutions," which attempts to prove the cultural relativity of the Oedipus complex and thus suggest that it is not entirely determining of adult behavior. Both Hall and Mead use a discussion of adolescence as a way of facilitating these criticisms. It is perhaps no surprise that adolescence was invented at the time that Freud's ideas were being disseminated throughout Western society. As with Hall and Mead, adolescence became a way of questioning the Freudian conception of human development. The argument that this conception was too "deterministic" was, in a sense, bolstered by introducing adolescence as a developmental stage in which the individual could attain new beliefs and posturings. The discomfort with infantile sexuality was, in a sense, answered by adolescence, which became a way of shifting the most sexually active period closer to adulthood.

But on a broader scale, Hall's and Mead's work spoke to something deeper than just anxiety about determinism and infantile sexuality; Freud to a certain degree served as a symbol of sexual permissiveness, modern sexual attitudes, and one of the "problems" of adolescence was the threat that sexuality could get out of control. Hall's recapitulation approach leads him to conclude that sexuality, if not contained and controlled, will simply prevent the individual and the species from evolving. For example, on the topic of "the secret vice," he says:

> These effects [of masturbation] might perhaps be summed up as phenomena of arrest. Growth, especially in the moral and intellectual regions, is dwarfed and stunted. There are early physical signs of decrepitude and senescence. . . . While it can not, of course, be mathematically demonstrated, it is nevertheless probable that worse and earlier than any of these psychic effects are those that appear in offspring. Beginning with the gradual descendance rather than ascendance of the long line of posterity in proportion as the evil has become more intense, its effects are manifest, nearer, perhaps, in the incomplete maturity of mind and body in the next generation.[49]

Indeed, no math is needed to understand this equation: adolescents will masturbate and therefore humanity will fail to evolve.

And as with the various other characteristics of adolescence, ultimately Hall layers a moral imperative on this "biological truth." As Gail Bederman has observed about Hall in her book *Manliness & Civilization,* adolescence, as a theoretical construct, provided him with a way to come to terms with anxieties about sexuality that plagued many men at the turn of the century. How could a man be the virile and passionate pioneer of his race but not waste this vital energy through sin and decadence? The answer appeared in adolescence:

> Here, then [in the stage of adolescence], Hall had found a solution to the problem of manly self-restraint, which had tormented him since his own adolescence. Sex was not dirty; it was holy. It was God's means of creating healthier human specimens and more advanced races. In *Adolescence,* Hall waxed lyrical about the ecstatic, almost holy, pleasures of sex and orgasm, which he described as "the sacred hour of heredity." . . . Hall believed that for healthy, married adults, God was love, and love was Godly. Sex was designed for pro-

creation; procreation was the mechanism of evolution; and evolution was God's way of progressing towards the millennium.[50]

Sexual desire, according to Hall, is a "natural" part of adolescence, from both a biological and a philosophical perspective. But such desire must be contained and used for a proper purpose, if the race is to evolve in the right direction.

The "primitive" villages visited by Mead in her studies of adolescence would appear to be Hall's worst nightmare. Communities such as Samoa, where masturbation, homosexual relationships, casual affairs, and sex in public settings are commonplace and accepted as the normal way of life, would undoubtedly serve as fodder for Hall's racist conclusions about the enlightened path of Western, Christian civilization. Mead draws conclusions from her observations of this sexual permissiveness, and its contrast with America, that are quite the opposite of Hall's. For her, it is the conflicting standards of morality in America that ultimately cause neurosis in the adolescent. About sixteen-year-old American girls, she observes: "It is at about this time that sex begins to play a role in the girl's life, and here also conflicting choices are presented to her. If she chooses the freer standards of her own generation, she comes in conflict with her parents, and perhaps more importantly with the ideals which her parents have instilled. The present problem of the sex experimentation of young people would be greatly simplified if it were conceived of as experimentation instead of as rebellion, if no Puritan self-accusations vexed their consciences."[51] Such experimentation is the norm in the "primitive" societies that Mead visits, and she makes it appear quite harmless. In contrast to the tortured logic of Hall's high moralism, Mead's liberal attitude must have rung true to many of her more progressive readers.

But it's important to note that such experimentation in these societies is framed within a conservative narrative of heterosexual marriage. If there is experimentation, it takes place during the teen years and ceases during marriage. Consider the following passage on homosexual relationships in Samoa:

> The general preoccupation with sex, the attitude that minor sex activities, suggestive dancing, stimulating salacious conversation, salacious songs and definitely motivated tussling are all acceptable and attractive diversions, is mainly responsible for the native attitude to-

wards homosexual practices. They are simply play, neither frowned upon nor given much consideration. As heterosexual relations are given significance not by love and a tremendous fixation upon one individual, the only forces which can make homosexual relationship lasting and important, but by children and the place of marriage in the economic and social structure of the village, it is easy to understand why very prevalent homosexual practices have no more important or striking results.[52]

Sexuality is polymorphous in Samoan culture, but ultimately such "play" is subsumed by the more important work of marriage and childbearing. So while sexual experimentation has its benefits in that it relaxes a Puritan morality that creates neurosis in the American adolescent, it is still sexual experimentation, appropriate only in a specific time and place. Along the same lines, it's important to note that this time and place in Mead's work is adolescence. Even though Mead attempts to demonstrate in her work that adolescence is a culturally constructed category that shapes the behaviors of teens, sexuality, in all its wild and exotic forms, becomes an essential quality of this developmental stage; it is essentialized in her observations of its existence in "primitive" cultures.

The Raw and the Cooked, the Real and the Ideal

As they react both to recapitulation theories of childhood on the one hand and "modern" notions of sexuality on the other, G. Stanley Hall and Margaret Mead look back to the nineteenth century and forward to the twentieth century. Their theories of adolescence provide a path that, if followed correctly, will help adolescents develop in the "right" direction, but this path is based upon a theoretical construct, an idealized adolescent. Furthermore, this idealized adolescent implies a "real" adolescent who is just as fictional and is everybody's worst nightmare. The ideal adolescent acquires moral traits for his or her species, is controlled, and always does the right thing. The real adolescent, as much a fiction as his or her counterpart, is out of control, a physical threat, and overtly sexual. Like Jekyll and Hyde, the two constructs need one another to survive and are locked in a dance that has remained endlessly fascinating for readers, propelled forward by both adoration and fear. As we shall see in the following chapters, the ideal adolescent is the inspiration for a blossoming of youth organizations, social movements, and books that inspire good behavior.

The real adolescent looms in the shadows of these texts as the hooligan, the cheat, and the savage. It's not until the middle of the century that the real adolescent comes into his or her own, enjoying a renaissance in young adult literature and flaunting his or her own moniker: "the teenager." At that point, the ideal adolescent takes the form of the "square," the "geek," and the "nerd," and the whole process starts all over again.

3
Every Vigorous Race
Age and Indian Reform Movements

Kill the Adolescent, Save the Man

In an autobiographical account of the founding of one of the first and most prominent American Indian boarding schools, Richard Henry Pratt describes how far the Carlisle Indian Industrial School and the movement it represented had come by 1904, the year he retired as superintendent:

> In 1875 the total enrollment of Indian youth in Government and church schools, exclusive of the Five Civilized Tribes, was 6,101. . . . In 1904 . . . there was a total enrollment in schools from these tribes of nearly five times as many. . . . In 1875 practically all the tribes stumbled along in their business affairs and intercourse with whites through paid interpreters. . . . In 1904 young Indians from all the tribes taught in the schools to speak English had removed all necessity for paid interpreters. . . . In 1875 few Indians ever ventured beyond their tribal limits. . . . In 1904 multitudes were so living among the whites, and hundreds had entirely separated from their tribes and gone into employments among whites in city and country throughout the United States, many of them highly esteemed in the communities in which they lived for their industry, skill, and good character.[1]

Although history would take issue with the positive effects of schools such as Carlisle, Pratt was correct in regard to their popularity. By the turn of the century, twenty-five Indian boarding schools were in operation in the United States, and Pratt's philosophy of assimilation—encapsulated in his infamous goal to "kill the Indian, save the man"—had been by and large the standard of government policy for at least two decades.

The sudden and pronounced rise of these Indian boarding schools is rarely mentioned in association with the broader educational reforms discussed in chapter 1, but these movements had much in common. Although, as many critics have argued, Indian boarding schools used education as a guise for racial discrimination and, in some instances, genocide, they were motivated by many of the same fears that fueled the expansion of the American high school and college and the renaissance of American youth movements at the turn of the century. The expansion of Indian boarding schools was largely informed by prevailing social evolutionary theories that justified the superiority of white, Protestant culture over the supposed "barbarism" of the American Indian. This methodology was also greatly informed by age and, as such, the evolutionary paradigm became an appropriate developmental paradigm, which naturalized certain conceptions of the child, adult, and adolescent. Pratt's goal to "kill the Indian, save the man" is an age paradigm as much as it is an evolutionary paradigm, whereby becoming a "man"—which in this case meant a specific type of white man—was symbolic of movement into the stable adult position and therefore in direct contrast to what comes before, what must be killed.

The process of becoming an adult was a type of artificial adolescence imposed upon Native American youth, who were taught how to behave and therefore defined as potentially ungovernable, volatile, and a threat. Native Americans and adolescents were asked to save themselves, but ultimately boarding schools, rehabilitative as they were, intended to save society from a new generation that threatened traditions and beliefs that were at the root of this country's national identity. Such a rehabilitative program was far from seamless, however, and gave rise to a type of "crisis of identity" in the assimilated Native American. This crisis can most explicitly be seen in the many autobiographical accounts written by students in these schools.

Savagery and the Simple Child of Nature

Richard Henry Pratt was a Civil War veteran and career army officer. In spring of 1875, he was put in charge of seventy-two prisoners from the Arapaho, Cheyenne, Kiowa, and Comanche nations who were being transported from Fort Leavenworth in Kansas to Fort Marion in St. Augustine, Florida. Convinced that "the duty of the Government to these

Indians seems to me to be the teaching of them something that will be permanently useful to them," Pratt engaged his captives in a variety of enterprises, from fishing to instructing the local townspeople in archery.[2] He also insisted that they cut their hair and dress in old army uniforms, and eventually brought a local schoolteacher to the prison to teach them to read and write. In 1878, supposedly due to Pratt's successful reforming efforts, the prisoners were set free. At their behest, Pratt enrolled seventeen of the newly freed prisoners in the Hampton Institute, an agricultural school for African Americans in Virginia. These students did so well that the War Department enlisted Pratt as a recruiter.

But Pratt had his sights set on an entirely separate school for Native Americans. The realization of his dream came in 1879 when the army allowed him access to the vacant cavalry barracks in Carlisle, Pennsylvania. Pratt's first recruits were from the Sioux tribes. He reveals in his memoirs that this was a choice made by the government, which hoped the "children, if brought east, would become hostages for tribal good behavior."[3] His first class of 147 students arrived on October 9, 1879. The education at Carlisle was largely industrial; in addition to learning to read and write, the students learned trades: blacksmithing, wagon building, and harness making for the boys; cooking, sewing, and laundry for the girls. Pratt's assimilationist approach was centered on three basic tenets. First, the youth who attended the school were entirely cut off not only from their families but also from their culture. They were forbidden to speak their native language and given new names. These restrictions were designed not only to achieve a total immersion in Anglo culture but also to instill a type of individualism. As Pratt wrote in a 1908 tract on the school, the individual "is the unit and all development throughout the history of the world has been and must continue [to be] an individual process."[4] Second, students had their hair cut and were made to wear matching military-style uniforms, based upon a belief that a physical transformation was the first step toward an internal transformation. Third, students were encouraged to socialize with society outside of the institution through "outings," during which they lived with families and worked in homes, businesses, or on farms.

Pratt was a master of public relations and word of the Carlisle Indian School spread fast. His infamous before-and-after pictures of "reformed" Indian youth were disseminated to local publications and members of Congress, and he developed extracurricular activities for the school that provided access into mainstream American culture. The Carlisle marching band, for instance, become a popular feature at local events, including

the October 1892 parade in New York City commemorating the quadri-
centennial of Columbus's discovery of the New World. And the Carlisle
School football team earned certain notoriety when Pratt invited college
teams such as Harvard, Yale, and Cornell to the Carlisle field for scrim-
mages. To publicize these accomplishments, Pratt instituted a magazine
for the school: the *Indian Craftsman*, which would later be renamed the
Red Man. This publication, which proudly proclaims on the first page to
be "a magazine not only about Indians, but mainly by Indians," was ostensibly for alumni but was also disseminated to friends of the school and
prominent American media outlets, which often picked up its stories.

As these stories, which appeared in *Outlook* and *Harper's Weekly*, would
proclaim, Pratt seemed to have reached a solution to the vexing "Indian
problem." But, as many scholars who have written about Carlisle and
similar boarding schools have since revealed, the results of such education more often than not led to a kind of crisis of identity for the Native American students. Even though the students at Carlisle learned
the trades that were becoming the lifeblood of the modern American
economy, lingering racism often prevented skilled Native Americans from
getting the jobs for which they were trained. In his autobiography, *My
People the Sioux*, Luther Standing Bear, who was a member of the first
class at Carlisle, describes this conflict: "Vacation time was coming and
they were going to close the boarding-school for the summer. . . . I wanted
to continue my work at the store, as I was interested in it. . . . I tried very
hard to find a suitable place, but when I would find something that seemed
suitable, and the people discovered my nationality, they would look at
me in a surprised sort of way, and say that they had no place for an Indian boy."[5] Because of this lingering racism, many Carlisle graduates "returned to the blanket," as Pratt called it, but this only posed more problems. Through years of military-style training, many had not only lost
touch with the traditions of their tribes, but they had been taught to look
on these traditions with disdain. Furthermore, many were seen as traitors
to their family and tribe. Despite these problems, Pratt's school and others like it continued to thrive. The Carlisle Indian Industrial School stayed
open for thirty-nine years. During the twenty-four years that Pratt ran the
school, he saw 4,903 youth from seventy-seven different Indian nations
pass through its doors.[6]

The popularity of schools such as Carlisle, I would argue, can be attributed to three cultural factors, all of which ultimately relate to age and
the burgeoning developmental stage of adolescence. We have seen how a

fear of juvenile delinquency inspired and shaped the concept of adolescence. A similar fear of crime informs the justification for Indian boarding schools as well. Such a "natural" connection between Native Americans and delinquency can be seen in many of the popularly quoted treatises about the plague of homeless and wayward youth that were circulated in late nineteenth-century American society, such as Charles Loring Brace's well-known depiction of the corrupt children of the streets of New York discussed in chapter 1. Brace notes:

> There seemed to be a very considerable class of lads in New York who bore to the busy, wealthy world about them something of the same relation which Indians bear to the civilized Western settlers. They had no settled home, and lived on the outskirts of society, their hand against every man's pocket, and every man looking on them as natural enemies; their wits sharpened like those of a savage, and their principles often no better. Christianity reared its temples over them, and Civilization was carrying on its great work, while they— a happy race of little heathens and barbarians—plundered, or frolicked, or led their roving life, far beneath.[7]

The fact that Brace could use this negative portrayal of Native American culture as an object of comparison to enforce his point about homeless youth in New York testifies to how widely accepted and naturalized such beliefs about Native Americans must have been.

Although, as many critics have noted, the expansion of Indian boarding schools was seen by many reformers as meeting a desperate need to preserve a seemingly dying Native American society, I would argue that it was also largely motivated by fear. As Shari Huhndorf has demonstrated, even though, as the nineteenth century came to a close, the Indian was reimagined as an object of conquest, depictions of criminality persisted well into the twentieth century: "Until the mid-nineteenth century, captivity narratives describing the horrifying fates of noble settlers, often women, at the hands of violent savages typified accounts of European-American interactions with Natives. Later, dime novels adapted these conventions, titillating vast audiences with stories of Indian brutality inflicted upon hapless settlers. Beginning around the turn of the century, Western novels and films . . . supplied further opportunities for Indian-hating, justifying Europe's bloody conquest of the Americas with fictions of Native people's aggression and inherent malevolence."[8]

Informed by such mythologies, Indian boarding schools were developed partially out of fear of what might happen if Indians, and in particular Indian youth, were left to their own devices. For example, in an 1888 address to the Lake Mohonk Conference for reformers who called themselves "the Friends of the Indian," the Reverend Lyman Abbott makes the following plea:

> A great deal has been done toward the education of individual Indians, something, perhaps, toward the education of single tribes, but no plan has been agreed upon; and it is hardly too much to say that no plan has even been proposed for solving the educational problems of the Indian race,—for converting them from groups of tramps, beggars, thieves, and sometimes robbers and murderers, into communities of intelligent, industrious, and self-supporting citizens. . . . Put an ignorant and imbruted savage on land of his own, and he remains a pauper, if he does not become a vagrant and a thief. Open to him the courts of justice, and make him amenable to the laws of the land, and give him neither knowledge nor a moral education, and he will come before those courts only as a criminal; but inspire in him the ambition of industry, and equip him with the capacity of self-support, and he will acquire in time the needful land and find a way to protect his personal rights.[9]

As we saw in chapter 1, prevailing bioevolutionary approaches to the proposed epidemic of juvenile crime informed such popular notions, which clearly had nothing to do with actual crimes committed by Native Americans and everything to do with fear of "uncivilized" races and their "natural" propensity for crime. In any case, the justification for assimilation here is predicated upon the fear of what will happen if it doesn't take place, which in the case of the Indian is theft and ("sometimes") murder.

Along these lines, it's important to emphasize that the successful and well-publicized "experiment" undertaken by Pratt involved captured Indian criminals. Their transformation became the case study that gave rise to the Carlisle School and others like it: the belief being that what was effective with the criminal is clearly effective with any Indian youth because they are all, by and large, "naturally" criminals. This image very much worked in Pratt's favor, because it made his before-and-after pictures seem all the more significant. As with many manifestations of adolescence, the greater the storm and stress, the more stable the adult identity achieved.

As Pratt once reflected on the group he "transformed" at Fort Marion: "Having been the worst, because the most active of their people, they are capable for the same reason of becoming the best."[10]

As with the teen demographic and juvenile delinquency, such connections between Indians and crime are greatly informed by social evolutionary thought, spawned by the works of Herbert Spencer and others. In his book on American Indian autobiography, David Brumble exposes the ways in which such notions shaped conceptions of the Indian by white and Native American authors at the end of the nineteenth century. "By the mid-nineteenth century," he explains, "scientific and popular opinion had moved decisively away from the eighteenth-century ideas about the essential unity of the human race that had inspired the Jeffersonian declaration that 'all men are created equal.' . . . It was Spencer who did most to teach Americans that what was happening to the Indians was the inevitable— sad, of course, but certainly inevitable—working out of the laws of nature. And such ideas powerfully influenced those who concerned themselves with Indian affairs during these years. . . . This kind of thinking produced a curious blend of fatalism and nostalgia."[11] In this case, Native American culture was situated as the lowest point on an evolutionary scale that culminated in the "enlightened" civilization of Western, white Protestantism. Such scientific "fact" became the justification, of course, for speeding this inevitable evolution along.

This social evolutionary philosophy was greatly informed by notions of age as well. Such an influence can be seen in Pratt's famous goal to "kill the Indian, save the man," but also in much of the rhetoric that surrounded the establishment of boarding schools in general. The 1880 annual report of the Board of Indian Commissioners, for example, begins with the following statement: "As a savage we cannot tolerate him any more than as a half-civilized parasite, wanderer, or vagabond. . . . The Indian, though a simple child of nature with mental faculties dwarfed and shriveled, while groping his way for generations in the darkness of barbarism, already sees the importance of education."[12] Tempering social evolutionary thought with an age paradigm in this case offers a way to empty the savage of all threatening qualities but still sustain these qualities as a potential threat if the child is not raised correctly. The "simple child of nature" implies a certain vulnerability that makes the Indian more approachable, but most important the age paradigm invoked here implies that this child is amenable to change. This change could happen in the span of a few years because it is in the context of individual human development, rather than development of the race. Such age-inflected theories of evolution can be seen throughout the literature surrounding the development of boarding schools at the time. They perhaps reach their sentimental best in an address by Thomas J. Morgan, the commissioner of Indian Affairs, who said, poetically, in 1889: "At last, in the midst of our bustling, busy life: the din of business, the clatter of machinery, the thunders of commerce; the whirl of pleasure, and the passion of politics, we have heard the cry of the Indian baby, 'An infant crying in the night, An infant crying for the light.'"[13]

Social evolutionary philosophy tempered with notions about age categories was used to justify a space wherein Indians could be transformed into upstanding adults. Although it was not described as such, this space is a precursor to adolescence and reveals a great deal about the late nineteenth-century belief systems that accommodated this new developmental stage. G. Stanley Hall makes this connection between adolescents and Native Americans himself. In the final chapter of the second volume of *Adolescence,* entitled "Ethnic Psychology and Pedagogy; or, Adolescent Races and Their Treatment," he provides an overview of the "nearly one-third of the human race" that are "in a relation of greater or less subjection to a few civilized nations." Lumping together American Indians with other "savages" such as Hawaiians and Filipinos, he argues that "[m]ost savages in most respects are children, or, because of sexual maturity, more properly, adolescents of adult size. . . . Their faults and their virtues are those of childhood and youth. They need the same careful and painstaking study, lavish care, and adjustment to their nature and needs." Interestingly, in this same chapter, Hall takes Richard Henry Pratt to task for being so hostile "to the tribal system that he would stamp it out and prevent the young brave from returning to his tribe." But even though Hall argues against the extermination of Native American culture, his theory of recapitulation still, for all intents and purposes, reaches the same end, as the Indian as adolescent will eventually evolve into the "higher race." He focuses on this association and thus broadens his theory of adolescence to include races and not just individuals; the final sentences of his massive work on adolescence reads: "[E]very vigorous race, however rude and undeveloped, is, like childhood, worthy of the maximum of reverence and care and study, and may become the chosen organ of a new dispensation of culture and civilization. Some of them now obscure may be the heirs of all we possess, and wield the ever-increasing resources of the world for good or evil somewhat perhaps according as we now influence their early plastic stages, for they are the world's children and adolescents."[14] Such an adolescence, I would argue, was played out in Indian boarding schools at the turn of the century. This can be seen most prominently through the autobiographical accounts—both real and fabricated—of the youth that made their way through these schools. I would like to take a look at two of these accounts, both narratives of adolescence: one a fabricated narrative that functioned as a tool of rehabilitation for the Carlisle Indian School, and the other an interrogation of the belief system that kept this school in power.

These autobiographical accounts are interesting for a study of adolescence on a number of levels. They demonstrate in narrative form how this rehabilitative tool that was later called adolescence could be used in a variety of contexts. In this case, an age-informed paradigm of development is imposed upon a teen who is offered a prescribed evolutionary path to become an adult. The narratives also demonstrate the ways in which social evolutionary theory and notions of recapitulation informed texts well into the twentieth century. Although, as mentioned earlier, such theories are usually associated with the "bad-boy" books of the nineteenth century, they informed many other texts as well, including these two sketches of the lives of Native American girls.

Strange Summers

As mentioned earlier, part of the industrial training at Carlisle included work on the school's magazine, the *Red Man*. This publication, which was distributed not only to students and alumni but also donors and government officials, became a venue through which the school was publicized and its pedagogical beliefs and approaches were voiced. Included were "real-life" stories about students after they left the school and returned to the reservation. One such story—entitled "How an Indian Girl Might Tell Her Own Story if She Had the Chance"—was serialized in the school magazine beginning in the September 20, 1889, issue. The story was so popular it was later published, in 1891, as a book entitled *Stiya: A Carlisle Indian Girl at Home*. Although it is told from the perspective of its title character, the story, and later the novel, was actually written by Marianna Burgess, a teacher and superintendent of printing at Carlisle, under the pen name of Embe, a phonetic spelling of her initials, M.B. Burgess appropriated the narrator's name from an actual student at Carlisle, Stiya Kowacura, but tells us in the book's preface that "[t]he story of Stiya and her trials is woven out of the experiences of girls at various times members of the Indian Industrial School at Carlisle, Pa. The fundamental facts, therefore, are true."[15] Like many narratives documenting the return of boarding school students to their reservations, the story of Stiya portrays a crisis of identity, as the "reformed" individual finds she no longer identifies with her native culture but has not yet assimilated into the society she has been asked to emulate. But as a direct product of the Carlisle School, this narrative provides a solution to this crisis, in the form of the "adult" identity of the assimilated Indian.

The narrative opens with Stiya excitedly returning home to her family after five years of study at the Carlisle School. As her homebound train reaches the station, her excitement soon turns to disappointment as she finds her mother and father, with "grimy faces" and their hair looking "as though it had never seen a comb." She turns about and rushes into the arms of her "school-mother" and begs her to return to "old Carlisle," but her school-mother tells her to "be a woman! Make the best of these people, and go to your mother."[16] Thus, within the first few pages of the narrative, the central conflict of the story is set. Stiya experiences a conflict between her identities as Indian and as student at Carlisle. This crisis is contextualized in terms of age: her Indian identity is the childhood she has worked to leave behind during her training at Carlisle, and her prospective adult identity is what she will achieve if she succeeds in this challenge to "be a woman!" Interestingly, becoming an adult here does not mean only resisting the temptation to de-evolve into her former childhood self, but also to "make the best of these people": which is to say, become a mother to her own parents and guide them out of their state.

This age paradigm is informed by the social evolutionary philosophy so commonly expressed in the assimilation rhetoric of the time and the recapitulation rhetoric commonly associated with adolescence. When Stiya returns to her home—via a burro—she literally and figuratively returns to the dawn of humankind, to a pueblo "black with age and smoke as well as very dirty," its floor visited by the occasional scorpion, centipede, or tarantula. But these broader narratives are always personalized by Stiya and her own development as an individual. "Well," she sighs as she surveys her old home, "this is still my home, is it? No improvement upon what it was when I went away? Then I was a child, now I am a young woman."[17]

In a chapter appropriately entitled "Unsettled," Stiya lies awake the first night at home, unable to sleep because of the thick air of the pueblo and the hard floor, but most important because her entire identity has been thrown into question. "Would that I had never been at school!" she thinks to herself; but then a moment later rejoins: "I do not wish anything of the kind," because "[w]e must learn to feel disgust for these things.

If we have not disgust for them we will never try to make them better." The use of the possessive "we" here is very telling, as she parrots what has been taught to her at Carlisle, taking on the group identity of the institution. Stiya resolves to make things better, but then worries that her family will make fun of her. Peppered with exclamation points, the voices inside her head represent the various identities she has internalized: "And thus I plunged and struggled, asserting and contradicting myself." She misses Carlisle and decides she must return, but then remembers the words of her school-mother again: "Be a woman!"[18] The best—or perhaps more accurately the only—path becomes clear to her: she resolves not to return to childhood nor to Carlisle, but to move forward by enacting the role she learned at Carlisle and, most important, by passing on this identity to those around her.

Such a resolve not only provides a path for Stiya, it also has the effect of solidifying her identity, making the inside and outside cohesive. The next day, she takes a trip to the local store to purchase the tools for her transformation, which include a washtub, washboard, flatiron, bedstead, mattress, and table. When she and her parents arrive, the shop owner immediately recognizes her as a "Carlisle girl," because, he tells her, with some Indian youth, "Carlisle is stamped on their very faces."[19] The fact that he recognizes her as a "Carlisle girl" and not "Carlisle woman" means, of course, that Stiya is evolving in the right direction, but the development is not complete.

The final challenge comes when the community attempts to cover up this Carlisle "stamp" with some traditional Indian clothing. The corrupt governor of the tribe, who, Stiya observes, "seems to be trying to lead them back where they were in the first place," orders the tribe to perform a dance in which everyone is required to wear traditional Indian dress. The order throws Stiya's identity into question once again, as she is strong-armed by her mother, father, and the governor himself to acquiesce. But using this crisis as a chance for her to show "what [she] was made of," Stiya holds true to her resolve, which is charged not only by the narratives of age and social evolution, but by national patriotism as well. She reflects: "Is this the way my liberty is to be taken from me? Having been educated out of and away from this superstition, am I still to be a slave to it? Must I submit?" Submit she does not. As a result of her rebellion, Stiya is alienated from the tribe, as she is whipped and thrown in jail for her resistance. During this trial, Stiya questions: "This is what a Carlisle school-girl must endure, is it, if she wishes to follow the RIGHT?"[20] The answer is, of course, a resounding and inspiring yes, because the only real path out of the crisis that Stiya is placed in is the one she takes.

Interestingly, while Stiya's father joins in her resistance and later tells her how proud he is of her commitment to follow the right path, her mother sides with the governor, talking back to her husband "in such manner as is possible for an uncivilized Indian woman only under proper conditions." This misbehavior opens up the mother position in the family structure, offering a place for Stiya to occupy as she finally becomes a woman at the end of the novel. As such, the traditional age categories and family roles are disrupted according to the more "natural" and "right" evolutionary scheme that has been established. Stiya becomes the head of the family; her father relinquishes the role, telling her, "I believe you have with you the white man's God. I intend more than ever to follow you. I am your father and should be able to lead you, but the old Indian way is not good." At the end of the novel, when Stiya's father helps earn some money to support their quest to buy a home, Stiya tells us that he looked "as delighted as any boy." Under Stiya's tutelage, he develops within him "the spirit which we at Carlisle had been so earnestly advised to cultivate,—COURAGE."[21]

Evoking a sense of patriotism and, interestingly, abolitionism, this complex narrative of age and social evolution ends with Stiya, now a grown woman, speaking to the reader, advising and inspiring him or her to take the right path. "And, indeed, I have never regretted having braved the first hard steps that led me out of the accursed home slavery and made me a free woman," she tells the reader. "If every returned girl could resist the first efforts of her home friends to drag her back into the old Indian ways, and make them feel in a kind but decided way that they were no longer right for her, she would eventually enjoy untold satisfaction and happiness."[22] This book thus becomes a tool of rehabilitation, a function that, as we have seen, characterizes so much of the literature surrounding adolescence at the turn of the century and in many ways is fundamental to this developmental stage itself.

Not all narratives about students returning to their tribes provided such a seamless movement into adulthood, however. The February 1900 edition of the *Red Man* contains a review denigrating one such account. "We do not for a moment believe that 'Zitkala-Ša' desires to injure the cause of her own people, whose title to the blessings of enlightenment and civilization has so lately found a general recognition," the author proclaims, "but we do feel that the home-sick pathos—nay, more, the underlying bitterness of her story will cause readers unfamiliar with Indian schools to form entirely the wrong conclusions. Her pictures are not, perhaps, untrue in themselves, but, taken by themselves, they are sadly misleading."[23] The story was "The School Days of an Indian Girl," which had appeared in the February issue of *Atlantic Monthly.*

Born Gertrude Simmons on the Yankton Reservation in South Dakota in 1876, Zitkala-Ša spent the first eight years of her life on the reservation with her mother, her father having deserted the family before her birth. Against her mother's wishes, she left the Yankton Reservation at age eight to study at White's Manual Institute in Wabash, Indiana. She returned to Yankton at age eleven and stayed for four years before finishing her education at White's and studying at Earlham College in Richmond, Indiana, between 1895 and 1897. She taught at Carlisle from 1898 to 1899. In 1900 she published three autobiographical essays in the January, February, and March issues of the *Atlantic Monthly:* "Impressions of an Indian Childhood," "The School Days of an Indian Girl," and "An Indian Teacher among Indians." The anonymous reviewer at Carlisle had good reason to take offense at her autobiographical account of her days at White's because the narrative ultimately subverts many of the fundamental beliefs upon which Indian boarding schools were founded.

The developmental arc that Zitkala-Ša presents in these three essays is similar to but also significantly different from what we have seen in the story of Stiya. As with Stiya, the movement is from a childhood/Indian stage to an adolescent stage that is characterized by a conflict between native and white identity. Significantly different in Zitkala-Ša's text is the way in which childhood is characterized. Whereas in the story of Stiya, childhood is a "primitive" and "uncivilized" state that one must leave behind in one's evolution to a "higher" stage, in Zitkala-Ša's text, childhood is an idealized state, characterized by a connection with nature that is lost in the assimilation process. In the opening pages of "Impressions of an Indian Childhood," Zitkala-Ša establishes the connection between childhood and unspoiled nature in her description of herself: "Loosely clad in a slip of brown buckskin, and lightfooted with a pair of soft moccasins on my feet, I was as free as the wind that blew my hair, and no less spirited than a bounding deer." Although this idyllic natural childhood space is constructed as a prelapsarian space before the corrupting influence of the boarding school, the reservation is depicted as already threatened by the influence of white civilization. Descriptions of the young Indian and her friends playing "like little sportive nymphs on that Dakota sea of rolling green" are contrasted with foreboding tales of loss, often told by the young girl's mother. In the first section of the essay, when questioned about her tears, the mother points toward a nearby hillside and tells a quite different story about the relationship of humankind and nature: "There is what the paleface has done!" she tells her daughter, pointing to a hill where her uncle and only sister are buried. "Since then your father too has been buried in a hill nearer the rising sun. We were once very happy. But the paleface has stolen our lands and driven us hither. Having defrauded us of our land, the paleface forced us away."[24]

Despite this foreshadowing, the young girl experiences a oneness with nature that reflects a cohesive, singular identity that makes no distinction between the self and representations of the self and/or roles that one must play. Within these three essays, Zitkala-Ša sets up a sophisticated series of metaphors that narrates an evolution of identity formation: from a singular identity experienced in childhood to a bifurcated identity experienced during adolescence to a series of multiple identities that will constitute the narrator's adulthood. The childhood experience of self is richly captured in a moment wherein the young Indian girl chases her own shadow as it is reflected back to her by the blank canvas of the Dakota countryside: "On one occasion I forgot the cloud shadow in a strange notion to catch up with my own shadow. Standing straight and still, I began to glide after it, putting out one foot cautiously. When, with the greatest care, I set my foot in advance of myself, my shadow crept onward too." This game symbolically captures a uniquely "childlike" relationship with the self, as the young girl is both separate and one with nature, recognizing this external representation of herself but also able to integrate it into one larger sense of who she is. Zitkala-Ša frames this important moment with a reflective paragraph told from the adult's perspective: "Before this peculiar experience, I have no distinct memory of having recognized any vital bond between myself and my shadow. I never gave it an afterthought."[25] Such a moment, framed as it is by the author, could be seen as the beginnings of the young girl's self-consciousness. But it is an idealized self-consciousness that is, as we shall see, severely contrasted with her reconnection with the shadow many years later.

Having been taken from her homeland and mother—with the promise of "a land of red apples"—and stripped of her native clothing and her long hair, the narrator is made to submit to the "civilizing machine" of the boarding school in the second of the three essays, "The School Days of an Indian Girl." As with Stiya, the agenda of the boarding school experience is to obliterate Indian identity and replace it with what was seen as the more "evolved" values of white Protestantism. The process here is exposed more for its hypocrisy and cruelty than lauded for its success, however. Such hypocrisy reaches a climax for the narrator when she witnesses the death of a classmate: "At her deathbed I stood weeping, as the paleface woman sat near her moistening the dry lips," the narrator sadly recalls. "Among the folds of the bedclothes I saw the open pages of the white man's Bible. The dying Indian girl talked disconnectedly of Jesus the Christ and the paleface who was cooling her swollen hands and feet. I grew bitter, and censured the woman for cruel neglect of our physical ills." This moving moment is framed by the second mention of the shadow. Reflecting upon her experience in school, she writes, "The melancholy of those black days has left so long a shadow that it darkens the path of the years that have since gone by."[26] In this case, the shadow earlier associated with nature is subsumed by the shadow of the boarding school identity forced upon the narrator.

The next section of the second essay, appropriately titled "Four Strange Summers," narrates the four years the narrator spends back on the reservation after her experience at the boarding school. Separated both formally and metaphorically from the childhood she experienced on the reservation and at the boarding school and the adulthood that will follow, these years—from eleven to fourteen—become an adolescence as the narrator experiences a crisis imposed upon her by her boarding school experience. In one of the great early twentieth-century glimpses into the drama of this middle stage, the narrator tells us: "During this time I seemed to hang in the heart of chaos, beyond the touch or voice of human aid. My brother, being almost ten years my senior, did not quite understand my feelings. My mother had never gone inside a schoolhouse, and so she was not capable of comforting her daughter who could read and write. Even nature seemed to have no place for me. I was neither a wee girl nor a tall one; neither a wild Indian nor a tame one. This deplorable situation was the effect of my brief course in the East, and the unsatisfactory 'teenth' in a girl's years."[27] Caught between the natural identity of her early childhood and the mechanical identity imposed upon her at boarding school, between "wild Indian" and "tame one," the narrator experiences a literal crisis of identity. This crisis reaches an apex when she is unable to attend a dance with the "civilized" youth of her tribe because she is not "properly" dressed, having thrown away her school shoes to wear soft moccasins.

As the narrator tells us, this adolescence is a direct effect of her boarding school experience, which has created the crisis not only by opposing her native identity with a white one but also by imposing a script that argues that the only way out of this crisis, the only way to become an adult, is to assimilate. This is the same exact situation that Stiya had found herself in when asked to participate in the native dance, a situation that was solved by her becoming a "woman." Zitkala-Ša becomes an adult herself, but in quite a different way. As with the author Zitkala-Ša, the narrator once again leaves the reservation to finish her schooling. After a last, disappointing, visit to her mother, she makes what appears to be the final step into adulthood, becoming a teacher at, of all places, the Carlisle Indian Industrial School. But instead of her finding the peace that was promised with the end of the journey, this step only brings more crisis as she realizes the hypocrisy and cruelty inherent in this path: "As months passed over me, I slowly comprehended that the large army of white teachers in Indian schools had a larger missionary creed than I suspected. It was one which included self-preservation quite as much as Indian education. . . . At this stage of my own evolution, I was ready to curse men of small capacity for being dwarfs their God had made them."[28] The narrator's use of the terms "evolution" and "dwarfs" is particularly telling here, as she recognizes the falsity of the adult position she has been asked to occupy and the social evolutionary philosophy that has been used to essentialize it as the "natural" and "right" path.

Zitkala-Ša's markedly negative exposé of Carlisle caused significant backlash from the administration and Pratt himself. Zitkala-Ša's interrogation of the adolescence imposed on Native Americans resonates on more than a political level, however. Although the falsity of the adult position offered to her results in an extension of the crisis, there is a sense at the end of these three essays that some kind of stability is reached: "Now a cold bare pole I seemed to be, planted in a strange earth. Still, I seemed to hope a day would come when my mute aching head, reared upward to the sky, would flash a zig-zag lightning across the heavens. With this dream of vent for a long-pent consciousness, I walked again amid the crowds. At last, one weary day in the schoolroom, a new idea presented itself to me. I was a new way of solving the problem of my inner self. I liked it. Thus I resigned my position as teacher; and now I am in an Eastern city, following the long course of study I have set for myself."[29] If we take these essays to be reflective of the life of Zitkala-Ša, then the "new way" she took was to take up residence in Boston and pursue her career as a writer.

In her recent study of the boarding school experience and its representation in American Indian literature, Amelia Katanski suggests that through her writing Zitkala-Ša (and writer Charles Eastman) constructed an identity that somehow broke free of the strict binary offered up by the assimilationist tale of Stiya:

> Zitkala-Ša and Charles Eastman point toward the multivalent identities that so-called representative Indians inhabited at the turn of the century. . . . Unwilling and unable to be classified as assimilated or tribal, these writers sought to create versions of Indian identity that would enable them to achieve (sometimes provisional) reforms without locking them into a single essentialized identity. . . . Rather than being trapped between worlds, they inhabited several worlds simultaneously. By refusing any simple classification and by choosing expressive codes to represent themselves situationally, Eastman and Zitkala-Ša encourage us to question our own critical assumptions concerning Indian identity and its representation in autobiography.[30]

Her ability to represent herself situationally and inhabit several worlds simultaneously also questions many critical assumptions about age that were prevalent at the turn of the century, most important the common construction of adolescence as a search that resulted in a singular, stable adult identity—an assumption that both essentialized and privileged the white adult identity in texts such as *Stiya*.

Identity in Crisis

In his book *Rebels: Youth and the Cold War Origins of Identity*, Leerom Medovoi makes the persuasive argument that the notions of the "search for identity" and "identity crisis" that have become so synonymous with our contemporary understanding of the teenager actually did not enter popular discourse until the middle of the twentieth century, largely as a result of the work of Erik Erikson and a cultural/political environment that made his theories of adolescence resonate with an American audience. "Identity discourse rapidly permeated postwar U.S. culture in no small part through its now largely forgotten relation to two key terms: 'youth' and the 'Cold War,'" Medovoi asserts. "It is rarely remembered that Erikson erected the concept of identity as part of his influential model of the stages of human development, with adolescence playing the pivotal role. Moreover, Erikson relied heavily on the ideological terrain of Second World War and Cold War geopolitics to promote his understanding of the identity concept as part of what would soon become an emergent postwar common sense."[31]

Interestingly, as with the two theorists in the early twentieth century who did so much to define the stage of adolescence, Erikson's construction of the stage can also be seen as a response to Freud. Reacting mainly to Freud's emphasis on childhood development and on his portrayal of a "defensive ego"—which is to say, according to Erikson, an ego whose main purpose is to control and regulate biologically determined instincts and drives—Erikson's work provides a life-span theory of psychosocial development that emphasizes how human beings must categorize and integrate their experience into an "ego-identity." In *Identity: Youth and Crisis*, Erikson comments on Freudianism: "Instead of accepting such instinctual 'givens' as the Oedipus trinity as an irreducible schema for man's irrational conduct, we are exploring the way in which social forms codetermine the structure of the family."[32] Erikson challenges Freudianism by arguing that "social forms" affect the various "instinctual givens" that Freud outlines in his theory of the Oedipal. The effect of these social forms can be found, according to Erikson, in individuals' "ego identity"—how they perceive themselves in society.

The developmental stage of adolescence is crucial to Erikson's theory of human development. The time when the individual begins to view him- or herself as a product of his or her previous experiences entails a synthesis of these experiences and a formulation of a sense of self-identity. Erikson says of this process: "In their search for a new sense of continuity and sameness, which must now include sexual maturity, some adolescents have to come to grips again with crises of earlier years, before they can install lasting idols and ideals as guardians of final identity."[33] Erikson's notion of this "coming to grips with crises of earlier years" and installing "lasting idols and ideals" as the adolescent develops a sense of identity is the origin of what contemporary society refers to as the adolescent "identity crisis."

The term *identity* is entirely absent from the work of Hall and Mead. Perhaps, as rehabilitative paradigms, the early constructions of adolescence could not posit an individual identity discovered because it would destabilize the relationship between the individual and the species—to use Hall's terminology—and call into question the unstated moral agenda of these constructions of adolescence, which clearly privilege traits acquired as being "good" or "bad." So, even though their work gestures toward the notion that adolescents "search for identity"—as can be seen in Hall's notion of the "new birth" and Mead's call for a moratorium on choice—the adolescent is never really allowed any independence. As Medovoi puts it in his overview of how adolescence was constructed at the turn of the century: "This new category of transitional age placed its subjects (who formerly had exited childhood directly into the position of young adulthood), in a formalized state of legal, economic, and intellectual subordination to their elders. . . . The very meaning of adolescence, associated as it was with sexual, moral, and intellectual immaturity, precluded youth from the rights of personal autonomy that liberal enlightenment doctrine granted to the mature individual."[34]

Although the "formalized state" constructed in these turn-of-the-century texts of adolescence serves to preclude any sense of "personal autonomy," this paradigm was far from seamless, and thus we can find examples of adolescents struggling with this issue of identity well before the appearance of Erikson's work. The "formalized state" becomes particularly unstable when it is applied to populations that were marginalized from the largely white, Protestant middle class it was aimed at controlling. The peculiar aspect of many turn-of-the-century conceptions of adolescence is that even though they posited adolescence as a "universal" experience, they had a very specific population in mind. Indeed, promoting the idea of the universality of adolescence was often a way of demonstrating how this specific population could become "the other" if it was not controlled properly. Adolescence was a universal stage in theory, but in practice it became a form of discrimination. These contradictions and paradoxes often become unmanageable when dealing with the complex identity politics of marginalized groups. The "crisis of identity" experienced by Stiya and Zitkala-Ša, I would argue, is a crisis created by problems inherent in the paradigm of development they are being asked to follow. There is, of course, the crisis between the Indian and white conceptions of identity, which is ultimately "solved" in the story of Stiya by the identity of the assimilated Indian. But more profoundly, there is a crisis in the sense that even though the adult identity of the assimilated Indian is promised to have the same cultural currency as the white identity, it turns out to not be the case; in fact, it often is perceived as no different from the initial Indian identity it was supposed to subsume. The identity of the assimilated Indian is an adult identity that has no currency in the adult society of either the Indian culture or the white culture. The "formalized state" breaks down because the status of its product (the adult) interrogates the very developmental paradigm and process (adolescence) that enabled the individual to come of age. This is the nature of the crisis experienced by Zitkala-Ša, which she solves by renegotiating the terms of identity formation, taking herself outside of the adolescent paradigm entirely—a rare and inspiring move for an adolescent at the turn of the century.

4
Playing Indian
The Rise and Fall of the Woodcraft
Youth Movements

Getting the Treatment

If the young hooligans who vandalized the property of Ernest Thompson Seton in the spring of 1901 had only known that their behavior would directly inspire the largest youth movement in American history, they probably would have lobbied for some honorary mention, but to this day they remain largely unknown. Although the fact is not included in any of the official histories, the original impetus of Seton's Woodcraft Indians, who would later become the Boy Scouts of America, was a desire to protect what was his by keeping the neighborhood bullies busy and thus out of trouble. As Seton tells the story in his 1928 piece, "The Rise of the Woodcraft Indians," his dream of partitioning off a small tract of woodland outside of New York City, to use for experiments in conservation and restocking, was consistently frustrated by a gang of neighborhood boys who saw fit to destroy his fence, shoot his animals, and paint "wicked pictures" on his gate—pictures, mind you, "not even a Sunday paper would have dared to print." Frustrated, Seton sought advice from a learned friend who informed him there was simply no other option but to arrest the whole ugly lot and pray that the worst of them would get sent to jail. But "knowing something of boys," indeed, being "much of a boy myself," Seton resisted the temptation for lockdown and instead proceeded to buck conventional wisdom by inviting the young lads to spend a weekend camping, "Indian-style," on the very patch of land they had so sorely abused. After two days of hollering, skinny-dipping, gorging, and participating in the establishment of a basic constitution and governing structure, come Monday morning, "instead of forty-two little reprobates, doing all the mischief they could to me and mine, I had forty-two staunch friends" who all turned out to be "high-class citizens" in the end.[1]

News of Seton's miracle treatment for the characteristically troubled years of adolescence spread quickly. In 1902 a series of seven articles in the *Ladies' Home Journal,* entitled "Ernest Thompson Seton's Boys," described his success.[2] Within a year there were fifty other "tribes," consisting of fifty members each, scattered throughout the country.[3] In 1906 Seton's official manual of the Woodcraft Indians, *The Birch-bark Roll,* was co-opted by British war hero Lord Robert Baden-Powell and turned into *Scouting for Boys,* the book that launched the Boy Scout youth movement. Seton's ability to subdue the seemingly unruly and irresponsible adolescent appealed to a society that was becoming increasingly concerned about this new and frightening segment of the population. His talent for instilling a sense of adventure into the youth organization—or "picturesqueness," as he was fond of saying—appealed to a nation of "modern" youth who, in Seton's opinion, were being ruined by city life, and just plain needed to get outside.

Seton's solution offered a way of keeping this segment of the population busy and out of trouble and addressed as well broader anxieties over urbanization and industrialization. On the one hand, the Woodcraft Indian, as constructed by Seton, allowed a return to nature that cultivated those qualities of self-reliance and virility that many believed were concomitant with American greatness, qualities that had been lost as America moved into the modern age. In addition, the Woodcraft Indian instilled a devotion to the "tribe" that would counteract the selfishness that characterized capitalist society. The texts surrounding the Woodcraft Indians were so popular and read by so many boys and their parents because they both articulated prevailing anxieties and appeared to provide a solution to them. Such an attempt to monopolize and systematize the social activities of teens was the common structural feature of youth organizations at the turn of the century. Seton's youth movement, and its sister organization the Camp Fire Girls, can be seen as a solution to a rise in juvenile delinquency and, more broadly, as an answer to the widespread anxiety over what this new and characteristically unruly segment of the population would do if left to its own devices. Years later, as the Woodcraft Indian is eclipsed by the much more popular figure of the Boy Scout, and Seton's early writings are reconfigured by Baden-Powell and others, this unique cultural moment comes to an end; American society becomes much more concerned with hooligans abroad than at home and, like England, begins to prepare its youth for war.[4]

The Lure and the Lash

As we saw in chapter 1, the problem that Ernest Thompson Seton was having with his local gang of hoodlums was not an unusual one in American society at the turn of the century. Even though the statistical evidence was lacking, the conclusion reached by experts such as Charles Loring Brace, Jacob Riis, and W. Douglas Morrison was that juvenile delinquency was a growing epidemic in American cities. Whether directly informed by the work of these theorists/alarmists or not, the popular newspapers and magazines of the time echo the same sentiment. For example, a January 14, 1904, *New York Times* article on the release of the first annual report of the newly established juvenile court in New York City shockingly reveals that 4,360 boys and 430 girls were convicted of crimes in 1903: "Total arrests [of children] between [one and seven years old] number 432; between seven and twelve, 949; between twelve and fourteen, 1,437, and between fourteen and sixteen, 1,952." Concern over this seeming increase in juvenile crime colors the many lengthy articles on delinquency-related issues published by the *Times* during this period. For example, a piece describing the recently renovated New York Juvenile Asylum, printed on Sunday, December 17, 1905, begins with the observation that "[t]he child of the street, homeless, lawless, original, is just as much in evidence to-day as he was in the days of Gavroche and Oliver Twist." Similarly, an April 8, 1906, article on a debate between a local juvenile court judge and the board of education as to the reasons behind the plague of juvenile crime in New York City begins: "Ignorance, depravity, indifference, and supineness of parents and deplorable home conditions are cited as the chief causes of the incorrigible child problem as it exists in New York."[5]

This "incorrigible child problem" was not unique to New York City. A series of articles in the national magazine the *Outlook* during the first decade of the century, for example, examines various aspects of the "growing" epidemic, including the attempt to rehabilitate juvenile delinquents by their local pastors ("Getting at the Boys"), how home life and lack of social training lead to crime ("The Causes of Juvenile Crime"), the effect of new laws in Massachusetts on delinquency ("Delinquent and Wayward Children"), and the large number of inmates in penal institutions who came from unhappy homes ("The Defective Home and Juvenile Delinquency").[6] Similarly, the *Ladies' Home Journal* published articles by experts in juvenile delinquency on how impulsiveness can lead to a life of crime ("Why Boys Go Wrong") and how a young boy's primitive instincts and spirit of adventure need to be curbed (or redirected) or they will get out of hand ("The Bad Boy of the Street").[7] All of these articles emphasize the common fear that juvenile crime had reached new and alarming proportions; for example, the *Outlook* article "Delinquent and Wayward Children" begins with the observation that "[t]he police know that the tide of lawlessness is rising in Boston, and that almost daily there is a new high-water mark." Perhaps even more ominous, the author of "The Causes of Juvenile Crime" opens his piece with these words: "The delinquent child has always been a problem. The parent in the home and the teacher in the school have often tried in vain to fathom the causes of the child's offenses and the courts and officers of the law have frequently acknowledged that their methods were wholly inadequate to deal with the steady growth of juvenile delinquency."[8]

Seton's problem was part of an unsubstantiated but still quite frightening "incorrigible child problem" thought to be plaguing the nation, but what made it different for him was that he had an answer. As Seton explained in his popular *Ladies' Home Journal* series and many other articles he wrote about the Woodcraft Indians movement, there were two qualities that characterized the boy: a reversion to the state of primitive man and an innate desire for the gang. In "The Rise of the Woodcraft Indians," Seton bluntly states, "The boy is a caveman till he is sixteen or seventeen. At this time, he is in the clan period. Loyalty to his clan or gang is his religion, far overpowering any loyalty he may feel to church or state."[9] The boy is experiencing a "primitive" stage of human development wherein he has no sense of morality, no sense that a person's right to property is to be respected. He simply takes or destroys. Along the same lines, accompanying his "caveman" instinct is his desire for the "clan." Simply put, if left to his own devices, he will "naturally" gravitate toward the gang because this is what characterized the human species during the "primitive" stage of development.

As H. Allen Anderson has maintained in his biography of Seton, these recapitulation-based notions of childhood that pepper Seton's writings were gleaned from G. Stanley Hall, whose work Seton knew quite well.[10] Such conceptions spoke directly and strongly to Americans who, like Seton, were searching for an explanation of this assumed rise in juvenile delinquency. For example, in the article from the *Ladies' Home Journal* cited earlier, on "The Bad Boy of the Street," the author notes that "[i]n the life of each boy there comes a time when primitive instincts urge him to action, when he is himself frightened by their undefined power." Along the same lines, in "Why Boys Go Wrong," the author describes a case of theft that resulted from a boy who had "simply yielded to a sudden wild and unaccountable impulse."[11] Why is juvenile delinquency seemingly on the rise? Because juveniles are reverting back to their savage nature.

As was discussed earlier, such recapitulation-based approaches to the problem of juvenile delinquency were attractive because they essentialized crime as an instinct and thus superseded any actual data on crime or any much more troubling sociological explanations—adolescent crime was as natural as pubic hair and masturbation. This logic spoke to the American fear of delinquency, which, of course, was more about the fear of adolescence than any actual rise in crime committed by teens. However, Hall's ideas must have been particularly attractive to those, like Seton, who were involved in "boys work" at the turn of the century not only because they essentialized certain adolescent traits, such as "wild" and "unaccountable" impulses, but also because they made the theoretical connection between such instincts and the history of the race, as Hall described it, and thus established adolescence as a distinct "stage" with identifiable characteristics that could be explained and policed. This logic opened the door for the types of broad generalizations about adolescents that formed the theoretical bases of the many youth movements that appeared at the turn of the century and justified their activities by asserting that they were expressions of the "natural" tendencies of the individual and the race. As David Macleod has argued in his work on American youth movements, there were organizations—such as boys' clubs, the Boys' Brigade, and the early incarnations of the YMCA—that predated Seton's "scheme," but such movements had only moderate success, largely because they had no theoretical basis for attracting, understanding, and cultivating their members. This theoretical basis came in the form of recapitulation theory and most important in the theories of adolescence proffered by Hall and his followers. "After floundering in confusion, unsure even what age group to serve," Macleod argues, "[the organizers of youth movements] found an ideology to explain their efforts—based upon the notion that boys recapitulated the development of the race as they grew older, progressing upward as instincts implanted during each past culture epoch emerged in sequence. Character builders now promised recreation and training adapted to the boys' cultural level. These ideas took hold among YMCA boys' workers around 1900, spread from there to Boy Scouting, and ushered in two decades of rapid expansion during which character building agencies rose to prominence on the American scene."[12] Seton and others borrowed recapitulation theories from an earlier era that essentialized the boy's savage nature, and took from Hall the notion that such impulses could be directed into a morally productive theater, which would enable children to evolve. Their youth movements thus became an adolescent stage of development.

Thus, according to the prevailing characterization of adolescence, as "caveman" impulses take charge, the adolescent reverts back to a childhood state of incivility, and it is no surprise that "wicked pictures" result. However, all is not lost. What is needed is a stabilizing force that will correctly funnel these savage impulses into a morally productive arena. Clearly, according to Ernest Thompson Seton, the modern city was not accomplishing this task. In a 1910 article in *Success* magazine entitled "Organized Boyhood," Seton begins by pondering the reasons why America was able to win the Revolution. Was it because "we were not drilled soldiers, but self-reliant men"? Indeed it was. And, according to Seton, one of the problems with our "modern society" is that "[s]ince the Revolution, some great and regrettable but inevitable changes have come about. The decay of small farming, the growth of large cities, the enormous increase of the manufacturing classes, have tended to the elimination of the self-reliant boy with his adaptable knowledge of handicraft."[13] According to Seton, life in the city, and work in the factory, has compounded the problem of the wayward youth because it precludes any possibility of being an individual, of being "self-reliant." What is needed, then, is a wholehearted return to nature. Seton opens the official manual of the Woodcraft Indians, *The Birch-bark Roll*, with these prophetic words: "This is a time when the whole nation is turning toward the outdoor life, seeking in it the physical regeneration so needful for continued national existence—is waking to the fact long known to thoughtful men, that those live longest who live nearest the ground, that is, who live the simple life of primitive times."[14]

Seton is correct in his observation that Americans took a particular interest in outdoor life at the turn of the century. This interest is evidenced by events such as the founding of the Sierra Club in 1892, the establishing of the Federal Forest Reserves in 1897 and, of course, Teddy Roosevelt's famous White House Conference on Conservation in 1908. But, as many critics have observed, concomitant with a turning toward the outdoor life was an anxiety about the rise in urbanization and a fear of the disappearance of the American frontier. Roderick Nash, for example, has illuminated the significant change in the American attitude toward the "wilderness" that took place at the end of the nineteenth century: "The census of 1890 only gave statistical confirmation of what most Americans knew first hand: the frontier was moribund, wilderness no longer dominant. From the perspective of the city streets and comfortable homes, wild country inspired quite different attitudes than it had when observed from a frontiersman's clearing. . . . The average citizen could approach wilderness with the viewpoint of vacationer rather than conqueror." According to Nash, this new attitude toward the wilderness resulted in two very significant changes in American culture: first, a negative stance toward the effects of city life became common, and second, a belief was fostered that a return to nature was a way of returning to the strength and independence that had made the country great. As a result of these shifts in attitude and perception, getting out of the city and back to nature meant recapturing an idealized past, a "pioneer past that was believed responsible for many unique and desirable national characteristics," and reclaiming traits of "virility, toughness, and savagery—qualities that defined fitness in Darwinian terms."[15] Seton's movement was popular not only because it solved the (seemingly) expanding problem of juvenile delinquency, but also because it soothed growing fears of a loss in national virility resulting from urban expansion and industrialization. As was discussed in chapter 1, the problems of urban expansion and juvenile delinquency were inexorably linked at the turn of the century, and adolescence became both a symbol of and a solution to both of these problems. Youth movements such as Seton's link this symbol to anxieties about masculinity and nationalism that were of concern to Americans as they moved into the modern age.

In Seton's miracle treatment, the adolescent's primitive desires and need for the gang find a "natural" solution in the form of the Woodcraft Indian, who both lives in a primitive state and bands together with others into a tribe. However, Seton makes clear in his *Ladies' Home Journal* series that although he has chosen the Woodcraft Indian as the model for his youth movement, this Indian should be clearly distinguished from the "savages" that roamed the Americas in the past. In the June 1902 installment of "Ernest Thompson Seton's Boys," he observes: "I suppose that every boy in America loves to 'play Injun.' It was one of my greatest pleasures and I often wished for someone who could teach me more about it. That does not mean that I wanted to be a cruel savage, but rather that I wanted to know how to live in the woods as he does, and enjoy and understand the plants and living creatures that are found there." Indeed, in the opening pages of *The Birch-bark Roll,* Seton indicates that the model for his movement may not have existed at all: "The ideal Indian," he explains to his readers, "whether he ever existed or not, stands for the highest type of primitive life, and he was a master of Woodcraft, which is our principal study."[16] But if the "ideal" Woodcraft Indian never existed, then what is he, exactly, and what did this image have to do with the developmental stage of adolescence?

Seton wrote a great deal about Native American culture—or what he referred to as the "Redman"—most specifically in his 1936 work *The Gospel of the Redman.* As his wife, Julia Seton, explains in her introduction, this work was spawned by a meeting Seton had with a mahatma from India who informed him that he was the Red Indian Chief, reincarnated to give the message of the Redman to the white race. Seton took this prophecy to heart and makes it clear in the opening pages of the work that "the Redman is the apostle of outdoor life, his example and precept are what the world needs to-day above any other ethical teaching." Interestingly, however, most of *The Gospel of the Redman* is devoted to emphasizing the similarities between the rules of the Redman and the fundamental precepts of Western Judeo-Christian religion. In the foreword, for example, Julia Seton describes how the text is endorsed by a Jewish rabbi and two Presbyterian ministers, who have acknowledged that it consists of the same principles taught in their own respective religions. Along these lines, the "Indian Creed" outlined in chapter 1 of this work prescribes that there is one Great Spirit, that the soul of man is immortal, and lists twelve commandments that are markedly similar to the ten in the Bible—in particular, the worship of the single Great Spirit, the honoring of the father and the mother, and the prohibition of idolatry, false testimony, murder, adultery, and coveting property.[17]

On the other hand, Seton is quick to point out the characteristics of Indian life that are lacking in "modern" American society. One important thing we can learn from the Redman, for example, is his respect for nature; according to "The Ancient Way," no man owns the land and he has a right only to as much of the wood, water, and soil that he can gather in his own hands. Seton asserts that in addition to a healthy relationship to nature, the key to the happiness and productivity of the Redman was that he was a successful socialist. "Sociability as a fundamental of human nature," Seton explains, "is fully recognized in all Indian Tribes—even the nomads—and is the inevitable solution of many of the troubles that are harassing the White race in America."[18] In contrast to modern American society, the socialistic society of the Redman provides for the sick and the aged and does not inspire any avarice among its citizens.

Placing *The Gospel of the Redman* beside Seton's writings on the Woodcraft Indians, one can easily see why he chose the Redman as the symbol of his youth movement and recognize the way in which his writings inform and reflect one another. Pieced together from published accounts of trappers, traders, and missionaries, with a little of Seton's own personal testimony thrown in, the Indian configured in *The Gospel of the Redman* represents some idealized past—literally a "native" America—and a set of hypothetical characteristics that not only once made this country great but will assure its survival as it moves into the modern age. What America needs, according to Seton, is not only a return to nature to counteract the negative effects of urbanization and industrialization, but also a renewed socialist devotion to the tribe to combat the selfishness inspired by capitalist culture. The qualities that Seton associates with the Redman are the basis of the laws that govern his Woodcraft Indians, and, later, will comprise the laws of the Boy Scouts of America. The fundamental qualities of cleanliness, bravery, cheerfulness, honesty, kindness, and love for country that characterize the Indian in *The Gospel of the Redman* are the essence of the ten laws of the Woodcraft Indians as stated in *The Birch-bark Roll:* "Don't rebel; Don't kindle a wild fire; Protect the song-birds; Don't make a dirty camp; Don't bring firearms of any kind into the camps of those under fourteen; Keep the game laws; No smoking (for those under eighteen); No firewater in camp; Play fair; Word of honor is sacred."[19] These ten laws will ultimately become the nine points of "the Scout Law" as introduced by Seton—with a bit of help from Lord Robert Baden-Powell— in his 1910 *Boy Scouts of America: A Handbook of Woodcraft, Scouting, and Life-Craft:* "A scout's honor is to be trusted; a scout is loyal; a scout's duty is to be useful and to help others; a scout is a friend to all; a scout is courteous; a scout is a friend to animals; a scout obeys orders; a scout smiles and looks pleasant; a scout is thrifty."[20]

As Philip Deloria has made clear in his book *Playing Indian,* the Redman constructed in the texts surrounding Seton's youth movement is part of a long tradition of portrayals of "Indianness" that have served to define American identity since the days of the American Revolution. In his chapter devoted to Seton's Woodcraft Indians and Daniel Beard's youth organization, the Sons of Daniel Boone, Deloria correctly asserts that early twentieth-century American youth movements such as Seton's "set out to reimagine the frontier experience through scouting, wilderness, and nature study. Even if one could no longer pursue rugged individualist destiny on the frontier, a rustic week of Indian camping in a national park or a scouting expedition in the country might prove a reasonable substitute."[21] The "primitive" nature of this substitute was particularly well suited to the out-of-control adolescent and served to ease anxieties about juvenile delinquency in American society at this time. Part Fenimore Cooper, part Longfellow, and part a figment of the collective imagination, the Woodcraft Indian, as he is constructed in Seton's writings, is an idealized figure that appeals to the boy's sense of adventure and also enables Seton to negotiate the many contradictions at the heart of his youth movement. The idealized Indian has a savage need to run wild in the forest, but he also has a respect for property not his own. He is markedly self-reliant, but he has an undying devotion to the tribe. Ultimately, Seton is aware of these contradictions and argues that they are irrelevant in light of the true intent of the movement, which is, of course, to keep these young hooligans out of trouble. Toward the end of "The Rise of the Woodcraft Indians," Seton concludes by observing that "[t]here was sanity in every part of the scheme, because it had picturesqueness; it made the boys govern themselves, and it gave them definite things to do; but, above all, it never failed to play on the master power of the savages, the love of glory—that was always kept in mind. It was used as the lure, the lash and the motive power to get these boys into different ways of life and thought."[22] Given the immense popularity of the movement, it is apparent that the lure and the lash were not only an effective way to sway young hoodlums away from an innate propensity for painting "wicked pictures" on the fences of their unsuspecting neighbors, but also became a vehicle for both expressing and soothing anxieties about this new and seemingly destructive element of society.

Peace and War, Indians and Scouts

Although Ernest Thompson Seton would have liked to take credit for founding the largest youth movement in American history, most official histories of the origin of the Boy Scouts of America award this honor to William D. Boyce, a millionaire publisher from Chicago. As the story is told by Robert Peterson in *The Boy Scouts: An American Adventure,* the official seventy-fifth-anniversary history of the Scouts, "Boyce was in London on business in August 1909 en route to British East Africa for

a photography and shooting expedition. One afternoon the city was en-
shrouded in a pea-soup fog. Boyce lost his bearings in the murk and was
approached by a boy of about 12 carrying a lantern who offered to guide
him to the address he was seeking. When Boyce proffered a shilling up,
the boy replied: 'No, sir, I am a Scout. Scouts do not accept tips for courte-
sies or Good Turns.' The American publisher was intrigued, and after he
had completed his business, the lad led him to the new British Scout office
nearby." Inspired by the "Unknown Scout," Boyce spoke with a number
of scouting officials while in London and upon returning to the United
States called together a wide variety of educators and leaders of American
youth movements in order to begin an official scouting organization in the
United States. In 1911 the first "official" guide, *Boy Scouts of America: The
Official Handbook for Boys,* was published. By 1915 the total membership of
the Boy Scouts of America was 182,303; by 1920 the total membership was
490,911; and by 1930 it was 847,051.[23]

As Betty Keller explains in her biography of Seton, three years before Boyce's legendary trip, Seton himself had visited England. During
his visit, he was introduced to some pamphlets on the training of military
scouts written by Lord Robert Baden-Powell, a popular hero in British society for his defense of the small city of Mafeking during the Boer War.
Entitled "Reconnaissance and Scouting" (1885) and "Aids to Scouting"
(1899), these pamphlets had only a slight influence on military thought
but, much to their author's surprise, they were immensely popular with
British youth. Upon learning of their popularity, Baden-Powell began re-
searching the possibility of forming a youth organization based upon the
tenets he had outlined in his pamphlets. While in England, Seton con-
tacted Baden-Powell and sent him a copy of his *Birch-bark Roll.* The two
met on October 30, 1906, and agreed that Baden-Powell would contrib-
ute to the scouting portion of the *Birch-bark Roll,* but he would not help
with Seton's "scheme" because, it turned out, he had plans for one of his
own. When Baden-Powell came out with the first official guide to the Boy
Scout youth movement in 1908, *Scouting for Boys: A Handbook for Instruction in Good Citizenship,* Seton was astonished and annoyed to discover
the uncanny similarities between this manual and the one he had sent to
Baden-Powell years earlier. As Keller describes it: "When Baden-Powell
brought out his *Scouting for Boys* in 1908, Seton 'was astounded to find all
[his] ideas taken, all [his] games appropriated, disguised with new names,
the essentials of [his] plan utilized and not a word of acknowledgment . . .
and not a word of explanation about why [he] should be left out of the

movement [he] began.' Seton could find nothing in Baden-Powell's book that he had not already published in *Two Little Savages, The Birch-bark Roll*, or his woodcraft and scouting articles, and, so far as he could see, the only changes Baden-Powell had made were to rename things and assume their authorship."[24] Thus ensued a series of angry letters between Seton and Baden-Powell in which Seton expressed his concern over Baden-Powell's refusal to acknowledge his contribution to his *Handbook*.

But Seton's problems did not end there. On June 15, 1910, after William D. Boyce's trip to London, representatives from a wide variety of American youth agencies met for the first time in New York City with the intent of establishing a Boy Scout movement in the United States. Although Seton was included in the negotiations and was given the position of "Chief Scout," that post, he soon realized, entailed largely symbolic duties. A lawyer and personal friend of Theodore Roosevelt, James E. West, was named the executive secretary of the Boy Scouts of America and clearly wielded most of the power over the early direction of the movement. Borrowing from his own *Birch-bark Roll* and sections of Baden-Powell's *Scouting for Boys*, Seton composed the first *Boy Scouts of America Handbook for Boys* in 1910, but the National Council heavily revised it and published the "official" *Handbook for Boys* in 1911. This created one of the many conflicts between Seton and West that resulted in Seton's ultimate resignation as Chief Scout in 1915.

As can be seen, the process of establishing the Boy Scouts of America was characterized by a fight for power on a par with some of the great corporation mergers of the twentieth century. But more important, the founding of the movement, and the way it constructed adolescence, reflects a broader shift in American cultural values as the twentieth century progressed. Central to this shift is the change from Woodcraft Indians to Boy Scouts. Seton himself had commented upon the significance of this change in "Organized Boyhood." Speaking of how Baden-Powell had "incorporated" the principles of the Woodcraft Indians into his own more popular movement, Seton observed that "[l]argely through the superior attraction of the name, [the Boy Scout movement] has been more successful than my 'Woodcraft Indians.' . . . Indeed, I find now that many were repelled by the name 'Indian.' They imagined we were teaching boys to imitate Indians."[25] Seton's assertion that the popularity of the Boy Scouts was due to its name is most certainly a jab at Baden-Powell, who, Seton believed, contributed nothing original to his "incorporation" except the new name. On the other hand, Seton clearly realized the popular appeal of the scout and acknowledged the problems inherent in his choice of the Indian to serve as the figurehead of his movement. As mentioned earlier, Seton had always expressed concern over the public's misinterpretation of the Woodcraft Indian. He was not espousing that boys become "cruel savages" but rather that they learn how to live in the woods and glean knowledge of its plants and animals. The image of the Woodcraft Indian appeals to the savage, primitive part of adolescent nature and lets the adolescent act out, but the governing structure of the movement and its rituals makes certain that this savage impulse is tamed by Christian morality—the lure and the lash. Seton feared that this configuration was too subtle for the public to comprehend, and the popularity of the Boy Scouts suggests that he may have been right.

However, as Betty Keller has pointed out in her biography of Seton, while these changes were taking place, and while the conflict between Seton and James West was reaching its zenith, war was breaking out in Europe. Although the United States was not involved in the conflict, there must have been a certain anxiety in the culture at large as to how well our young men would fare if called to battle. This anxiety was expressed by Roosevelt himself, who wrote a letter to James West questioning the ultimate intent of the Boy Scouts of America. On the issue of militarism in the movement, Roosevelt emphatically states, "A Boy Scout who is not trained actively and affirmatively that it is his duty to bear arms for the country in time of need is at least negatively trained to be a sissy, and there cannot be anything worse for this country than to have an organization of boys brought up to the mushy milk-and-water which is the stock and trade of the apostles of pacifism."[26] Keller quotes this letter in full in her biography and correctly identifies the "apostle of pacifism" here as being none other than Ernest Thompson Seton.

This movement from a peaceful, communistic Indian to a war-ready Scout is evidenced by the contrasting sections of the early manuals of the Boy Scouts written by Seton and Baden-Powell. Seton was clearly attempting to continue his focus on a return to nature and a socialist devotion to the tribe, or in this case, troop. He opens his 1910 *Boy Scouts of America: A Handbook of Woodcraft, Scouting, and Life-Craft* with these words:

Every American boy, a hundred years ago, lived either on a farm or in such close touch with farm life that he reaped its benefits. He had all the practical knowledge that comes from country surroundings;

that is, he could ride, shoot, skate, run, swim; he was handy with
tools; he knew the woods; he was physically strong, self-reliant, resourceful, well-developed in body and brain. In addition to which he
had good moral training at home. He was respectful to his superiors,
obedient to his parents, and altogether the best material of which a
nation could be made.

We have lived to see an unfortunate change. Partly through the
growth of immense cities, with the consequent specialization of industry, so that each individual has been required to do one small spe-
cialty and shut his eyes to everything else, with the resultant perpetual narrowing of mental horizon.[27]

The "unfortunate" changes are, of course, the urban expansion that sev-
ers the healthy tie between adolescent and nature and a capitalist morality
that forces the boy to "shut his eyes" to anything but his own self-serving
ends.

Whereas Seton was continuing with a philosophy of adolescence he
had developed many years earlier, Baden-Powell was clearly focusing on
something else. According to Baden-Powell, the Boy Scouts were developed in response to a national crisis: namely, the weakening of youth. In
a section of *Scouting for Boys* that compares his contemporary England
to Rome on the brink of collapse, Baden-Powell emphatically makes
his case:

The main causes of the downfall of Rome is similar to that which
resulted in the downfall of other great empires, such as the Baby-
lonian, Egyptian, Greek, Spanish, and Dutch, and that cause may
be summed up in each case as the decline of good citizenship and
the want of energetic patriotism. Each nation, after climbing labo-
riously to the zenith of its power, seemed then to become exhausted
by its effort, and sit down in a state of repose, relapsing into idleness,
studiously blind to the fact that other nations were gradually pushing up to destroy it. . . .

[M]y heart sickens at the reverse of the medal—thousands of
boys and young men, pale, narrow chested, hunched up, miserable
specimens, smoking endless cigarettes, numbers of them betting, all
of them learning to be hysterical as they groan or cheer in panic
unison with their neighbors [at football matches]—the worst sound
of all being the hysterical scream of laughter that greets any little trip

or fall of a player. One wonders whether this can be the same nation which had gained for itself the reputation of being a stolid, pipe-sucking manhood, unmoved by panic or excitement, and reliable in the tightest of places.

Get the lads away from this—teach them to be manly, to play the game, whatever it may be, and not be merely onlookers and loafers.[28]

As exemplified in this markedly caustic condemnation of British youth, the problem with England, according to Baden-Powell, is a problem with citizenship. In this case, the "pale, narrow chested, hunched up, miserable specimens" of British youth make poor citizens and thus add up to a weak nation. This "reverse of the medal" has resulted from the evil influences of "modern" culture, with its general lack of hygiene and unhealthy so-cial habits, and the boys' lack of desire to "play the game." According to Baden-Powell, the boys don't participate; they sit on the sidelines as "on-lookers and loafers" because they lack patriotism, have no knowledge that they are part of a thing bigger than themselves, and thus feel no respon-sibility for the whole. Thus what is needed is a type of paradoxical solu-tion: the individual boys must be taught to take care of themselves in order to take care of the nation of which they are a part. Individual work *on* the self ultimately means collective work *for* the nation. This mission is par-ticularly crucial because of the specter of war on the horizon, and the pos-sibility that "other nations were gradually pushing up to destroy" England and take its place as the foremost international power.

One point of agreement between Seton and Baden-Powell, however, was an emphatic belief in the need for society to get back to nature. As with Seton, returning to nature in Baden-Powell's eyes meant enacting qualities of virility and self-reliance that he believed had been lost in the modern age. But this belief in returning to nature took on some unique characteristics in light of Baden-Powell's emphasis on preparing youth for war. On this point, Robert H. MacDonald has shown that

the frontier, and its stereotypical hero, the war scout, provided Brit-ish society at the beginning of [the twentieth] century with an alter-native ethic, answering this general fear about the condition of the nation's virility. Though in hindsight we might think that the period of imperial expansion was over by the turn of the century, the idea of the frontier was still potent and romantic to many Edwardians, and it came to symbolize an attractive solution to a set of increasingly complex problems at home. War was on the horizon; to make sure future combatants were virile and strong seemed the only way to keep the peace.[29]

According to MacDonald, the image of the frontier and the war scout became a way to elide a fear of loss of national virility and to reinvigorate people's confidence in England as an imperial country, spreading its message of God and freedom to the unenlightened, subduing and taming the primitive and unruly. MacDonald continues: "In the period that produced Scouting, the narratives of adventure matched nicely with the 'plot' of imperialism: the frontier was the unknown land, the hero was the frontiersman, the conquest of territory or native the heroic deed. The Empire itself was the scene of adventure, and its proof."[30] Much as getting back to nature in American society meant recapturing an idealized past, getting back to nature in British society reflects a broader desire to recapture a time when England was the moral and cultural center of the world. In both cases, the return to nature becomes a strategic psychological mechanism for eliding fears of the loss of individual and national virility in the face of a new century, but in the Boy Scout literature written by Baden-Powell this fear is more directly associated with the seeming inevitability of war and his lack of confidence in the "miserable specimens" who may be called upon to defend British interests at home and abroad.

Once Seton was forced to resign and the National Council revised his manual, few differences remained between the American and British movements and the texts that surround them. The Boy Scout motto in both cases is the famous "Be Prepared." The scout oath in the British manual is: "I give my word of honor that I will do my best: 1. To do my duty to God and the King; 2. To help others at all times; 3. To obey the Scout Law." In the American version, "the King" is simply changed to "my country." Baden-Powell's original Scout Law covers nine points: the virtues of trustworthiness, loyalty, helpfulness, friendliness, courtesy, kindness, obedience, cheerfulness, and thrift. The council added three points to the American version of the Scout Law: "be brave, clean, and reverent." This reference to "reverence" is perhaps the most significant difference between the British and American movements; although the texts of the American and British movements are similar in their use of religious thought, the Boy Scout movement in America has been sponsored more adamantly by religious organizations. But ultimately, the similarities in the handbooks of the British and American movements speak to a similar concern in the respective cultures.

As historians such as Gail Bederman and Anthony E. Rotundo have made clear, England was not alone in its imperialistic mission at the turn of the century. In a discussion of the popularity of Theodore Roosevelt and his auspiciously "virile political persona," Bederman has persuasively argued that "Roosevelt drew on 'civilization' to help formulate his larger politics as an advocate of both nationalism and imperialism. As he saw it, the United States was engaged in a millennial drama of manly racial advancement, in which American men enacted their superior manhood by asserting imperialistic control over races of inferior manhood. To prove their virility, as a race and a nation, American men needed to take up the 'strenuous life' and strive to advance civilization—through imperialistic warfare and racial violence if necessary."[31] Commenting on a related shift in how masculinity was conceived in American culture at the turn of the century, Rotundo has made the argument: "By the dawn of the twentieth century, then, old prescriptions for manhood were being replaced. Since the colonial era, ideas of manliness had expressed concern with the government of passions; since the revolution, manhood and independence had been closely linked. Now, male impulse was nurtured, manly reason was redefined, and bonds of dominance and submission between men became respectable." As part of this change, Rotundo cites a new emphasis on the "military ideal," which emphasized competition and "fighting virtues."[32]

Whether American culture was exhibiting a popular interest in imperial expansion, as exemplified in the popularity of Roosevelt, or was involved in a shift in how manhood was valued and conceived, or both, clearly the image of the Woodcraft Indian did not hold the popular appeal of the war scout. The specter of war on the horizon gave rise to a concern over national virility and a fear that the nation's adolescents would not be able to hold their own if they were called to the mat. By 1911, the year that the "official" Boy Scouts of America manual was published, the shift from Indians to Scouts is complete, and the danger is somehow shifted away from the threat of adolescents and their seeming propensity for crime to the threat of national security abroad.[33] After his resignation from the Boy Scouts of America in 1915, Seton focused all of his energy on his Indians, which he often presented as an alternative to the "militant Boy

Scouts."[34] In 1916 he attempted to revitalize the movement by renaming it the Woodcraft League of America, but his Indians never regained the popularity they once had, and the organization slowly fell into obscurity.

Fire Starters

By titling their movement the Boy Scouts, the founders in both America and England were quite clear that they had only male adolescents in mind, but much to their surprise by 1909 there were already six thousand girls registered in the movement.[35] This inspired Baden-Powell's sister, Agnes, to institute an entirely separate organization for girls. Titled the Girl Guides, the female version of the Boy Scouts came out with its own manual, *Handbook for Girl Guides,* in 1912. As would be expected, the motto, oath, and laws in the *Handbook for Girl Guides* are almost identical to those in *Scouting for Boys.* And indeed, the reasoning behind the movement echoes that of the Boy Scouts. The Girl Guides movement is structured upon the same tension between a return to nature and a commitment to playing the game. As summed up in the opening pages of the manual: "To be a Guide out there means you are one who can be relied upon for pluck, for being able to endure difficulty and danger, for being able cheerfully to take up any job that may be required, and for readiness to sacrifice yourself for others. Girls can be just as good as men in these points if they like."[36]

On the other hand, while the basic laws of the movements and their rationales seem to transcend sexual difference, the basic rituals that enforce these laws and goals are highly gender specific. Whereas *Scouting for Boys* is divided into sections on "Tracking," "Woodcraft," "Camp Life," and "Campaigning," the *Handbook for Girl Guides* is divided into sections on "Finding the Injured," "Tending the Injured," "Frontier Life," and "Home Life." Whereas, in general, the Boy Scouts are learning how to track men and animals, how to fell trees, and how to predict the weather, the Girl Guides are learning how to nurse invalids, how to cook, and how to care for children. Thus traditional gender roles are strictly enforced. This is perhaps best exemplified in a section of the *Handbook for Girl Guides* entitled "Be Womanly," which concludes that an

> imitation diamond is not as good as a real diamond; an imitation fur coat is nothing like as good as a real fur. Girls will do no good by imitating boys. Do not be a bad imitation. It is far finer to be a real girl, such as no boy can be. One loves a girl who is sweet and ten-

der, and who can gently smooth when wearied with pain. Some girls like to do scouting, but scouting for girls is not the same as for boys. The chief difference in the training of the two courses of instruction is that scouting for boys makes for MANLINESS, but the training for Guides makes for WOMANLINESS, and enables girls the better to help in the battle of life.

In this case, a "real girl" is the ideal companion for the "real boy"—someone who keeps the house in order and is there to care for him when he is injured. As the manual sums it up, "her place is not as the rival to man, but as the complement or helpmate."[37]

When these two manuals are placed side by side one sees a paradoxical view of gender. It is apparent that both of the Baden-Powells tried to construct this space of the Boy Scout and Girl Guide, this space of adolescence, as genderless. According to the authors, regardless of gender, the problem for the adolescent was simply that life in the city did not allow him or her to become an individual. But in a paradoxical fashion, when this adolescent is taken outside of his or her preconceived role in the city and placed in nature, he or she must be contained. The Baden-Powells are ultimately not willing to keep adolescence "plastic" in terms of gender identity and ultimately fall back upon the most traditional, and most restrictive, gender distinctions and binaries.

The concept of the Girl Guide made its way across the Atlantic through the work of Juliette Gordon Low, who founded the Girls Scouts of America in 1912.[38] Interestingly, Seton's ideas about adolescence were most influential on the rival to the Girl Scout movement, the Camp Fire Girls. The Camp Fire Girls youth movement was the brainchild of Luther H. Gulick and his wife, Charlotte. As president of the Playground Association of America, chairman of the Russell Sage Foundation's Playground Extension Committee, and the YMCA's first international secretary for Physical Work, Dr. Gulick had a distinguished record of youth work. He and Seton had worked together in a number of capacities, including the Executive Committee of the Boy Scouts of America. Much like the Woodcraft Indian youth movement, the Camp Fire Girls started with a series of impromptu camps held for girls by the Gulicks beginning in 1909. After consulting with Seton, Mrs. Gulick decided that Indian lore and ceremony would be the theme of the program. At the experimental camps, the girls donned Native American gowns and braided their hair; like the Woodcraft Indians, they adopted Indian names that reflected physical or personality traits. Seton and his wife, Grace, attended meetings for the initial planning of the movement and served on committees. He also helped craft the requirements for the three ranks of the Camp Fire Girls, including a recommendation that the girls "abstain forever from the damnable and swinish, filthy, ruinous habit of chewing gum."[39]

On a deeper level, Seton's philosophy permeated to the core of the movement and informed its adoption of the symbol of the Indian. In a passage that could just as easily have been in Seton's *Birch-bark Roll,* the manual of the girls' movement, *The Book of the Camp Fire Girls,* summarizes the focus on the Indian: "The names and symbols of the Camp Fires or of the Camp Fire Girls may be suggested from any source, especially from folk-lore of the different countries, but are perhaps more often taken from the Indian lore, because it is suggestive of the spirit of the out-of-doors, of the ingenious use of the materials at hand, and is so distinctly American."[40] As with Seton's work, the Indian in this case is both essentialized as "distinctly American" and placed in opposition to urban expansion and industrialization. The Indian is premodern in every sense of the word. Much of the appeal of the symbol to the Gulicks and the appeal of the movement to Americans must have been due to this seemingly logical solution to the "problem" of modern girlhood.

Like Seton's, Gulick's conception of adolescence was strongly influenced by G. Stanley Hall, who was a teacher and personal friend. From Hall, Gulick clearly received the recapitulation-based logic that both explained the storm and stress of adolescence and justified the use of Indian activities for girls in this stage. Gulick's writing is peppered with phrases from Hall, such as this remark, taken almost directly from Hall's work: "Adolescence is intended by nature to be the second birth for every individual. That second birth is the discovery of one's inner emotional nature. That inner emotional nature is the hope of life and it is life's fate." Essentializing adolescence as a "discovery of one's inner emotional nature" became a way to justify both the historical connection to the Indian—as "distinctly American"—and to position this developmental stage as an accessible and universal phenomenon. It also became a way to contain the "problem" of adolescence, as it served as a theoretical justification for the tasks and lessons that comprised the movement. Discovering one's inner emotional nature meant playing Indian, but through this play the girl learns to be a "woman," which had very specific connotations. As recounted in the official history of the Camp Fire Girls, during the first formal meeting of the organization, Dr. Gulick laid down the fundamental basis for all activities to come: "Some twenty years ago I was compelled to discover if possible what was meant by womanly and manly. . . . I believe that the keynote to the organization which appears to be before us is a clearer vision of this question. This organization ought not to be based on numbers, but upon something that is way down deep in the very nature of human individuals and the nature of human society, because only thus will it fit in with human nature and human society. . . . I believe the keynote is here—that we wish to develop girls to be womanly as much as we desire men to be manly."[41] Gulick's choice of words here is very telling. "Developing" girls to be womanly, as opposed to "teaching" them to be womanly, implies a kind of discovery of qualities that are already there and therefore essential and true.

Not surprisingly, perhaps, these qualities, however primal, are markedly domestic. In one of the many addresses he gave explaining the theoretical basis of his youth movement—a 1912 speech delivered to the Connecticut Valley Public Recreation Conference—Gulick outlines what he sees as these fundamental traits: "Now, during all the ages, woman no less than man has had a distinct group of occupations. The activities of the home have been woman's concern—all those activities that center about the fire, the cooking and serving of food and the social ceremonies connected with eating together. . . . Woman has been concerned with form and color; with the making of beautiful things, of pottery and of dress; with the decoration of the person; with all that group of personal relationships that cluster about the child." In this speech, Gulick goes on to explain how these traits have been seriously threatened by "modern life," which has made the home no longer the center of production and thus the space where a young girl may "pass through the race history of woman."[42] The answer is, of course, to reproduce such activities in the form of a youth movement. Moving from the entry stage of "Wood Gatherer" to "Fire Maker" on this path toward womanhood involved such tasks as preparing meals, mending a pair of socks, and knowing the principles of elementary bandaging. Such tasks were interspersed with activities that would help free girls from the yoke of urban industrial life, of course—such as sleeping with the windows open for at least a month, refraining from candies and sodas, learning to tie a square knot, and knowing what to do when someone is drowning.

As with the Woodcraft Indians and the many other youth movements at the turn of the century, the Camp Fire Girls is a movement rich in complexity and contradiction, at once stressing a return to a more "natural" life and attempting to adapt to the socioeconomic realities of the new millennium. Such richness is perhaps best captured in its central image. Burning at the center of the movement, the fire is a suggestive symbol, both commonplace and fleeting, familiar and exotic. As with adolescence, it burns with an almost primal energy, but put to good use it becomes the motivating force that orchestrates both individual and human evolution. It is both wildly natural and reassuringly domestic. It illuminates each individual but serves as the meeting place for the community. Ultimately, to become "womanly," Camp Fire Girls made their way through the levels of "Wood Gather," "Fire Maker," and "Torch Bearer"—a process of adolescence—learning the meaning of the fire in all of its many forms.

David Macleod has made the point that American culture was less alarmed about adolescent girls than boys at the turn of the century, which is evidenced by the fact that girls' youth organizations such as the Camp Fire Girls and Girls Scouts started later than boys' and were less extensive.[43] However, the later start and fewer recruits in the girls' movements might more accurately be explained by sexist attitudes in American culture that made it more difficult for women and girls to organize such movements and to the direct opposition of leaders such as James E. West and Baden-Powell, who were initially threatened by "copycat" movements for girls. It is apparent that the alarm that existed in American society was an alarm about adolescence in general. As we have seen, the threat of juvenile delinquency was not a specifically gendered threat. Indeed, the question of gender may have forced the experts to be a little more discriminating with their statistical evidence; it was much easier and more effective to speak in broader, nonspecific terms. Similarly, the earliest treatments of adolescence, such as Hall's and Mead's, argued that the "problem" of adolescence was as innately female as male—storm and stress was an abstract malady inflicted upon all members of the race. Along the same lines, Seton and Gulick, and arguably the initiators of the many other youth movements that were invented at the turn of the century, were in agreement that both adolescent boys and adolescent girls would find a natural affinity for playing Indian. The difference between boys and girls would be seen in the forms this natural attraction would take. The clear gender distinctions appear in the solutions to the problem rather than the problem itself. As such, gender roles became a powerful tool for controlling the seeming threat of this new population—the traditionally gendered adolescent was the "good" adolescent. But as with the many other scripts created for individuals in their teens at the turn of the century, these roles were a double-edged sword. No matter how womanly or manly they become, the Woodcraft Indian or Camp Fire Girl is still an Indian. And behind every good little Indian, a savage lurks in the shadows.

5
Teen Reading at the Turn of the Century (Part I)
Horatio Alger

Cheap Books and Their Readers

Late nineteenth-century American society experienced a remarkable increase in the production and consumption of printed texts. The expansion of the industry that took place after the Civil War has been attributed to a steady increase in literacy rates, the growth of the public library system, and new printing technologies and methods of distribution that made reading materials of many forms available to Americans from all socioeconomic classes.[1] Taking center stage in this expansion was the increase in "cheap books" made available to the public roughly between the 1870s and the enactment of the International Copyright Act in 1891. Such a "literary revolution," as Madeleine Stern has termed it in her book on the subject, consisted of cheap reissues of English and French novels—which were unprotected by copyright laws—story papers, series books, and the dime novel, which Stern deems "perhaps the first uniquely American form of literature."[2]

A natural connection has often been made between this "revolution"—in particular the dime novel—and children's literature, especially in regard to juvenile literature and the early origins of the young adult novel. In her recent book *The Dime Novel in Children's Literature*, for example, Vicki Anderson traces "the early writings [of children's reading] as a background to what eventually became the dime novel and thereafter the basis of today's paperback books," placing the dime novel within a history that includes broadsides, chapbooks, penny dreadfuls, series books, story papers, comics, and pulp fiction. In her well-known history of juvenile literature, *American Children's Literature and the Construction of Childhood*, Gail

Schmunk Murray devotes a section to the dimes, which she claims had "profound implications on the public's reception of such bad boy fiction as *Tom Sawyer* and *Huckleberry Finn,* and ensured that serial books would continue to entice young readers well into the twentieth century." In their popular textbook *Literature for Today's Young Adults,* Kenneth Donelson and Alleen Pace Nilsen identify dime novels along with domestic novels as the two most popular types of novels that emerged for young adults in the nineteenth century.[3]

However, before we rush to make this connection between "cheap books" and adolescent readers, it's important to consider that most of these books were not consumed exclusively or even predominantly by teens. In his detailed study of the dime novel, for example, Michael Denning specifically dismisses the argument that dime novels were children's literature, suggesting that the bulk of the reading audience of this immensely popular material were "workers—craft workers, factory operatives, domestic servants, and domestic workers."[4] Indeed, there is little evidence to support the notion that the dime novels, newspapers, and magazines that comprised this "literary revolution" were in any profound way oriented toward or consumed by teens. This is perhaps best captured by a notice from the publisher in one of the first Beadle dime novels, which expresses the firm's hope "to reach all classes, old and young, male and female, in a manner at once to captivate and to enliven."[5]

Interestingly, even though there is no data to suggest that "cheap books" such as the dime novel were exclusively or even largely read by teens, the many negative reactions to them at the time are often predicated upon the serious threat they posed to (innocent) teen readers. Indeed, even though Denning makes a convincing argument about age not being a factor in the audience for the dime novel, in the section he devotes to the censorship of these controversial texts almost all of the references he cites use age as an argument for banning. At the center of all of these calls to censor is Anthony Comstock, who established the Society for the Suppression of Vice, which campaigned against immoral and obscene books and materials and lobbied for the enforcement of the 1873 "Comstock Law" prohibiting the mailing of such material. In his analysis, Denning includes an oft-quoted passage from Comstock's 1882 book *Traps for the Young,* in which he has this to say about cheap books and their readers: "[T]he editor of the blood-and-thunder story papers, half-dime novels, and cheap stories of crime ... [is] willingly or unwillingly, [among] Satan's efficient agents to advance his kingdom by destroying the young." Comstock's influence was significant, and Denning implies that he was the motivating force behind an 1886 bill passed by the Massachusetts legislature that "forbade the sale to minors of books or magazines featuring 'criminal news, police reports, or accounts of criminal deeds, or pictures and stories of lust and crime.'"[6] The relationship between cheap books and teens in these reactionary tracts was apparently used as a rhetorical device to incite fear in the American public. This rhetoric feeds off of emotionally charged notions of the "innocent child" that were common in nineteenth-century culture, but also such characterizations show a new conception of the teen, who was quite distinct from the innocent child and who was apparently seen by Comstock and others as having a newfound economic freedom and power to get in some real trouble if not handled properly.

As Beverly Clark has demonstrated in her book *Kiddie Lit,* a similar discourse of value informed much of the critical reception of American children's literature in the late nineteenth and early twentieth century, including the juvenile. "The many reasons why twentieth-century literary critics have looked down on children's literature," she argues, "include an urge to dissociate America and American literature from youthfulness and an insistence on cultural independence from the parent country. They include an urge to achieve 'institutional maturity,' as Renker puts it. Also suspect are the popularity and profitability of much children's literature."[7] In terms of the juvenile, such popularity and profitability must have been an especially worrisome issue. The exact relationship between cheap books and this emerging demographic is an extremely complex issue, but what is apparent is that like "juvenile delinquency" and "wayward youth," "cheap books" became a way to articulate fears about an adolescent population that was becoming more conspicuous at the end of the nineteenth century. Even though it's not clear to what extent teens actually consumed these books, the two categories have a symbolic connection that has remained with us to this day.

The novels of Horatio Alger and Edward Stratemeyer were linked in very complicated ways with this literary revolution and fears about the effects of cheap books on teens. Although Alger's novels precede those of Stratemeyer by a generation, their works—spanning the turn of the century—show many commonalities and can tell us a great deal about the cultural environment that invented adolescence. Sharing an awareness of the great potential of the teen demographic, the work of these authors served to create a new teen readership and at the same time to control and shape this readership. As with the other inventors of adolescence, the space carved out for this teen population, as reflected in the characters and implied reader in the works of these two authors, was rehabilitative in nature and thus predicated upon the perceived threat this audience posed. Furthermore, the same economic discourse that has framed discussions of cheap reading by critics then and now shaped the narrative qualities of the works of these two authors and served as a way to censor what many feared about the modern generation. In part, the economic focus reflects an anxiety over the cheap reading both Alger and Stratemeyer had devoted their careers to producing, but it also represents the ultimate solution to the problem of adolescence. While the word *cheap* framed such discussions in economic terms, *economic* was broadly defined to include moral value as well and thus served as a method of controlling the main character and the implied reader. As we have seen in chapter 1, material changes in American society made teens more conspicuous and there was a marked anxiety about what this population might do if its members were left to their own devices. In general, the work of Alger and Stratemeyer seeks to put this disenfranchised and dangerously idle demographic back to work. Adolescence began as an economic problem, so it is perhaps no surprise that its solution might be figured as an economic one as well.

The Natural Science of Child Saving

Horatio Alger is a particularly complex figure in regard to the relationship between the teen population in the nineteenth century and the revolution of cheap books. A writer of over one hundred "juveniles," Alger is, of course, commonly seen as being one of the first authors to capitalize on the teen reading public that was becoming a growing market in the later half of the nineteenth century, but it's not clear whether his readership was wholly or even partially teens. A number of times in his career he spoke out against the negative influences of cheap books, dime novels in particular, but his works were published with some of the same firms that made these texts available to the reading public, and since many of his novels were sold in cheap reprints after his death—two situations over which he had no control—he has become closely associated with this revolution. What is clear is that he often focused on this teen demographic in his fiction and, as I will argue here, created a type of adolescence in his implied reader.[8]

Early in his life, Alger actually had moderate success writing fiction and poetry for adult magazines and literary weeklies, but, as Gary Scharnhorst describes it in his biography of Alger, the author had a significant change of heart in 1864 when he decided to "abandon his dream of literary distinction" and devote his energies to a "'humbler department which would pay . . . better.' He would henceforth write for children."[9] Scharnhorst's characterization of this critical moment in Alger's career is an interesting one on many levels. That Alger's decision was conceived not only in terms of economic value but also social value, where he had to sacrifice the lofty field of literature for the "humbler department" of writing for children, tells us a great deal not only about the (questionable) status of juvenile literature in the middle of the nineteenth century, but also much about people's attitudes toward the teen population. Because teens became synonymous with the growing publishing market, particularly the expansion of cheap books, one could not, it seems, write about and for them without being seen as more of a capitalist than an artist. The value of the author in this area was defined by the status of the genre itself, which is to say it was thought of in terms of economic and not literary value. The former, as can be seen in the quote from Scharnhorst, was commonly thought of in much less noble terms than the latter. Indeed, the two were united in the broader theater of status, in which the literary producer was valued far less than the literary author.

The teen demographic that Horatio Alger took such an interest in was not so much growing as just becoming more conspicuous in the late nineteenth century, and even though such an awareness of this population was profitable for Alger and his publishers, it was by no means unique. As we have seen, anxiety about the expanding teen population was articulated in many different forms in late nineteenth-century American society. Alger actually became good friends and associates with one of the strongest voices about the potential threat of this expansion, Charles Loring Brace, whose 1872 work *The Dangerous Classes of New York and Twenty Years' Work among Them,* as was discussed earlier, was one of the common sources for the dissemination of the notion of the rise in juvenile delinquency in nineteenth-century American consciousness.

Alger, of course, made a career out of writing about children on the streets of New York. His most popular series, Ragged Dick, was inspired by boys he met at the Newsboys' Lodging House, a dormitory for homeless boys developed by Brace and his society in 1854.[10] In his 1868 preface to this series he made clear his hope that the works would not only entertain but also enlist "the sympathies of his readers in behalf of the unfortunate children whose life is described, and of leading them to co-operate with the praiseworthy efforts now made by the Children's Aid Society and other organizations to ameliorate their condition." The series is peppered with references to the society and its work, and we even get a grand tour of "the Lodge" in the third installment of the six-volume series.[11] As such, Alger and Brace shared the common goal of wanting to create a space for these unkempt urchins of the street. Such an enterprise involved first defining who they were, describing their peculiar behaviors, and then proposing a plausible plan to save them. This scheme was all predicated upon the belief, of course, that the "street Arab" was a problem in the first place. Like Brace—and Hall and Mead, for that matter—Alger's work is rehabilitative, and, as such, it was posited as a way to contain a seeming threat.

But what was this threat? And what does Brace and Alger's approach to it reveal about nineteenth-century attitudes toward the teen population that would soon be known as adolescence? As reflected in his many writings on the subject, at the root of Brace's approach to the growing problem of the street Arab was a belief that environment shaped behavior. In his biography of Brace, Stephen O'Connor notes that much of Brace's notion of the rehabilitative ideal came from Darwin's *Origin of Species*, which he claimed, on a number of occasions, to have read thirteen times in his lifetime. For Brace, Darwin became scientific proof that environment could influence the development of the species.[12] To change the species, one simply needs to change the environment. To change the delinquent, one simply needs to put him or her in a new environment that would force the good traits to develop instead of the bad. In *The Dangerous Classes*, for example, Brace says the following about the effect of environment on this problem: "At heart we cannot say that [the "Arab of the streets"] is much corrupted; his sins belong to his ignorance and his condition, and are often easily corrected by a radical change of circumstances. The oaths, tobacco-spitting, and slang, and even the fighting and stealing of a street-boy, are not so bad as they look. Refined influences, the checks of religion, and a fairer chance for existence without incessant struggle, will often utterly eradicate these evil habits, and the rough, thieving New York vagrant make an honest, hard-working Western pioneer."[13] In Brace's mind, radically changing circumstances to more "refined influences" would "utterly eradicate" habits learned and enable the street boy to evolve into the "Western pioneer" instead of something here not stated, but clearly far worse—something degenerative. Such a Darwinian approach to the problem of wayward youth became the rationale behind the many programs of the Children's Aid Society, most famously the "Orphan Trains" that would cart the homeless out of the inner city and put them up for adoption in the country. Darwin was of particular interest to Brace because his theories offered an indisputable, scientific basis for the efficacy of such work.

But, of course, Brace molded Darwin to his own ends. In the case of the "Arab of the streets" mentioned above, the "struggle for existence" does not naturally select the optimum traits for the species, but rather the struggle is "corrected" by the Children's Aid Society, put in check, and, for all intents and purposes, evolution is reprogrammed by the society itself. Throughout Brace's work, the Darwinian struggle for existence is presented not as natural fact, but rather as a negative circumstance that can be corrected by Christian charity. Often in his work, Brace justifies such a misapplication of the natural laws of Darwin by reading him in broad, quasi-religious terms, seeing the evolution of the human race as a movement from evil to good. As he states in a telling writing on the topic of natural selection: "The current of all created things, or of all phenomena, is towards higher forms of life. Natural selection is a means of arriving at the best. . . . Nature moves physically towards perfection, and morally there must be the same unseen but necessary motion. For if the Darwinian theory be true, the law of natural selection applies to all the moral history of mankind, as well as to the physical. Evil must die ultimately as the weaker element in the struggle with good. The slow consent of the world's history is in the direction of moral goodness, as its physical development is ever towards higher forms."[14] In this case, the natural law becomes more of a religious truth than a scientific one. Removing children from the street was justified and "natural" because it was aiding the human race's evolution from savagery to civilization, evil to good. Brace read Darwin thirteen times not only because he provided scientific justification for the change in environment his society was providing for children of the street, but also because he saw in his work a paradigm for the moral and religious beliefs upon which such work was based.

Such an interpretation of Darwin was, of course, very convenient for Brace, but it was by no means unusual. Indeed, it is in close proximity to Herbert Spencer's unified evolutionary theory, with which Brace was most certainly familiar. In his study of the influence of Darwin and Spencer on American intellectual thought, Richard Hofstadter has made the very convincing case that much of the appeal of Spencer is that his attempt to link Darwin's biological observations to a unified evolutionary theory made his work adaptable to almost any intellectual context and thus very appealing to many thinkers who, like Brace, were searching for scientific proof to make their work more convincing and appealing to their intellectual peers and potential donors. "Spencer's philosophy was admirably suited to the American scene," Hofstadter explains. "It was scientific in derivation and comprehensive in scope. It had a reassuring theory of progress based upon biology and physics. It was large enough to be all things to all men. . . . It offered a comprehensive world-view, uniting under one generalization everything in nature from protozoa to politics."[15]

As such, it is tempting, of course, to align Brace's philanthropic enterprise with social Darwinists such as William Graham Sumner and American businessmen like Rockefeller and Carnegie who saw Spencer's infamous phrase the "survival of the fittest" as a blank check for capitalist industry. This is particularly tempting because in addition to getting teens out of the struggle for existence that characterized their life on the streets, training them in the "habits of industry," Brace tells us a number of times throughout his work, was key to their ability to evolve in the right direction.[16] But I think such an alignment is a simplification of the work of Brace. Brace borrowed from Darwin the notion that environment can shape behavior. What he borrowed from Spencer and what he shared with social Darwinists like Sumner and Carnegie was the belief in a unified theory of evolution and the intellectual prowess to connect biology with economics and issues of morality. This did not come in the form so much of an application of survival of the fittest to economics—which would have been at odds with the moral implications of his work—but in the use of the general structure of Darwin's thought as a way to bridge the gap between economics and morality and a comfortableness in using economic language to describe moral issues. As such, capitalism was not so much the ultimate end of the work of Brace as it was a convenient and persuasive means to express it. Such a unified model provided the context for the seeming threat of a growing teen population that, homeless or not, was becoming more conspicuous on the American landscape. The first step was always a change in environment. Such a change aligned the individual with the moral evolution of humankind. The rewards for evolving down this path were always economic, not only because such "pioneers" would be well trained in industry, but because the moral and economic were intimately related, and moral "value" could be easily calculated in economic terms.

In one of the final chapters of *The Dangerous Classes*, in which Brace discusses the decrease in juvenile delinquency in New York since the founding of his society and the amount of money such a decrease has saved the city, he concludes: "If our readers will refer back to these dry but cheering tables of statistics, they will see what a vast sum of human misery saved is a reduction, in the imprisonment of female vagrants. . . . How much homelessness and desperation spared! How much crime and wretchedness diminished are expressed in those simple figures! . . . The same considerations, both of economy and humanity, apply to each of the results that appear in these tables of crime and punishment. No outlay of money for public purposes which any city or its inhabitants can make, repays itself half so well as its expenses for charities which prevent crime among children."[17] Scientific figures are united with moral good and ultimately economic prosperity. The return on the investment, unlike the "outlay of money for public purposes," can be seen in the context of both economy and humanity, because the two are one, united in the broader scope of human and humane evolution.[18]

Working the Right Way in Ragged Dick

As revealed in the introduction to the Ragged Dick series, Charles Loring Brace and Horatio Alger shared a common goal of ridding the streets of New York of juvenile delinquents, but close examination of the novels in this series reveals that they were united in other ways as well. A close reading of the Ragged Dick series demonstrates that the books contextualized the "problem" of the new teen population in much the same terms and took the same theoretical approach to it. It is not clear whether Alger read Darwin and Spencer, but such a model, a unified theory of evolution that drew together biology, ethics, religion, and economics, I would like to argue, was turned into an entire universe by Alger, who used it as a central tenet of his books about and for this teen audience. This made sense to Alger as a worldview, but also it worked for him as a fictional paradigm. By putting his heroes in such a developmental stage, Alger allowed his characters and his readers to see firsthand how their behavior could be either an asset or a liability, could help them either evolve or devolve.

This developmental stage was an early form of adolescence and, for Alger, it was intimately tied up with moral economics. In her book *The Fictional Republic: Horatio Alger and American Political Discourse,* Carol Nackenoff makes the argument that this adolescent paradigm is reflective of a broader crisis in American society at the turn of the century. "Alger's basic story may be read as an allegory," she points out. "The trials of the young are the trials of the Republic. In the success of the former lies the triumph of the latter. Entering its adolescence, facing Civil War, immigration, urbanization, industrialization, increasing polarization of rich and poor, corruption, greed, materialism and selfishness—all of which threaten to tear it apart—the Republic's triumph lay in the preservation of virtue, meaning its integrity, identity, independence, and freedom. Alger's fiction does battle for the Republic."[19] Published in between the nineteenth and twentieth centuries and inhabited by characters in between childhood and adulthood, Alger's work attempts to negotiate conflict on many different levels; as such, it certainly fits a common paradigm of adolescence. But more important, I believe, is the attempt in these texts to craft a workable path out of this crisis and into the seemingly stable space of adulthood.

Alger actually promoted the cause of the Newsboys' Lodging House and the work of the Children's Aid Society a number of times before he introduced the institution and its inhabitants into popular consciousness through the Ragged Dick series. In an 1867 article in the *Liberal Christian*, for example, he gives a detailed account of a visit to "the Lodge" and ends with an appeal that could just as easily have come from *The Dangerous Classes:* "Just think what it is to pluck a boy out of the perils and pitfalls of a great city," he concludes in a Darwinian fashion, "and save him from a career of vice and crime to one of usefulness and honesty, and you will not hesitate to engage in the great work of practical beneficence."[20]

As noted above, such an appeal is continued in the preface to the Ragged Dick series, but further examination of the series indicates that Alger hoped that defining and explaining this strange breed would do more than enlist sympathy on the part of his readers and motivate them to open their pocketbooks. By the time of the second book in the series (*Fame and Fortune; or, The Progress of Richard Hunter*), Alger's preface reveals that he sees his books as a way of rehabilitating the very street Arabs he is describing. "The author has sought to depict the inner life and represent the feelings and emotions of these little waifs of city life," he claims, "and hopes thus to excite a deeper and more widespread sympathy in the public mind, as well as to exert a salutary influence upon the class of whom he is writing, by setting before them inspiring examples of what energy, ambition, and an honest purpose may achieve, even in their case." In order to better "exert a salutary influence" upon this readership, Alger even goes so far as to instruct his publisher to send gratuitous copies of the first two volumes of the series to "any regularly organized Newsboys Lodge within the United States."[21]

Fiction here for Alger was a way of changing the environment, of inciting an existence without struggle, and thus a way of rehabilitating in the image of what he saw as the model youth. Alger's fictional world becomes, then, the new environment that will naturally select the positive qualities and help the individual evolve in the right direction. But clearly these "little waifs of city life" were not the only ones who were to be rehabilitated through this tool. In the opening pages of the first volume of the series, Alger has this to say about his hero: "I have mentioned Dick's faults and defects, because I want it understood, to begin with, that I don't consider him a model boy. But there were some good points about him nevertheless. He was above doing anything mean or dishonorable. He would not steal, or cheat, or impose upon younger boys, but was frank and straight-forward, manly and self-reliant. His nature was a noble one, and had saved him from all mean faults. I hope my readers will like him as I do, without being blind to his faults. Perhaps, although he was only a bootblack, they may find something in him to imitate."[22] Alger's work is rehabilitative not only because he literally used it as a device to help the "Arab of the street," but also because he saw it as a way to reform the implied reader, who would "imitate" the "good points" of its hero. Dick was not a "model boy," but his positive qualities (frank, straightforward, manly, self-reliant) could form an abstract representation of a model boy that the reader could become through the reading process. Alger's implied readers, then, become both the "little waifs of city life" and those who might find something in Ragged Dick to imitate, those not, perhaps, in his circumstance but much like him just the same. Such a construction is, of course, based upon the natural premise that the reader—who, we would assume, is approximately the same age as Ragged Dick and thus still able to evolve in a good or bad direction—is in need of some guidance in the first place. As such, it reveals a great deal about attitudes toward teens, who were perceived as much less "model boys" and much more Ragged Dicks.

The rehabilitative focus of the series and its intended effect on the reader is perhaps most apparent in the fifth volume (*Ben the Luggage Boy; or, Among the Wharves*), which recounts the "true history" of a young boy from a well-to-do family who, when unjustly punished by his father, runs away to New York for six years. Though he decides to swallow his pride and return home to his family in the end, the time he spends selling newspapers and "smashing baggage" has a positive effect on Ben who, once home, "would run a chance of being spoiled by over-indulgence, if his hard discipline as a street boy had not given him a manliness and self-reliance above his years."[23] Such a plot universalizes the experience of the

Arab of the street, making it accessible to all teen readers. It also says a great deal about the fear of the street Arab, a category that is broadened here to mean not only the homeless waif of the street but all teens because all teens have the potential to turn to a life of crime. Concomitantly, as readers identify with Ben and perhaps emulate him, the plot provides a path to follow, behavior to practice, in order to evolve in the right direction.

Alger's texts, then, enact the very philanthropic enterprise they describe. If Alger's fiction is the method through which this change of environment will occur, then Alger himself, as author, is the benefactor who instigates and funds such a change. Models for such a benefactor figure, of course, fill his works. In Darwinian terms they are the impetus behind the change in environment that allows evolution to flow in the correct direction. In the third volume of the series, *Mark, the Match Boy,* on the character of the "numerous class of improvident boys," the narrator notes that these teens are "not naturally bad, they drift into bad habits from the force of outward circumstances."[24] These outward circumstances are changed for our hero Ragged Dick in the first two volumes of the series through the kindness of Mr. Whitney, who gives Dick a new suit; Mr. Greyson, who invites him to church; Mr. Rockwell, who gives him a high-paying job; and Mr. Murdock, who helps Dick with his investments. Dick himself becomes a benefactor when, in volume 3, he takes the homeless Mark under his wing and becomes his "guardian." Dick arranges to have Mark stay at his boarding place, starts him on a course of study, assists him in getting a job and, of course, takes him to church. Becoming the ultimate benefactor, and "model boy," at the end of the novel, Dick donates the one thousand dollars he is paid for his services to the Newsboys' Lodging House. The long list of benefactors continues in volume 4, *Rough and Ready,* with Mr. Turner, who gives Rufus a position in his firm; in volume 5, *Ben the Luggage Boy,* with the nameless reporter who gives Ben the money he needs to get started in his newspaper business; and in volume 6, *Rufus and Rose,* with Mr. Vanderpool, who gives Rufus not only a place to live but some bonds that turn out to be worth fifty thousand dollars.

The philanthropic interest the benefactor takes in the prospective hero is a staple in almost all of Alger's fiction. Michael Moon has argued that such an interest is a type of seduction, and the capitalist narrative in Alger's novels both facilitates and rewards a taboo relationship between benefactor and boy. "The 'magic trick' that the Alger text ultimately performs," Moon reasons, "is to recuperate the possibility of a man's taking an intense interest in an attractive boy without risking being vilified or persecuted for doing so—indeed, this 'interest' is taken in a manner that is made thoroughly congruent with the social requirements of corporate capitalism on the sides of both parties: boy and potential employer alike 'profit' from it."[25] Given the focus on the external looks of the heroes in Alger's work and the economic framework of their moral/economic rise, Moon's reading of the hero/benefactor relationships is persuasive. I would add that such an interest must also on some level be motivated by fear as well, a fear of what might happen to the "gentle boy from the dangerous classes"—to borrow a phrase from Moon—if he were left to his own devices, without the path of adolescence offered by the benefactor and the path that these texts offer the implied teen reader.

However we frame this relationship between hero and benefactor, the success that follows is testimony to the power of environment in shaping character. Indeed, even the worst possible specimen of boyhood in the Ragged Dick series, Roswell Crawford, has hope if his environment is changed. In the third volume, Roswell, who, as he constantly reminds everyone, was once the "son of a gentleman" but has fallen upon hard times, takes the path of all those boys aboard the "Orphan Trains." "Let us hope that, away from the influences of the city," the narrator tells us, "[h]is character may be improved, and become more manly and self-reliant. It is only just to say that he was led to appropriate what did not belong to him, by the desire to gratify his vanity, and through the influence of a bad advisor."[26]

It is very telling that the problem teen that Alger's fiction is purportedly hoping to save becomes the model to be emulated by his implied reader. Alger often glosses over this seeming paradox by claiming that he is simply being more realistic. In the fourth volume in the series, *Rough and Ready; or, Life among the New York Newsboys*, for example, after frankly listing some of the chief faults of the book's protagonist—a tactic he repeats in most of the other books in the series as well—Alger provides the following justification for his focus on such suspect characters: "In fact, one reason why I do not introduce any model boys into my stories is that I do not find them in real life. I know a good many of various degrees of goodness; but most of them have more failings than one,—failings which are natural to boys, springing oftentimes more from thoughtlessness than actual perverseness. These faults they must struggle with, and by determined effort they will be able, with God's help, to overcome them."[27] Such a focus on "real-life" boys with problems to overcome eliminates the distance between the waifs of the street in New York and all other teens by joining them in their "failings which are natural to boys." This focus also has the effect of centering the plot on the development of the protagonist and thus explores what he can become when he follows the right path. As such, although he often argues to the contrary, the world that Alger describes here is just as much about the model youth the hero aspires to be—and, ultimately, will become—as the homeless child of the street. Alger may not portray any "model boys" in his fiction, but always implicit in the rise of the flawed character is a model of behavior that can and should be practiced by any youth who wants to develop in the right direction.

Although Alger provides the reader with a "realistic" glimpse into how some flawed characters can redeem themselves if placed in the right environment, he clearly was not totally convinced of the Darwinian notion of natural selection. Although there may be no model boys in his work, there are some that have greater potential than others, thus implying that there are some innate, essential qualities that one must be born with, a "noble nature" that will bloom if put in the proper environment. Such innate goodness is often recognized by the benefactor, who becomes a type of weather vane to judge who might be able to make it in the new environment and who is simply a lost cause. As Mr. Greyson tells Dick in the first volume of the series when inviting him to church, "You evidently have some good principles to start with, as you have shown by your scorn for dishonesty." And if the benefactor doesn't notice, then Alger himself makes sure we don't miss the point, offering friendly qualifications now and then, like "Dick was a naturally smart boy" or "Of religious and moral instruction he had then received none; but something told him that it was mean to steal, and he was true to this instinctive feeling."[28]

Such "natural" and "instinctive" qualities, as essential as they are, are not predominant in all youth, however. Ragged Dick's foil character, Micky Maguire, for example, is placed in a new, positive environment in the second volume of the series when he secures a job—due in large part to Dick's influence—in the firm of Rockwell & Hunter. But void of any "noble nature," he is not destined for such great things as Dick is. "Micky has already turned out much better than was expected," Alger tells us, "but he is hardly likely to rise much higher than the subordinate position he now occupies. In capacity and education he is far inferior to his old associate, Richard Hunter, who is destined to rise much higher than at present."[29] Dick is superior to Micky in "capacity," that illusive quality that, when combined with the correct environment, enables him to rise, which is to say evolve in the right, good direction. Micky is not bad per se—but not as sure of an investment as Dick.

As many critics have noted, such "capacity" often comes with good looks, which serve as a key to the benefactor as to who has the ability to better themselves and who does not. Gary Scharnhorst, for example, has shown that such a correlation between capacity and beauty was inspired by Alger's familiarity with the pseudosciences of phrenology and physiognomy, which he used to distinguish between both good and evil characters in his work.[30] Alger actually makes direct references to such theories, as is the case in *Ben the Luggage Boy,* when he tells us that even though Ben had a pleasant face, "there was a flash in his eye, when aroused, which showed that he had a quick temper, and there was an expression of firmness, unusual to one so young, which might have been read by an experienced physiognomist."[31] Alger's use of these paradigms in relation to these waifs of the street is quite appropriate given, as we have seen in chapter 1, that such theories, and in particular the work of Cesare Lombroso, were the predominant way to understand juvenile delinquency in this time period.

Applying an economic gloss to this, however, I think it's important to note that Alger does not exactly describe Dick's beauty, but rather emphasizes how his external qualities are consistent with his inner, moral nature—in other words, there is balance between what he advertises and what he delivers. For example, at the beginning of Dick's rise, his benefactor, Mr. Whitney, agrees to invest in him not because he is good-looking—although no doubt that plays a part—but because he "looks honest" and has an "open face."[32] Such descriptors are consistent with how Dick and other heroes are described throughout the series; and, lest we forget, Alger reminds us again and again that Dick looks "frank," "straight-forward," "open," and "honest."[33] Such qualities imply that there is no discrepancy between what Dick believes and what he does—the inside is consistent with the outside. This includes spending habits, too. You must spend in accordance with what you make, you must charge what you are worth, and you must look what you believe—there can be no inconsistency between the two. This is part of Alger's economic understanding of character. A business is successful by balancing its spendings and earnings. This is how people are financially successful, but also it is the way that they are morally successful. They have a realistic understanding of their strengths and weaknesses and do not advertise in any other way.

In contrast to Dick is James Travis, for example, who is not only a "coarse-looking fellow," but his physical appearance is clearly linked with the fact that "he had no great fancy for work at all, and would have been glad to find some other way of obtaining money enough to pay his expenses,"[34] or, even worse, the woman on the bus in the first volume who accuses Dick of stealing. She is wrapped up in a particularly bad exterior (her "sharp visage and thin lips did not seem to promise a very pleasant disposition"), not only because she's lazy but also because she doubts the axiom that you can indeed tell if someone is honest by that person's appearance. "You can't tell by looks," she says when someone points out that Dick could not have stolen her pocketbook because he does not have the proper countenance for a criminal. "They're deceitful; villains are generally well dressed."[35] Contrary to this opinion, the villains in the Ragged Dick series, and arguably in Alger's work in general, are fairly well marked. Mark's abusive guardian, Mrs. Watson, in *Mark, the Match Boy,* for example, is appropriately described as a "coarse-looking woman"; Mrs. Waters's obnoxious daughter in *Rough and Ready* is described as "a short, dumpy little girl, of extreme plainness"; and the evil counterfeiter in *Rufus and Rose* is "a man of middle age, with bushy whiskers, and a scar on his left cheek. He wore a loose sack coat, and a velvet vest. His thick, bunch fingers displayed two large showy rings, set with stones, probably imitation."[36]

Given this natural correlation between the physical and the moral, arguably, the biggest crime that can be committed in the world of Alger is for there to be a discrepancy between external and internal, for someone to advertise something they cannot provide. In the first volume of the series, when Dick gives Frank a tour of New York City, really what he gives is a tour of false business, which is to say immoral practices. There is the tailor who claims to be selling suits at "less than cost," the "Grand Closing-Out Sale!" where everything seemingly costs a dollar, the stockbroker Samuel Snap who promises a "fortune" in shares of the Excelsior Copper Mining Company and, of course, the array of "swindlers" who offer them a lost pocketbook seemingly full of cash for twenty dollars and pass off a false check to an ignorant countryman. In each case, there is a discrepancy between advertisement and truth, and in each case, Dick, "frank" and "straight-forward" as he is, sees the truth and wittily exposes the lie. Like this walk through New York, the Ragged Dick series is filled with swindlers and confidence men, who attempt to profit by pretending to be something they are not. Such dishonesty perhaps reaches its pinnacle in the counterfeiter we meet in the final volume, described above, whose physical qualities symbolize his hypocritical nature and whose occupation is the worst form of false advertising.

If consistency between internal and external is the optimum state for an individual, both morally and physically, then nothing is more reprehensible than "putting on airs," acting like something one is not or advertising that one has more capital than one really has. The best example of this in the Ragged Dick series has to be Roswell Crawford. As mentioned earlier, Roswell's oft-touted status as the "son of a gentleman" is a sham that he parades to feel a sense of power over Dick and his "kind." His character flaw, then, is dishonesty, but in the world of Alger the moral and the economic are intimately related. In his short-lived position at Mr. Baker's bookstore, Roswell takes liberties that even the proprietors themselves rarely display: "To see the pompous air with which Roswell threw himself back in his chair," Alger tells us, "it might have been supposed that he was the proprietor of the establishment, though I believe it is true, as a general rule, that employers are not in the habit of putting on so many airs, unless the position is a new one and they have not yet got over the new feeling of importance which it is apt to inspire at first."[37] Roswell's problem is one of false advertising, but also one that implies a discrepancy between what one claims to be worth and what one is actually worth. As Alger tells us, "One who wants to climb the ladder of success must, except in rare cases, commence at the lowest round. This was what Roswell did not like. He wanted to begin half-way up at the very least."[38] Such a "putting on airs" is of course quite the opposite of Dick's "frank" character, where what you see is what you get. Even when in the early pages of the series, Dick is blessed with a new suit and may be accused of "getting above his business" from his fellow bootblacks, Alger assures us that "[t]here was nothing of what boys call 'big feeling' about him."[39]

In any case, the combination of innate goodness and external environment is a winning one for our hero, and whether it's in the form of a new suit, access to new society, a new job, or new skills, the benefactor creates a new environment where the good qualities can come to the surface.[40] The success of the new environment always, of course, comes in the form of capital. In the first volume of the series, the change of environment that Dick experiences as a result of his interaction with Mr. Whitney and his son is symbolized by the five dollars that he puts in his bank account. "He felt himself a capitalist," the narrator tells us, and it's a feeling that grows by leaps and bounds as Dick puts his nose to the grindstone, as it were, and rises in his new environment. "In the boot-blacking business, as well as in higher avocations, the same rule prevails, that energy and industry are rewarded and indolence suffers," the narrator relates, and Dick's energy and industry turn his 5 dollars quickly into 117 dollars.[41]

According to Carol Nackenoff, such a connection between cash and virtue was a way for the Harvard Unitarian–educated Alger to adapt his characters to a world threatened by the profit motive: "A cash reward or transfer cements and reinforces fellow-feeling—that 'something extra' inclining people to be virtuous. People *must* be paid for their acts of kindness, or in a world increasingly dominated by the profit motive, acts of kindness and bonds of community will vanish. This economic incentive to justice cements Alger's tie to the language of the emerging era. Many in his audience would remember the payoff but not the moral message. It was only if the two could be conjoined that the old values could be successfully brought to the new era."[42] In addition to enforcing this economic incentive to justice, such a connection between cash and virtue also enables Dick to see the vital connection between economic development and moral development. As Dick will explain later in the series, the critical turning point in his "rise" was not the five dollars given him by Mr. Whitney, but rather the advice given him by Frank, which first "made him ambitious."[43] Frank's advice is as moral as it is economic: "And you must not only work hard, but work in the right way," he tells Dick, "You began in the right way when you determined never to steal, or do anything mean or dishonorable, however strongly tempted to do so. That will make people have confidence in you when they come to know you."[44] Working in "the right way" is the key to Dick's success because it guides him through a universe where the economic and the moral are intimately related. In the fictional world of Alger, hard work is rewarded, but "hard work" includes not being tempted to do anything "mean or dishonorable" and most important not being tempted to steal, because such behaviors create a discrepancy between one's market value and one's moral value. We are reminded again and again in the Ragged Dick series of the heroes' determination never to steal because this would be the ultimate crime in a world where the moral and the economic are so closely tied.[45]

Since stealing represents the ultimate crime, then it is perhaps no surprise that the drama of each novel hinges upon stolen property that must be returned to its rightful owner—as with Dick's stolen bankbook in the first volume of the series—or Dick himself being accused of stealing, as is the case when Dick is framed by Micky Maguire and Mr. Gilbert in the second volume. The latter, of course, is the most dramatic because it represents not only the breaking of the law of property but also of the law of character, the two being one and the same in the world of Alger. Mark is similarly framed in the third volume of the series by none other than Roswell Crawford. In volume 5, *Ben the Luggage Boy,* Ben's character is momentarily called into question when some money he is transporting is stolen, but he is able to track down the thief and return the property to its rightful owner, getting a hefty reward for his efforts. The theft of property is particularly dramatic in volumes 4 and 6 of the series, since Rufus's stepfather, Mr. Martin, steals not only a box of cash and bonds Rufus is transporting for his job, he also steals his sister, young Rosie, whom he uses as a beggar to get money; in this case, it's bad enough that she is kidnapped, but to be trained into a life of panhandling is just too much to bear.

Frank's advice that Dick work in "the right way" recontextualizes Dick's entire character, providing him access to a world where success could be measured in something other than a mansion on "Fifth Avenoo." As Mrs. Greyson explains Dick's status during one of his earliest ventures into such a world: "Dick cannot be called poor . . . since he earns his living by his own exertions."[46] She mixes up economic poverty with moral poverty. One can be poor only if one does not earn one's own money. But most important, Frank's advice shows Dick how to "rise" in this economy, in which capital is used as a gauge of moral behavior. And Dick takes this lesson to heart, rising from "rags to respectability" in a universe that respects his "frank" manner. As Alger tells us at the end of the first volume, "In more ways than one, Dick was beginning to reap the advantage of his self-denial and judicious economy."[47] Here the economic and the moral are cleft together in one sentence.

Many critics have commented on the role luck plays in the rise of the heroes in Alger's work, focusing in particular on how luck interferes with the capitalist system portrayed in this world.[48] As evidenced in the Ragged Dick series, such incidents are not about how lucky the heroes are as much as about how they capitalize upon the situations that luck furnishes for them, how they act in such a way that distinguishes them from other, less moral and less successful, boys. An excellent example of this is when Dick saves Mr. Rockwell's son at the end of the first novel. This event will, of course, be key in Dick's rise because it gets him the high-paying position at Rockwell's firm. But it's important to note that Rockwell gives Dick the job not only because he feels he owes him for the life of his son but because Dick's selfless act indicates some quality in him that Rockwell thinks is essential for success in the capitalist system. "[N]ot many boys would have risked their lives for a stranger," Rockwell tells Dick, and in the moral economy, such a risk on Dick's part puts Rockwell in his debt: "My brave boy," he tells him, "I owe you a debt I can never repay." Mr. Rockwell begins to pay this limitless debt, of course, with a position in his firm and a salary of ten dollars a week. Dick "honestly" admits, "It's more than I can earn," but such a discrepancy is explained by the fact that he's being paid not for the errands he will run for Mr. Rockwell's shop but for the "work" he performed and the risk he took in saving the drowning boy.[49] Saving Rockwell's son turns into the capital that ultimately saves Dick from a life on the street. Similar examples of luck can be found in the other novels in the series; for example, in *Rough and Ready,* Rufus just happens to overhear two thugs planning a robbery of Mr. Turner, but more important he is resourceful and brave enough to act upon the situation and save Mr. Turner from harm, an action that then leads to a high-paying position in his firm. Regarding the role that luck plays in this economy, Mr. Rockwell perhaps puts it best in *Fame and Fortune* when he explains to Micky Maguire, who is downcast for not enjoying as much luck as his more successful peer, that "Dick may have been lucky . . . but I generally find that luck comes oftenest to those who deserve it."[50]

During his lifetime, the Ragged Dick series was the most popular "juvenile" Alger wrote and technically his only "best seller." Oddly though, Alger's work was significantly more popular decades after his death in 1899. Alger, for example, estimated his total sales at about eight hundred thousand volumes, but by 1910, his novels were enjoying estimated annual sales of over one million. Gary Scharnhorst has attributed such a resurgence of popularity to an "intense nostalgia for an imaginary olden time of equal opportunity and equitable trade, because they satisfied the popular desire to reform institutions of business and government through a 'return to fundamental morality.'"[51] It's also interesting to consider how much of this resurgence was due simply to a more defined and definable teen readership. Such a readership is evident in turn-of-the-century authors like Edward Stratemeyer who made an industry out of adolescence. But Stratemeyer and Alger shared many things besides just an expanding teen market, as will be discussed in the next chapter.

6
Teen Reading at the Turn of the Century (Part II)
Edward Stratemeyer

The Rockefeller of Juvenile Literature

Written four years after his death, a 1934 article in *Fortune* magazine ("For It Was Indeed He") commemorates the legacy of one of America's most prolific writers of fiction. Evaluating his success not in terms of international prizes awarded or the ability to "capture the soul of his generation," but rather in terms of numbers of titles produced and subsequent income gained, the article concludes that the million-dollar estate he accumulated during his lifetime "was his reward for discovering in the late nineties that, like many another natural resource of the time, the reading capacity of the American adolescent was limitless. As oil had its Rockefeller, literature had its Stratemeyer."[1] An enormously prolific and successful writer of "juvenile fiction" at the turn of the century, Edward Stratemeyer was responsible as creator and/or writer for around one thousand books, including such classic series as the Bobbsey Twins, the Hardy Boys, the Rover Boys, Tom Swift, and Nancy Drew.[2] In the same way John D. Rockefeller mined the oil reserves of the American West, Edward Stratemeyer mined the "natural resource" of the American teen reading public. Also like Rockefeller, he expanded his small business into a miniempire whose development was as limitless as the resource he was exploiting; in 1905 Stratemeyer founded the Stratemeyer Literary Syndicate, which consisted of ghostwriters who would flesh out his cryptic outlines into two-hundred page books, enabling him to produce at an unusually prolific rate.

This characterization of Stratemeyer as literary "producer" has been applied by both his detractors and admirers, past and present. For example, a prominent 1914 article written for *Outlook* magazine by Franklin

K. Mathiews, the chief librarian of the Boy Scouts of America, exposed the "shocking" manner in which the "explosive material" of the Stratemeyer series books was "not written, but manufactured."[3] Using the same characterization to markedly different ends, in her 1986 book *The Secret of the Stratemeyer Syndicate,* Carol Billman titles her biographical chapter on Stratemeyer "The Man and the Literary Machine."[4] For good or ill, Stratemeyer's method of composition, his unusually high rate of production, and his association with a teen readership have informed his lasting image as successful literary producer, as opposed to an inspired creative genius. As these and many other analyses of his life and work have demonstrated, Stratemeyer is an interesting figure in American cultural history not only because of his contribution to juvenile fiction but also because of the manner in which he so effectively capitalized on a growing teen reading public.

As with Horatio Alger, the characterization of Stratemeyer as "literary producer" reveals a great deal about the status of juvenile literature at the turn of the century, which is tied to what then and now is called cheap reading. But also as with Alger, this "cheapness" carried a sharp moral and class edge, charged by fear of a new and growing danger. The phrase *cheap reading,* which was "not written, but manufactured," functions similarly to *juvenile delinquency* and *street Arab,* vaguely sketching out a threat that was as much about everything "modern" as it was about teens themselves. Additionally, as with Alger, such a characterization frames the potential threat of the Stratemeyer series books in economic terms. While certainly such terminology was playing on fears shared by many Americans about the modern industrial state and its faceless "producers," it also taps into a popular way of conceiving adolescence. As with Alger, moral economics inflect the works produced by Stratemeyer and, as such, serve as a way of rehabilitating the teen characters within them and the implied teen reader him- or herself. Stratemeyer saw adolescence largely in economic terms, and the developmental paradigm he constructed in all of his works is intimately tied up with property. If Horatio Alger was able to rehabilitate the lost waif of the street through a system of development that was as moral as it was economic, Stratemeyer turned such a model into an industry that not only paired his heroes with the latest in modern technology and engaged them in a complicated mystery but also used such "hooks" to teach them something about ownership and, perhaps most important, keep them out of trouble. Analysis of titles from four of the most popular of the Stratemeyer series books in the early decades of the twentieth century—Tom Swift, the X Bar X Boys, the Hardy Boys, and Nancy Drew—reveals not only a common thematic focus on the values of hard work and ingenuity but also a common plotline that connects moral development to property. Such a plotline also facilitates the redirection of desire away from a romantic love interest toward the more acceptable object of capitalist production, whether it is a boat, airplane, horse, or the latest clue in a complicated mystery. Moving from the story structure to the material qualities of the books themselves, the same system of capitalist censorship is imposed as the reader's desire for a single ending is perpetuated endlessly through ambiguously provocative chapter titles and references to other editions in the series. As with the characters' physical desire, readerly desire is redirected and sustained through the next adventure, which has already begun before the reader turns the final page. The series book in many ways is a uniquely adolescent genre, not only because it is synonymous with the origin of the young adult novel, but also because its structure both mirrored and shaped its reading public and reflected what this readership meant to American society at the turn of the century.

Moral Economics in the Stratemeyer Series Books

The depictions of how Edward Stratemeyer became a successful literary producer often make him out to be more of a Ragged Dick than a John D. Rockefeller. Summarizing Stratemeyer's career, Andrew Svenson, a ghostwriter and partner in the syndicate, has said: "As a young man he had a burning desire to write. This did not please his father, who wanted him to go into the commercial field. Edward secretly wrote his first short story on brown wrapping paper and sent it to *Golden Days*. His success in the field of children's literature was immediate. . . . Edward Stratemeyer was a man of simple tastes, fun loving and imaginative. He hewed straight to the line of the high moral concepts of integrity and loyalty, and, through the vast circulation of his books, instilled these ideas into the minds of millions of young readers."[5] A classic personification of the American work ethic—and a living tribute to the Algerian "rags to respectability" narrative—Stratemeyer, as recounted in these biographical accounts, had a unique gift for creating exciting and entertaining characters and stories, and also had the ingenuity to produce them in a marketable fashion. As mentioned earlier, at his death in 1930, Stratemeyer had amassed somewhere around a million dollars in assets. Perhaps even more impressive is the fact that the Stratemeyer formula has stood the test of time: after his death, his two daughters continued to run the family business and published more than 480 books; in 1984 the syndicate was sold to Simon & Schuster, which has since issued more than 290 new titles without markedly altering the formula.[6]

But what exactly is the Stratemeyer formula? Although each series has its distinctive "hook"—whether it is Tom Swift's latest invention or Nancy Drew's latest mystery—the underlying story structure of the majority of the series books is basically the same: there is usually a quest that entails the recovery of a stolen item from a crook; this quest is intermittently frustrated by various physically threatening situations; sometimes there is a love interest, but it always takes second place to the task at hand; there is little change in the main characters of the stories, but they always find that core values of hard work and ingenuity "pay off," sometimes in the form of a prize or a reward, but most often in the satisfaction of seeing property returned to its rightful owner. For example, in one of the early books of the Tom Swift series, *Tom Swift and His Motor Boat* (1910), Tom uses some reward money (given to him by Mr. Swift for retrieving some valuable papers from a gang of thieves in an earlier volume) to buy a secondhand motorboat. Happy Harry, a local tramp, and his "cronies" rob Mr. Swift's workshop, getting away with some inventions and Tom's boat, which we find out later has a diamond hidden in it. After many daring feats, including the rescue of a hot-air balloonist, Tom is able to locate his boat, capture the gang, and return the stolen property to its rightful owner. A similar situation unfolds in one of the early books of the X Bar X Boys series, *The X Bar X Boys on the Ranch* (1926). In this case, Roy and Teddy Manley and their father have their horses stolen by a gang of rustlers. After many long hours on the trail, including such adventures as an almost fatal fall off a cliff and a fight with a mountain lion, the Manley boys track down the rustlers. As a result of their infighting—a common characteristic of men with this type of evil nature—the rustlers reveal the location of the horses. In the first episode of the Hardy Boys series, *The Tower Treasure* (1927), career criminal "Red" Jackley goes on a crime spree in Bayport, stealing Chet Morton's yellow roadster, robbing the city steamboat office, and breaking into a safe at the Tower Mansion. Frank and Joe Hardy are able to piece together the connections between the crimes and track down Jackley himself, who confesses the location of the stolen property on his deathbed. Similarly, in the first book of the Nancy Drew series, *The Secret of the Old Clock* (1930), a missing will has usurped the rightful inheritance of the kindly Turner sisters and others. Some ingenious "sleuthing" puts Nancy hot on the trail of a stolen clock, which turns out to be the hiding place of the will. At one point Nancy is locked in a closet by some desperate thieves, but perseverance and quick thinking get her out of trouble and in possession of the lost will that makes certain justice is served.

In these cases, and typical of the Stratemeyer series books in general, the adolescent heroes—wealthy enough to have access to some opportunity, but not so wealthy that they do not know the value of a dollar—are put in the position of demonstrating the responsibilities of ownership. This position is often challenged by some villain, but through hard work and ingenuity and a basic moral sense, the hero is able to come out on top, while enjoying a great deal of excitement and adventure along the way. Enforcing the responsibilities entailed in the ownership of property and the values that will ensure success in a capitalist society (hard work and ingenuity), the formula of these texts emphasizes the very ethics that enabled their author to realize his million-dollar estate. The unusual circumstances surrounding the origin of these texts, in which so many titles were produced under the creative eye of one individual, resulted in many similarities in plot and characterization; also, interestingly, the same values that ensured the success of Stratemeyer have been imprinted upon the texts themselves.[7]

As such, Stratemeyer borrowed a great deal from the work of Horatio Alger. Interestingly, Stratemeyer, working as a ghostwriter, completed a series of Alger's unfinished manuscripts after his death in 1899 and has been seen by many authors as Alger's heir apparent.[8] As do Alger's, Stratemeyer's heroes have the "capacity" for success, which is as much a work ethic as it is a moral sense that instinctively despises people who pretend to be what they are not and situations where property does not go to its rightful owner. As in Alger's books, such an innate capacity often comes with good looks, while evil or conceit is accompanied by physical disfigurement. In the episode of Tom Swift's adventures related above, the villain, Happy Harry, is characterized by a tattoo of a blue ring on the little finger of his left hand; in *The X Bar X Boys on the Ranch,* the rustler has a scar on his chin; "Red" Jackley in *The Tower Treasure* is characterized by his penchant for wearing bright red wigs when committing his crimes; and in the first episode of Nancy Drew, lest we should get confused, the crooks are short, heavyset, and have big noses.

As mentioned earlier, in Alger's novels such a connection between the physical and moral becomes a way to essentialize moral goodness as a measurable, physical quality and to portray one of the most valuable characteristics of the model teen, which is that he or she demonstrate no discrepancy between what is on the inside and the outside. That such a system is at work in the Stratemeyer series books is no surprise, given the many turn-of-the-century attempts by Hall and others to essentialize adolescent behavior as biological. In the world of the Stratemeyer series books, hard work and ingenuity are essentialized as the "true" characteristics of adolescence, and the heroes in the books have the physical beauty to prove it. The specific definition of "beauty" in these texts can tell us a great deal about their readership, particularly in terms of race and class. Many critics have commented upon the racial stereotypes in the Stratemeyer series books. Donnarae MacCann, for example, has demonstrated how the portrayal of African American characters in the Nancy Drew books served to reinforce a myth of white supremacy and the inferiority of African Americans that was still quite prevalent in America during the time the books were written. Regarding class and the readership of these books, Nancy Romalov has made the interesting argument that the intense debate among librarians about whether to include the Stratemeyer books in the new and growing public library system in the early decades of the twentieth century was often drawn along class lines. One argument for the inclusion of the series books was that even though "[t]hey might not be desirable for every library . . . [they] were appropriate in libraries located at or near factories, where children of workers could enjoy them and perhaps graduate to better things."[9] Such a focus on the middle class is inscribed in the texts themselves and the characters that populate them.

In addition to revealing a great deal about readership, such racism and classism, I would argue, is concomitant with the static worldview of these books—in particular, their static portrayal of adolescence. Whereas in Alger, the accumulation of capital marks the "rise," both morally and economically, of the hero, in the Stratemeyer books, evolution is marked by the return of capital to its rightful owner. Whereas with Alger, the "rise" is in part a movement between social classes, in the Stratemeyer books, by and large, the teen hero is already thoroughly middle class and white; such a status gives the heroes access to commodities, and the plots typically affirm the rights of ownership. As such, the characters in the Stratemeyer books never age; they are caught up in a perpetual adolescence in which they are forever occupied in maintaining order. The teen in the Stratemeyer books is taken outside of any real developmental framework and is, for all intents and purposes, turned into an adult.

There are other significant differences between the fictional worlds of Alger and Stratemeyer, however. As Carol Billman has pointed out, whereas Alger often depicted sober youth, devoted to making a clean living, taking time off only to study their Bibles and bankbooks, "Stratemeyer's fiction depicted freewheeling youth who lived in the present and sported such contemporary luxury items as motor boats, automobiles, motorcycles, or . . . airplanes. There is no mistaking the old-fashioned, Algerian social and moral codes Stratemeyer maintained as underpinnings in his narratives; but, compared to preceding literature, these values did just that—underlay, or took a back seat to, the wonderful, superficial stories of adventure and suspense."[10] Indeed, a simple glance through the titles of the syndicate's books indicates that it was not character that was the selling point but rather the latest commodity to which these characters were attached—whether it is a motorboat, motorcycle, motorcar, airship, submarine, gun, horse, airplane, radio, or motion picture camera. Along the same lines, the lives of these youth would be of little interest if, within the first page and a half, they did not stumble upon a clue to an unsolved mystery.

I emphasize these two characteristics of the Stratemeyer formula not only because they differentiate the Stratemeyer books from Alger's work but also because this focus on the commodity and the retrieval of the stolen property at the center of the mystery plot is intimately tied up with notion of adolescent development in these texts. The mystery is a way of connecting moral development to property. Out of the roughly sixty-nine series that are attributed to the syndicate, thirty-seven include at least several mystery novels, including the most popular and longest-running series such as the Rover Boys, Tom Swift, the X Bar X Boys, the Hardy Boys, and Nancy Drew. As D. A. Miller has pointed out, the narrative structure of the classic detective story is predicated upon a paradoxical economy of meaning:

> On the one hand, the form is based upon the hypothesis that everything might count. . . . From the layout of the country house (frequently given in all the exactitude of a diagram) to the cigar ash found on the floor at the scene of the crime, no detail can be dismissed a priori. Yet on the other hand, even though the criterion of total relevance is continually evoked by the text, it turns out to have a highly restricted applicability in the end. At the moment of truth, the text winnows grain from chaff, separating the relevant signifiers from the much larger number of irrelevant ones, which are now

revealed to be as trivial as we originally were encouraged to suspect they might not be.[11]

Applying Miller's paradigm to these series books, one might argue that commanded by the economy of the mystery plot, objects become charged in how they relate to the crime and, perhaps more important, character "development" is possible only in how it facilitates this crime's solution. The mystery is introduced early and both character and reader are propelled forward by a desire to see justice done. Additionally, in the case of the series books, this mystery plot is always related in some way to the enforcing of the ethics of the capitalist economy because it always entails the returning of the property to its rightful owner. Thus the mystery plot and the capitalist ethics work in tandem, supporting and enforcing one another. Character "development" here is the solidification of a capitalistic morality that is marked by the possession of property. Along the same lines, in these texts in which capitalist ethics are so prominent, not only is it true that "everything might count," as Miller describes it, but certain objects become doubly charged because they both facilitate the solution to the crime and serve as receptacles for the romantic desire displaced along the way. Unlike in Alger's work, whose homeless waifs of the street were a vague symbol of the threat of adolescence, the nature of the threat in Stratemeyer's books is more succinct and direct; it is the threat of adolescent sexuality.

This censorship of desire can be seen in many of the Stratemeyer series books. In the Tom Swift, X Bar X Boys, Hardy Boys, and Nancy Drew series there are, of course, love interests, and sometimes these love interests play a significant role in the plot, but typically the initial desire for the love interest is redirected by the task at hand, which entails the returning of some property to its rightful owner. For example, in the episode of Tom Swift I mentioned earlier, Tom shows a distinct interest in Miss Nestor: "a flash from her brown eyes . . . made Tom's heart beat double time."[12] Tom plans to give Miss Nestor lessons with her new motorboat, but these plans are soon frustrated by the theft of his father's inventions and his own motorboat, and Tom has to devote his time and energy to the retrieval of the property.

Similarly, in the case of the Manley boys in the X Bar X Boys episode mentioned above, the arrival of Ethel Carew and Null Willis at the beginning of the book seems like a perfect setup for Roy and Teddy: "The boys now saw two young girls, of about their own age, who had just stepped from the train to the platform. Small hats were set over piquant faces; laughing eyes looked into those of Roy and Teddy. Somewhat in a daze, the boys acknowledged the introduction." But soon after the arrival of the girls, the horses are stolen, and although there are a number of references throughout the book to the two girls, any steps toward developing a relationship, any expressions of desire, are subsumed by the search for the horses. At one point in the book a dance is planned, and indeed, the reader expects to see some development in terms of the boys' initial desire, some expression of sexuality, but news arrives that the rustlers have been spotted and a censorship is imposed, a hierarchy established:

> "What do you say, boys?" Mr. Manley cried, turning to the punchers. "Do we go after 'em? Hey?"
>
> "You bet!" came his answer in a roaring chorus. "Let's go! Nick, throw that mouth-organ of yours out the window! We got business!"
>
> "All right, boys! On our way!"
>
> There was a rush for the door. Decorations were scattered ruthlessly. Chairs were tossed aside. And where, but a moment before, was a crowd of jostling, happy, overdressed cowpunchers, now stood only Mrs. Manley, Belle, Ethel, Null and Norine, looks of anxiety on their faces.[13]

Indeed, the mouth organ is thrown out the window and the boys do not even stop to change their clothes; they will greet their stolen horses in the same outfits they wore to enamor their sweethearts. The important "business" of the retrieval of property becomes the status quo as the "roaring chorus" heads out the door. The "looks of anxiety" on the faces of the women left behind might indicate concern for the danger facing the men, but more likely they indicate frustration, as, once again, they are marginalized by the task at hand.

From the very beginning of the Hardy Boys series, a reoccurring romantic interest is set up for both Frank and Joe. In the first episode, mentioned above, while searching for Chet Morton's yellow roadster, Frank's attention is momentarily diverted by an attractive girl walking down the street: "Frank's face lighted up, for he recognized the girl as Callie Shaw, who was in his own class at Bayport high school. Of all the girls at the school, Callie was the one most greatly admired by Frank. She was a pretty girl, with brown hair and brown eyes, always neatly dressed, and quick and vivacious in her manner." Though he isn't quite as romantically inclined as his older brother, Joe demonstrates a reoccurring interest in Iola Morton, a "plump, dark girl" who, we are told, "had achieved the honor of being about the only girl [he] had ever conceded to be anything but an unmitigated nuisance." As in subsequent books in the series, encounters with Callie and Iola are slightly charged but typically become a way to facilitate the solving of the mystery at hand. For example, in the scene quoted above wherein Frank encounters Callie on the street, only minutes earlier she was almost run over by the crook who has stolen Chet Morton's yellow roadster, so they interact just long enough to add some new information to the search. Frank is on his way, and Callie is understanding, saying, "I know you're anxious to chase that awful man."[14]

In the Nancy Drew series, Nancy's relationship with her reoccurring love interest, Ned Nickerson, is continually frustrated by the latest mystery. In episode 7 (*The Clue in the Diary*), when Ned makes his first appearance, there is clearly an interest on both parts. Their courtship becomes intimately tied up with the mystery, as the teens meet again and again to discuss leads and exchange clues. When Ned promises to drop by the Drew home to hand off an important clue, Nancy is ecstatic but is quick to attribute her emotion to the new developments in the case: "After Ned had hung up the receiver, Nancy fairly danced back into the bedroom. She sent one slipper flying toward the bed, and the other into the far corner of the room. She attempted to explain her jubilant spirits by telling herself that she was overjoyed at unearthing a possible clue to the identity of the person who had caused the Raybolt fire." When the mystery is solved and the property is returned to its rightful owner, Ned makes his first move by suavely suggesting that he may develop a diary of his own. In this (tension-filled) moment the teens' desire for one another, which has been redirected into the clues, is unmasked for what it is, but only briefly, as Nancy's friend George redirects everyone's attention back to the important issue, which is the mystery:

"It all came from the clue in the diary, too," Ned declared. "Say, I have a notion to start one of my own!"

"Why don't you?" Nancy asked lightly.

She became conscious that Ned's eyes were very tender as they rested upon her. In confusion she looked away, but her hand shook so that she nearly dropped the tray of empty glasses which she had gathered up to carry to the kitchen.

"I would if I thought it might bring me the happiness I want," Ned answered meaningly. "Do you think it ever would, Nancy?"

Nancy laughed and glanced quickly toward the other end of the dining room, where Bess and George were gathering up silverware and napkins. She understood well enough what Ned meant, but she preferred to give no indication that she did.

George, who had caught only one word of the conversation, saved Nancy the necessity of answering.

"Speaking of diaries," she called out cheerily, "I think it would be a good idea if Nancy kept one herself. The only trouble would be that she couldn't find one large enough to hold all of her exciting adventures."[15]

The quick-moving and exciting plots of the Stratemeyer series books left little time for anything but following the next lead. As Andrew Svenson has succinctly summarized the Stratemeyer formula: "A low death rate but plenty of plot. Verbs of action, and polkadotted with exclamation points and provocative questions. No use of guns by the hero. No smooching. The main character introduced on page one and slambang mystery or peril set up."[16] Slambang mystery, indeed! When you're an adolescent in the world of Stratemeyer, who has time for smooching?

This capitalist censorship of desire would perhaps not be quite so worthy of emphasis if it weren't for the charged quality of the objects that substitute for the object of desire. The object of production or property becomes charged in the sense that it displaces the initial object of desire. At one point in the ninth book in the Tom Swift series, *Tom Swift and His Sky Racer* (1911), in which Tom wins a ten-thousand-dollar prize for his speedy airplane the "Humming-Bird," Tom's chum Ted reminds Tom that this attention to his work has left little room for Miss Nestor:

"I saw Mary Nestor on my way over here. She was asking for you. She said you must be very busy, for she hadn't seen you in some time."

"Um!" was all Tom answered, but by the blush that mounted to his face it was evident that he was more interested in Mary Nestor than his mere exclamation indicated.

When Ted had gone Tom got out pencil and paper, and was busily engaged in making some intricate calculations. He drew odd little sketches on the margin of the sheet, and then wrote out a list of the things he would need to construct the new aeroplane.

The obvious interest in Miss Nestor, signified by the blush, is soon lost to the task at hand, that is, producing the best plane and winning the money. Throughout the book, as with the other episodes in the Tom Swift series, Tom's attention is directed toward his latest invention, which is legitimized in the capitalist society through the patent and is gendered with a feminine pronoun: "'She's just got to do it; that's all! But I know she will,' and he petted the big propeller and the motor's shining cylinders as though the machine was a thing alive."[17]

Similarly, in the opening pages of *The X Bar X Boys on the Ranch*, Teddy Manley is teasing his brother Roy about his unusual affection for his horse Star: "Do you tuck him in bed and kiss him good-night, Roy?" Although, as we have seen, the boys soon meet two girls, their attention is once again directed back upon the horses when they are stolen. Throughout the book, the girls are used by each of the brothers simply to divert the other's attention from the important desire, their affection for the horses: "Roy looked quickly at his brother. He knew the strain the younger boy had been under, and felt that the best thing to do was to take his mind off Flash and Checkered Shirt. 'Say Teddy,' he said in a loud voice, 'what do you think of those two girls dad met on the train?'" As we saw earlier, any expression of desire for the girls is taboo in the culture of capitalist production. In this case, capitalist ethics regulate sexuality to the point where there is an inversion: the fundamental desire for the girl is put in a secondary position and used to divert the boy's attention from the relevant desire, the desire to own, and the object of that desire, property (horse). The desire is legitimized in the text through the brand—"The X Bar X was proud of its mark. It stood for many years of upright, square dealing"—and therefore the expression of this desire is acceptable, in contrast to the unacceptable desire for the girl. A censorship is imposed, and thus the narrative ends with the reunion with the horses: "'Just like kids,' Nick said to Pop, with a grin, as the two brothers ran down the path toward the enclosure. 'They're crazy to get their ponies under them, an' I don't know as I blame 'em! Golly—watch 'em! Look at Roy! By jimminy, he's kissin' the bronc! Now he's on—so is Teddy! Yay, boy! See 'em go! Ride 'em, cowboy! Yay!'"[18] Kissing Ethel and Null is one thing; kissing Star, "the bronc," is quite another.

Many critics of the Nancy Drew series have noted a similar displacement of sexual desire. Bobbie Ann Mason, for example, has noted the manner in which sexuality is often sidelined by the mystery plot and (somewhat jokingly) has highlighted the often-masturbatory nature of the many searches for concealed treasure in the books. Lee Zacharias has suggested that sexuality in the Nancy Drew series is redirected not toward production but toward the consumption of food: "[Nancy and Ned's] lack of physical relationship is compensated for by the fact that the first thing they often do when together is eat: 'Oh, this has been a wonderful picnic!' Nancy declared as she finished her third sandwich. 'Ned, I have never tasted better meat.'"[19] While clearly the narrative descriptions reflect the sexual tension that is glaringly absent in the characters' relationship, I would argue that ultimately it is the mystery plot that censors such desires. As such, the clues become charged both in how they facilitate interaction between Nancy and Ned and in how they replace such interactions, as exemplified in the charged discussion about the diary cited above. Ultimately it is the stolen property that must be returned to its owner that diverts Nancy's attention.

The mystery plot censors desire in a similar way in the Hardy Boys series. For the most part, interactions with Callie and Iola become ways to exchange new clues about the crime or add an emotional layer to the need to solve the crime and return the property to its rightful owner. In the third episode of the series, *The Secret of the Old Mill* (1927), for example, Frank and Joe find themselves hot on the trail of a gang of counterfeiters. The search is inspired by Callie who, in an early scene in the novel, tearfully explains to Frank how her guardian has been cheated by one of the counterfeiters and now her business is in jeopardy. She is also able to facilitate the solving of the case by furnishing Frank with one of the bogus bills.

Although in this case, capitalist ethics regulate and, in a sense, censor desire, this desire does not disappear, and indeed the capitalist paradigm that takes over is quite sexual in its structure. As we have seen, within the text, the substitute object of desire or the clue becomes charged in how it stands in for the initial object of desire. Interestingly, moving outward from the plot and characterization to the structure and material qualities of the books themselves, it is not difficult to find echoes of this basic paradigm. In this sense, the book itself becomes charged as it promises and delays the reader's desire for an ending. In both cases, the desire is intimately tied up with the dollar value, the lifeblood of the capitalist economy. If, as Roland Barthes has pointed out, the linear narrative structure works by making "expectation . . . the basic condition for truth: truth, these narratives tell us, is what is at the end of expectation," then the mechanism of the Stratemeyer series book is to reinscribe the expectations of the reader so the desire for truth is never fulfilled and therefore the reader never loses interest.[20] In the case of the individual books in the series, this is done through the chapter titles. All of the syndicate books have chapter titles that give a slight tease as to the next twist in the plot. Short, minimal, yet powerfully ambiguous, the titles certainly point in an exciting direction but nonetheless leave a great deal of room for speculation. For example, the reunion of the Manley boys and their horses mentioned above appears in a chapter entitled "Round-Up." This title suggests to the reader that some type of closure is in store, but how this closure will be accomplished and whether it will involve a returning of the horses, or a meeting with the two young girls, for that matter, is left to the reader's imagination.[21]

But, of course, these books do not necessarily stand on their own; they are pieces of an overall series. Encoded within the text itself are references to other works, so as the reader moves forward, drawn by the expectations aroused by the illustrations and chapter heads, he or she encounters references to other books that create new expectations and the cycle is repeated ad infinitum. In *Tom Swift and His Motor-Boat*, Tom uses his motorcycle to get to the auction where he buys his motorboat—"Shortly before this story opens the youth had become possessed of a motor-cycle in a peculiar fashion. As told in the first volume of this series *Tom Swift and His Motor-Cycle*"—and with his motorboat he meets Mr. Sharp, with whom he plans to build an airship: "'We'll build it, however, as soon as we can solve that one difficulty.' They did solve it, as will be told in the next book of the series, to be called 'Tom Swift and His Airship; or, The Stirring Cruise of the Red Cloud.'"[22]

Ultimately, then, the imprint left by the literary production of these texts is more encompassing than one might initially suppose; capitalism regulates not only the desire of the adolescent hero but the desire of the reader as well. As with Alger, these texts are rehabilitative in the sense that they are predicated upon a type of adolescent sexual desire that must be regulated by the capitalist work ethic, which is both economic and moral. As the patent and brand legitimizes the love affair between character and invention, hero and property, perhaps the price of the books themselves legitimizes the love affair between the syndicate as producer, the book as product, and the reader as consumer. As the dollar amount is paid, the relationship is transferred from writer-product to reader-property. In this case, there is a type of marriage between inventor and invention, owner and property, producer and product, reader and book, but it is a marriage without much of a honeymoon.

This perpetuation of readerly desire is compounded by the fact that typically in the Stratemeyer series books the main characters do not age; thus, readers usually grow out of these books, moving on to more "adult" fare, before they read all of the volumes. This general characteristic of the Stratemeyer books, however, is altered in a few of the series, including the Tom Swift series, in which Tom eventually grows up and marries. In volume 32, *Tom Swift and His House on Wheels,* Tom finally marries Mary Nestor; but, needless to say, there is little expression of erotic desire and we are assured that his relationship with Mary will not draw his attention away from his inventions: "Nonsense! Nothing of the sort!" says Mr. Jackson when the suggestion is made. "Tom Swift will never stop inventing. I shouldn't wonder, now that he's married, but what he'll do the best work of his life."[23]

Additionally, the syndicate had an infallible technique for ensuring that the marriage of protagonists did not mean the end of their adventures, which was to endow them with children who exhibited the same appetite for adventure and reliance upon hard work and ingenuity as their parents—hence, Tom Swift Jr., a series begun in 1954. The Rover Boys also marry and have sons who turn out to be uncannily similar to their fathers. As Carol Billman has put it,

> Tom's boy Jack is the eldest and is the born leader of the next generation of cousins. Tom energetically sires twins, Andy and Randy, so the second series has a double dose of mischievous fun. Sam's Fred is as faceless as his father and, predictably, plays second-in-command to Jack. . . . Rounding out the Rovers' camp is a coterie of school chums whose primary function is to supply comic moments in the adventure drama. . . . The second batch of Rovers have a similar supporting cast, which includes the requisite fat boy, Fatty Hendry (Tubbs played this role earlier); the oafish German student, Max Spangler; and assorted others, some of whom are—no surprise— sons of the first crew of secondary characters. The Rovers' world, we can safely conclude, is full of corresponding places and people.[24]

Help Wanted

Regarding adolescent sexuality and how it can be "scripted" by reading material, Suzanna Rose has made the argument that romances, with their emphasis on themes such as "escape, security, desire for recognition, power over men, the mystery of the male, and passivity as an exulted state," and adventure stories, with their emphasis on "independence and conquest," pattern how women and men, respectively, express sexual desire.[25] While her analysis of adventure stories does not directly apply to the Stratemeyer series books, the idea of using adolescent literature to theorize about the dynamics of interpersonal relationships, deciphering the cues encoded in the script/book, could be quite telling in this case. Of course, Rose's notion of scripting desire describes just one of the many possible relationships between the readership and these texts, and sexuality is comprised of many influences above and beyond the pages of Tom Swift, but in terms of the series books we have looked at so far, it is not difficult to see how this script could play into (or is an interesting reflection of) early twentieth-century American culture. In this case, capitalism's censorship both feeds into the American work ethic and serves as a way of containing or regulating adolescence. An advertisement for the Tom Swift series claims that the purpose of these exciting stories is not only to entertain but also "to interest the boy of the present in the hope that he may be a factor in aiding the marvelous development that is coming in the future."[26] Interpersonal relationships and the expression of sexuality are recoded in the guise of technological development, production, hard work, and financial success. This script is one that leaves little room for direct expression of sexual desire and one in which the object of desire is always somehow moderated by the dollar value.

This instilling of values of hard work and ingenuity and the focus on the commodity might be reflective of the burgeoning of consumer culture that theorists such as Jean Baudrillard have identified with early twentieth-century American society. In his 1970 essay "Consumer Society," Baudrillard points out:

> We don't realize how much the current indoctrination into systematic and organized consumption is the equivalent and the extension, in the twentieth century, of the great indoctrination of rural populations into industrial labor which occurred throughout the nineteenth century. The same process of rationalization of productive

forces, which took place in the nineteenth century in the sector of production is accomplished, in the twentieth century, in the sector of consumption. Having socialized the masses into a labor force, the industrial system had to go further in order to fulfill itself and to socialize the masses (that is, to control them) into a force of consumption.

According to Baudrillard, the industrial system that characterizes so many aspects of modern Western culture controls the wage-labor force not only by instilling the values of production but also by creating a "system of needs" that scripts what we consume and how we determine value and status in our society.[27] Following Baudrillard's logic, one might argue that the censorship of desire, and perhaps more important the eroticization of the substitute object, portrayed in the Stratemeyer series books is part of a broader "system of needs" both instilled and perpetuated by consumer culture. Tom Swift's desire for Mary Nestor, Nancy Drew's desire for Ned, and the Manley and Hardy boys' desire for their sweethearts is literally transformed into a desire for commodity. This script creates a seamless relationship between production and consumption, and thus makes the commodity as desirable as the initial object of affection for which it substitutes. Adolescent development is moral development, which is realized through commodity. We have seen in chapter 1 how the invention of adolescence was largely a result of urbanization and industrialization; it is perhaps no surprise that in the teen literature at the turn of the century, adolescent development should be so intimately related to consumption. If, using Baudrillard's terminology, the turn of the century marked a movement from the indoctrination into industrial labor to an indoctrination of consumption, I would argue that adolescence has been central to such a shift.

However we theorize the relationship between adolescent development and capitalist culture, one thing is glaringly apparent: the most important goal in the early years of the twentieth century was simply to put adolescents back to work. Whether they are "inventors" or "cowboys" or assisting their fathers with the latest case, the teens in the Stratemeyer books are part of the adult workforce in one way or another. These exciting professions must have been just as much of a selling point as the latest commodities owned by the characters. Indeed, in many of the Stratemeyer series books, part of the quest of the main characters is their desire to prove to those around them that they are skilled enough to practice these professions, and they often must compete with adults to do so. The Hardy Boys series, for example, is framed by the question of whether Frank and Joe can become "real detectives" like their father. The opening pages of the first episode highlights this question. As the boys roll along the country-side on their motorcycles, they discuss their futures: "Like most boys, they speculated frequently on the occupation they should follow when they grew up, and it had always seemed to them that nothing offered so many possibilities of adventure and excitement as the career of detective." Their mother, of course, wants them to be doctors or lawyers, but Joe sniffs, "We were both cut out to be detectives and dad knows it." And this is proven by the end of the book when they find the missing tower treasure, and the owner, pleased to have her property back in her possession, acknowledges publicly that they are the "real detectives": "the Hardy boys received no compliment that they treasured so much as that remark of Adelia Apple-gate's."[28] In this case, what is most valuable to the Hardy boys, the true treasure, is not the reward money or the fact that property has been re-turned to its rightful owner, but that they have proven themselves wor-thy of and qualified for their dream job. However, their father is not com-pletely convinced, which means they must prove themselves again in the very next episode.

Proving that one is the right person for the job in these books often means competing with adults, but typically the adults are so incompe-tent that this is not a difficult task. A perfect example of this are detec-tive Smuff and police chief Collig from the Hardy Boys series. "Chief of Police Collig was a fat, pompous official who had never been blessed by a superabundance of brains," we are told in episode 2 of the series. "His chief satellite and aide-de-camp was Oscar Smuff, a detective of the Bay-port police force. As Chet was fond of saying, 'if you put both their brains together you'd have enough for a half-wit.'"[29] Like many of the adult offi-cials in these series books, whose distrust of authority must have been ap-pealing to their young readers, Collig and Smuff do more to hinder the work of the Hardys than facilitate it, but they do facilitate the boys' quest to prove that they are the true detectives. Unlike Collig and Smuff, the Hardys are good workers and deserve to be promoted.

American culture found the right, or perhaps only, answer to the "problem" of adolescence that had been vexing the popular conscious-ness since the middle of the nineteenth century. Ironically, the answer was simply to shackle teens with the most traditional sign of entrance into adult society—the job. Thus the answer to the problem of adolescence was simply to turn it back into adulthood, the category with which it had been conveniently confused before its invention at the end of the nineteenth century.

The first two decades of the twentieth century, in which the syndicate had the most series in production, witnessed many significant changes in how adolescence was conceived by American society. Part and parcel of this was the scripting of desire exemplified in these series books. A glance, once again, at the titles of the Stratemeyer series books reveals not only how often the characters are connected to some commodity, but also how often these commodities are modes of transportation: motorboats, motorcars, motorcycles, horses, and so on. These were teens who were going somewhere, always in motion, always on the move. But often the emphasis is shifted away from the goal to the journey itself—and, even more specifically, to the very invention that makes this journey possible. In a modern world filled with a seemingly limitless amount of mysteries to solve, crooks to catch, cars to race, horses to ride, planes to fly—and, of course, editions of series books to read—who has time to do anything else?

Notes

Introduction

1. "Mysteries of the Teen Years: An Essential Guide for Parents," special edition, *U.S. News & World Report*, 2005.

2. Meg Bostrom, *The 21st Century Teen: Public Perception and Teen Reality* (Washington, DC: FrameWorks Institute, 2001), 4–7; Meg Bostrom, *Teenhood: Understanding Attitudes toward Those Transitioning from Childhood to Adulthood* (Washington, DC: FrameWorks Institute, 2001), 18.

3. Mike A. Males, *Framing Youth: 10 Myths about the Next Generation* (Monroe, ME: Common Courage, 1999), 21. See also his *The Scapegoat Generation: America's War on Adolescents* (Monroe, ME: Common Courage, 1999) and *"Kids and Guns": How Politicians, Experts, and the Press Fabricate Fear of Youth* (Monroe, ME: Common Courage, 2001).

4. Philippe Ariès, *Centuries of Childhood: A Social History of Family Life,* trans. Robert Baldick (New York: Vintage, 1962), 25–32, 164, 240, 268; Joseph F. Kett, *Rites of Passage: Adolescence in America, 1790 to the Present* (New York: Basic, 1977), 158, 178.

5. Philip J. Deloria, *Playing Indian* (New Haven, CT: Yale University Press, 1998), 104–5.

6. Kenneth B. Kidd, *Making American Boys: Boyology and the Feral Tale* (Minneapolis: University of Minnesota Press, 2004), 67.

7. David I. Macleod, *Building Character in the American Boy: The Boy Scouts, YMCA, and Their Forerunners, 1870–1920* (Madison: University of Wisconsin Press, 1983), 108.

8. Marcia Jacobson, *Being a Boy Again: Autobiography and the American Boy Book* (Tuscaloosa: University of Alabama Press, 1994), 155, 151, 158.

9. In *The Adolescent in the American Novel, 1920–1960* (New York: Frederick Ungar, 1964), W. Tasker Witham also identifies the 1920s as the decade that gave birth to the "novel of adolescence" and mentions the same titles as Jacobson. Witham argues that these novels are characterized by a more "frank" attitude, contrasting with the "gen-

teel" tradition of novels published before this time. Such an association between adolescence and realism is an interesting precursor to the scholarship on young adult literature I discuss in this introduction.

10. Peter Stallybrass and Allon White, *The Politics and Poetics of Transgression* (Ithaca, NY: Cornell University Press, 1986), 191.

11. In *Youth and History: Tradition and Change in European Age Relations, 1770– Present* (New York: Academic, 1974), John R. Gillis reaches a similar conclusion about European society's relationship to adolescence. He states: "It seems, therefore, that the images of the innocent adolescent and the predatory delinquent have formed an historical dialectic for most of this century. They both originated in the same period; both were largely projections of the hopes and fears of a middle strata of European society struggling to hold its own against successive waves of social and political change. The notion of a stage of life freed from all the cares and responsibilities of a troubled civilization was their escapist dream, the vision of juvenile degeneracy their recurring nightmare" (182).

12. Steven Mintz, *Huck's Raft: A History of American Childhood* (Cambridge, MA: Belknap, 2004), 252–53.

13. Jon Savage, *Teenage: The Creation of Youth Culture* (New York: Viking, 2007), xv, 14. In his 1999 book *The Rise and Fall of the American Teenager* (New York: Avon, 1999), Thomas Hine also traces the "prehistory" of the teenager and makes some interesting connections between the teenager and the adolescent.

14. Sarah K. Herz and Donald R. Gallo, *From Hinton to Hamlet: Building Bridges between Young Adult Literature and the Classics*, 2nd ed. (Westport, CT: Greenwood, 2005), 9–10.

15. Marc Aronson, *Exploding the Myths: The Truth about Teenagers and Reading* (Lanham, MD: Scarecrow, 2001), 55–56. For similar histories, see also Michael Cart's *From Romance to Realism: 50 Years of Growth and Change in Young Adult Literature* (New York: HarperCollins, 1996) and Kenneth Donelson and Alleen Pace Nilsen's popular textbook *Literature for Today's Young Adults* (Boston: Pearson, 2004).

16. G. Stanley Hall, *Adolescence: Its Psychology and Its Relations to Physiology, Anthropology, Sociology, Sex, Crime, Religion and Education* (New York: D. Appleton, 1904), 1: xviii. For a more detailed discussion of America as adolescent, see Karen Halttunen, *Confidence Men and Painted Women: A Study of Middle-Class Culture in America, 1830– 1870* (New Haven, CT: Yale University Press, 1982).

17. Margaret Morganroth Gullette, *Declining to Decline: Cultural Combat and the Politics of Midlife* (Charlottesville: University Press of Virginia, 1997), 207.

18. The most famous example is, of course, the work of Erik Erikson. See, in particular, *Childhood and Society* (New York: W. W. Norton, 1964), *Identity: Youth and Crisis* (New York: W. W. Norton, 1968), and *The Life Cycle Completed* (New York: W. W. Norton, 1997).

19. James R. Kincaid, *Child-Loving: The Erotic Child and Victorian Culture* (New

York: Routledge, 1992), 17. See also his book *Erotic Innocence: The Culture of Child Molesting* (Durham, NC: Duke University Press, 1998).

 20. Hall, *Adolescence,* 1:xiv.

Chapter 1

 1. Ariès, *Centuries of Childhood,* 25.

 2. Ibid., 164, 240, 268, 30.

 3. Ross W. Beales Jr., "In Search of the Historical Child: Miniature Adulthood and Youth in Colonial New England," *American Quarterly* 27, no. 4 (1975): 379–98; Steven R. Smith, "The London Apprentices as Seventeenth-Century Adolescents," *Past and Present* 61 (November 1973): 149–61; Anne Yarbrough, "Apprentices as Adolescents in Sixteenth Century Bristol," *Journal of Social History* 13, no. 1 (1979): 67–81; Natalie Zemon Davis, "The Reasons of Misrule: Youth Groups and Charivaris in Sixteenth-Century France," *Past and Present* 50 (February 1971): 41–75; Richard C. Trexler, "Ritual in Florence: Adolescence and Salvation in the Renaissance," in *The Pursuit of Holiness in Late Medieval and Renaissance Religion,* ed. Charles Trinkaus and Heiko A. Oberman (Leiden, Netherlands: E. J. Brill, 1974), 200–264.

 For similar discussions of "adolescentlike" spaces in other time periods, see "Chapter 5: Troubled Youth: Children at Risk in Early Modern England, Colonial America, and Nineteenth-Century America," in Gerald F. Moran and Maris A. Vinovskis, *Religion, Family, and the Life Course: Explorations in the Social History of Early America* (Ann Arbor: University of Michigan Press, 1992), 141–80; N. Ray Hiner, "Adolescence in Eighteenth-Century America," *History of Childhood Quarterly* 3 (1975): 253–80; Lawrence Stone's analysis of "Attitude to Adolescent Sexuality" in his book *The Family, Sex, and Marriage in England, 1500–1800* (New York: Harper & Row, 1977), 512–18; Steven R. Smith, "Religion and the Conception of Youth in Seventeenth Century England," *History of Childhood Quarterly* 2 (1974–75): 493–516; Bernard Capp, "English Youth Groups and the Pindar of Wakefield," *Past and Present* 76 (August 1977): 126–33; Barbara A. Hanawalt's chapter "Growing Up and Getting Married" in her book *The Ties That Bound: Peasant Families in Medieval England* (Oxford: Oxford University Press, 1986), 188–204; and Thomas Hine's book *The Rise and Fall of the American Teenager.*

 For an overview of the critical history of Ariès's work, see Richard T. Vann's article "The Youth of Centuries of Childhood," *History and Theory* 21, no. 2 (1982): 279–97.

 4. Gillis, *Youth and History.*

 5. Aaron H. Esman, *Adolescence and Culture* (New York: Columbia University Press, 1990), 17; John Neubauer, *The Fin-de-Siècle Culture of Adolescence* (New Haven, CT: Yale University Press, 1992), 6. John Springhall reaches a similar conclusion about adolescence in British society in his book *Coming of Age: Adolescence in Britain, 1860–1960* (Dublin: Gill & MacMillan, 1986). Patricia Meyer Spacks provides an interesting

analysis of the adolescent in the eighteenth-, nineteenth-, and twentieth-century British novel in her book *The Adolescent Idea: Myths of Youth and the Adult Imagination* (New York: Basic, 1981).

6. See John Demos and Virginia Demos, "Adolescence in Historical Perspective," *Journal of Marriage and the Family* 31, no. 4 (1969): 632–38; Macleod, *Building Character*.

7. Kett, *Rites of Passage*, 243.

8. Ibid. See also his article "Adolescence and Youth in Nineteenth-Century America," in *The Family in History: Interdisciplinary Essays*, ed. Theodore K. Rabb and Robert I. Rotberg (New York: Harper & Row, 1971), 95–110.

9. A full genealogy of the term *adolescence* is beyond the scope of this project, but a preliminary investigation supports the critical consensus that adolescence made a sudden and pronounced appearance in a wide variety of discourses in America at the turn of the century and took on more specific, and markedly negative, connotations as the century progressed. For example, a search of the American Periodicals Series Online, a digital archive of over eleven hundred American periodicals that originated between 1740 and 1900, reveals a significant increase in the use of the term *adolescence* in the first decade of the twentieth century. The database lists 153 occurrences of the term in the citation or abstract of articles published between 1822 and 1940. The breakdown of the number of articles by decade is as follows: 1820–29 = 2; 1830–39 = 10; 1840–49 = 7; 1850–59 = 5; 1860–69 = 3; 1870–79 = 12; 1880–89 = 20; 1890–99 = 16; 1900–9 = 31; 1910–19 = 21; 1920–29 = 16; 1930–40 = 10. Two of the articles listed from between 1900 and 1909 were written by G. Stanley Hall, and five are about his work on adolescence. Before these articles, most of the references to adolescence are in passing, use the term synonymously with childhood or youth, or use it metaphorically. In fact, there are only two articles that focus on adolescence as a distinct stage: an 1875 piece entitled "The Insanity of Adolescence and the Climacteric Period," which discusses the negative effects of masturbation, and an untitled 1890 article that identifies adolescence as one of the three epochs in mental evolution.

A search of the ProQuest Historical Newspapers *New York Times* database, which includes every edition of the newspaper from its first issue in 1851 through 2004, also demonstrates that the term was used more frequently and with increased specificity at the turn of the century and evidences a progressive increase in the use of the term after that. This database lists 770 occurrences of the term *adolescence* in the citation or abstract of articles from 1877 to 2004. The breakdown of the number of articles by decade is as follows: 1870–79 = 2; 1880–89 = 2; 1890–99 = 2; 1900–9 = 6; 1910–19 = 4; 1920–29 = 15; 1930–40 = 42; 1940–49 = 54; 1950–59 = 65; 1960–69 = 64; 1970–79 = 88; 1980–89 = 158; 1990–99 = 205; 2000–4 = 63. As with the other periodicals mentioned above, there is no use of adolescence as a distinct stage until the four articles referring to Hall's work in the 1910–19 period.

Although the *Oxford English Dictionary* lists the earliest occurrence of "adolescence" in 1430 and cites appearances in 1647, 1760, 1865, and 1876, the uses of the term display few specific qualities. Before the latter decades of the nineteenth century, adolescence simply designated something other than childhood and adulthood. For example, as specified in the *Oxford English Dictionary* (1989), in 1760 Laurence Sterne, in *Tristram Shandy*, refers to a "[s]ystem of education, for government of my childhood and adolescence." Similarly, in 1876 *Rogers' Political Economy* states that "[a]n infant had its price which rose as the child reached adolescence." The vagueness of the word is exemplified by the *Oxford English Dictionary*'s definition, which reads: "The process or condition of growing up; the growing age of human beings; the period which extends from childhood to manhood or womanhood; youth; ordinarily considered as extending from 14 to 25 in males, and from 12 to 21 in females." Although the connotations of growing—as if one does not grow as a child or adult—will be inherited by more contemporary uses of the term, these early definitions mainly designate something that is not childhood and not adulthood and also indicate that the term *adolescence* was used interchangeably with the more common term *youth*. It is interesting to compare this definition with more contemporary dictionary definitions. For example, the *Random House Compact Unabridged Dictionary* (1996) defines adolescence as: "The transitional period between puberty and adulthood in human development, extending mainly over the teen years and terminating legally when the age of the majority is reached." The increase in specificity is apparent; not only is adolescence now a specific biological stage (marked by puberty and the teen years) and a legal stage (marked by the age when majority is reached), it is also a transitional stage that is characterized, specifically, by sexual development. Similarly, *The American Heritage Illustrated Encyclopedic Dictionary* (1987) defines an adolescent as "[i]mmature in attitude or behavior; puerile." In this case, adolescence has markedly negative connotations which, interestingly, define the adolescent as more "childish" than the child.

10. Theodore R. Sizer, *Secondary Schools at the Turn of the Century* (New Haven, CT: Yale University Press, 1964), 6.

11. Ibid., 8.

12. "Farming Life in New England," *Atlantic Monthly*, August 1858, 337. On the lure of the city for boys on the farm, see also Percy Wells Bidwell and John I. Falconer, *History of Agriculture in the Northern United States, 1620–1860* (New York: Peter Smith, 1941).

13. Kett, *Rites of Passage*, 152–53.

14. Ibid., 158, 178, 154. See also Sizer, *Secondary Schools at the Turn of the Century*, 7, for the influence of these new jobs on secondary school enrollments.

15. Forest Chester Ensign, *Compulsory School Attendance and Child Labor* (New York: Arno, 1969), 52. Ensign provides a detailed overview of the history of compulsory education laws in five states.

16. See Robert H. Bremner, ed., *Children and Youth in America: A Documentary History, Volume II: 1866–1932, Parts Seven and Eight* (Cambridge, MA: Harvard University Press, 1971), 1389, for the first state high school law, passed in 1827.

17. Kett, *Rites of Passage*, 123, 127.

18. Macleod, *Building Character,* 40.

19. "Public High School," *American Journal of Education* 3 (1857): 186, reproduced in Bremner, *Children and Youth in America, Volume II, Parts Seven and Eight,* 1385–87.

20. Kett, *Rites of Passage,* 125.

21. "The Proper School Age," *Pennsylvania School Journal* 12 (March 1864): 268. See also "Action and Reaction—School Discipline," *Common School Journal,* July 1, 1850, 196–98.

22. Kett, *Rites of Passage,* 126.

23. Sizer, *Secondary Schools at the Turn of the Century,* 35.

24. *Laws of the State of Illinois, Enacted by the Forty-first General Assembly at the Regular Biennial Session* (Springfield: Phillips Bros., 1899), 131–32. The law can also be found in Bremner, *Children and Youth in America: A Documentary History, Volume II, Parts One through Six* (Cambridge, MA: Harvard University Press, 1971), 506–11.

25. *Laws of the State of Illinois, Enacted by the Forty-fourth General Assembly at the Regular Biennial Session* (Springfield: Illinois State Journal, 1906), 153.

26. Robert M. Mennel, *Thorns & Thistles: Juvenile Delinquents in the United States, 1825–1940* (Hanover, NH: University Press of New England, 1973), 124. On the problems with these institutions, see also Julia C. Lathrop, "The Background of the Juvenile Court in Illinois," in *The Child, the Clinic, and the Court* (New York: New Republic, 1925), 290.

27. Harry Manuel Shulman, *Juvenile Delinquency in American Society* (New York: Harper & Brothers, 1961), 16.

28. John Peter Altgeld, *Our Penal Machinery and Its Victims* (Chicago: McClurg, 1886), cited in Bremner, *Children and Youth in America, Volume II, Parts One through Six,* 502. On the subject of public outcry over the mixing of juvenile offenders with adult criminals, see also Timothy D. Hurley, *Origins of the Illinois Juvenile Court Law* (New York: AMS, 1977), 69, a reprint of the 1907 edition published by the Visitation and Aid Society of Chicago; Louise de Koven Bowen, *Speeches, Addresses, and Letters of Louise de Koven Bowen, Reflecting Social Movements in Chicago* (Ann Arbor, MI: Edwards Brothers, 1937), 1:62, 288.

29. Charles Loring Brace, *The Dangerous Classes of New York and Twenty Years' Work among Them: Reprinted, with Original Illustrations from the Third Edition, 1880* (Montclair, NJ: Patterson Smith, 1967), 97.

30. Jacob A. Riis, *How the Other Half Lives: Studies among the Tenements of New York* (New York: Sagamore, 1957), 148. For a more complete discussion of Riis's work, see Keith Gandal's book *The Virtues of the Vicious: Jacob Riis, Stephen Crane, and the Spectacle of the Slum* (Oxford: Oxford University Press, 1997). For an interesting discussion of the work of Brace and Riis and their relation to boy work at the turn of the century, see Kidd, *Making American Boys.*

31. Sophia Moses Robison, *Can Delinquency Be Measured?* (New York: Columbia University Press, 1936), 9–10.

32. W. Douglas Morrison, *Juvenile Offenders* (New York: D. Appleton, 1897), 17.

33. Frederick H. Wines, *Report on Crime, Pauperism, and Benevolence in the United States at the Eleventh Census: 1890*, part 1: *Analysis* (Washington, DC: Government Printing Office, 1896), 213, 11. Joseph Hawes has made a similar observation about the lack of statistical evidence for the seeming increase in juvenile delinquency at the end of the nineteenth century in his excellent history, *Children in Urban Society: Juvenile Delinquency in Nineteenth-Century America* (New York: Oxford University Press, 1971); see in particular 219–20.

34. Riis, *How the Other Half Lives*, 140; Brace, *The Dangerous Classes of New York*, 245. For other examples of this belief in the connection between urbanization and the rise in juvenile delinquency, see Wiley B. Sanders, ed., *Juvenile Offenders for a Thousand Years: Selected Readings from Anglo-Saxon Times to 1900* (Chapel Hill: University of North Carolina Press, 1970), 437, 411; de Koven Bowen, *Speeches, Addresses, and Letters*, 1:115, 126, 145.

35. Morrison, *Juvenile Offenders*, 31.

36. Edward Crapsey, *The Nether Side of New York; or, The Vice, Crime, and Poverty of the Great Metropolis* (New York, 1872), cited in Sanders, *Juvenile Offenders for a Thousand Years*, 431–32.

37. A similar conclusion about the relatively small amount of delinquency in comparison to the bigger issue of wayward youth is reached by Peter Holloran in his history of the child welfare system in Boston, *Boston's Wayward Children: Social Services for Homeless Children, 1830–1930* (London: Associated University Presses, 1989).

38. Anthony M. Platt, *The Child Savers: The Invention of Delinquency* (Chicago: University of Chicago Press, 1969), 45.

39. Ibid., 107.

40. Hurley, *Origins of the Illinois Juvenile Court Law*, 14–15.

41. Ibid. For more examples of such laws, see Frederick B. Sussmann, *Law of Juvenile Delinquency* (New York: Oceana, 1950), 13.

42. Morrison, *Juvenile Offenders*, 295–98.

43. Ibid., 250.

44. Dorothy Williams Burke, *Youth and Crime: A Study of the Prevalence and Treatment of Delinquency among Boys over Juvenile-Court Age in Chicago*, United States Children's Bureau Publication 196 (Washington DC, 1930), cited in Bremner, *Children and Youth in America, Volume II, Parts One through Six*, 545–46.

45. Hawes, *Children in Urban Society*, 180.

46. Holloran, *Boston's Wayward Children*, 107.

Chapter 2

1. Esman, *Adolescence and Culture*, 4.

2. Sigmund Freud, *The Standard Edition of the Complete Psychological Works*, ed.

James Strachey (London: Hogarth, 1953), 2:244, 99. Freud uses the German word *Adoleszenten* in both cases. The first appearance in the German can be found in *Studien über Hysterie* (Leipzig and Vienna: Franz Deuticke, 1916), 214, and is actually attributed to Breuer. The second appearance of the term in the German can be found in *Sammlung kleiner Schriften zur Neurosenlehre* (Leipzig and Vienna: Franz Deuticke, 1911), 69.

3. G. Stanley Hall, *Life and Confessions of a Psychologist* (New York: D. Appleton, 1923), 409, 411.

4. Hall, *Adolescence,* 1:131.

5. Ibid., 203. For an interesting discussion of theories of recapitulation in nineteenth-century thought, see Cynthia Eagle Russett, *Sexual Science: The Victorian Construction of Womanhood* (Cambridge, MA: Harvard University Press, 1989).

6. Hall, *Adolescence,* 1:155, 364.

7. Herbert Spencer, *The Principles of Sociology* (New York: D. Appleton, 1905), 1:91.

8. Lewis Henry Morgan, *Ancient Society* (Cambridge, MA: Harvard University Press, 1964), 16.

9. Jacobson, *Being a Boy Again,* 13–14. On the persistence of theories of recapitulation in nineteenth-century depiction of children, see also Kidd, *Making American Boys.*

10. Hall, *Adolescence,* 1:viii.

11. Ibid., 1:128.

12. Ibid., 2:70, 58, 81.

13. Ibid., 1:xvii.

14. Ibid., 1:465.

15. Ibid., 2:94.

16. Ibid., 1:415, 418.

17. Ibid., 1:xiii.

18. "Stanley Hall on Youth's Problems, President of Clark University Discusses Adolescence—The 'Cave-Man' Period of Life," *New York Times,* September 28, 1907, BR581. See also "Youth: President Hall's Elaborate Discussion of the Psychology of Adolescence," *New York Times,* July 2, 1904, BR446; A. K. Rogers, "A Study of Adolescence," *Dial,* August 16, 1904, 82; N. P. Gilman, "Reviews: Dr. Stanley Hall on Adolescence," *Literary World,* September 1904, 248; Edwin E. Slosson, "Hall's 'Adolescence,'" *Independent,* November 24, 1904, 1206; untitled review, *Monist,* April 1905, 303; "For Teachers and Parents of Adolescent Youth," *Dial,* April 16, 1908, 249.

19. Margaret Mead, *From the South Seas: Studies of Adolescence and Sex in Primitive Societies* (New York: W. Morrow, 1939), x.

20. Margaret Mead, *Coming of Age in Samoa* (New York: W. Morrow, 1928), 74.

21. Margaret Mead, *Growing Up in New Guinea: A Comparative Study of Primitive Education* (New York: W. Morrow, 1975), 189.

22. Ibid., 195.

23. Margaret Mead, *Sex and Temperament in Three Primitive Societies* (New York: W. Morrow, 1935), 245.

24. Ibid., 76.

25. Ibid., 96, 98.

26. Ibid., 214, 212.

27. Ibid., 212.

28. Ibid., 249.

29. Margaret Mead, *Male and Female: A Study of the Sexes in a Changing World* (New York: W. Morrow, 1967), 108, 119.

30. Ibid., 112.

31. Ibid., 124.

32. Mead, *Coming of Age in Samoa,* 209.

33. Mead, *Growing Up in New Guinea,* 216, 240.

34. Mead, *Coming of Age in Samoa,* 235.

35. Hall, *Adolescence,* 2:645.

36. Mead, *Coming of Age in Samoa,* 235.

37. Hall, *Adolescence,* 2:610. For an excellent discussion of Hall's attitude toward women, see Russett, *Sexual Science.*

38. Hall, *Adolescence,* 1:xiii.

39. Mead, *Coming of Age in Samoa,* 137.

40. Derek Freeman, *Margaret Mead and Samoa: The Making and Unmaking of an Anthropological Myth* (Cambridge, MA: Harvard University Press, 1983), 100; Freda Kirchwey, "Sex in the South Seas," *Nation,* October 24, 1928, 427.

41. Hall, *Adolescence,* 1:325.

42. Ibid., 1:333, 364, 366.

43. Morrison, *Juvenile Offenders,* 60.

44. In his history of juvenile delinquency in American society, *Children in Urban Society,* Hawes argues that Hall "inspired the first American efforts to apply the teaching and techniques of criminal anthropology to juvenile delinquents" (208); this was done through some influential articles penned by two of Hall's students, George Dawson and Maximilian P. E. Groszmann. For a detailed overview of this relationship, see chapter 11 of Hawes's book. For another interesting example of the recapitulation approach to juvenile delinquency, see Edgar James Swift, "Some Criminal Tendencies of Boyhood: A Study in Adolescence," *Pedagogical Seminary* 8 (1901): 65–91. This journal was edited by G. Stanley Hall.

45. For a reference to juvenile delinquency, see Mead, *Coming of Age in Samoa,* 169.

46. Ibid., 144, 164–65.

47. Mead reaches similar conclusions about problems with family structure in *Growing Up in New Guinea.* See, for example, 239–42.

48. Nathan G. Hale, *Freud and the Americans: The Beginnings of Psychoanalysis in the United States, 1876–1917* (New York: Oxford University Press, 1971), xi.

49. Hall, *Adolescence*, 1:144.

50. Gail Bederman, *Manliness & Civilization: A Cultural History of Gender and Race in the United States, 1880–1917* (Chicago: University of Chicago Press, 1995), 104.

51. Mead, *Coming of Age in Samoa*, 166.

52. Ibid., 103–4.

Chapter 3

1. R. H. Pratt, "American Indians; Chained and Unchained: Being an Account of How the Carlisle Indian School Was Born and Grew in Its First 25 Years," *Red Man*, June 1914, 409–10.

2. Richard Henry Pratt, *Battlefield and Classroom: Four Decades with the American Indian, 1867–1904* (New Haven, CT: Yale University Press, 1964), 176.

3. Ibid., 202.

4. Frederick J. Stefon, "Richard Henry Pratt and His Indians," *Journal of Ethnic Studies* 15, no. 2 (1987): 91.

5. Luther Standing Bear, *My People the Sioux* (New York: Houghton Mifflin, 1928), 189.

6. Mary Kay Morel, "Captain Pratt's School," *American History* 32, no. 2 (1997): 26. For more information on the history of Carlisle and other Indian boarding schools, see David Wallace Adams's excellent work *Education for Extinction: American Indians and the Boarding School Experience, 1875–1928* (Lawrence: University Press of Kansas, 1995); Michael C. Coleman's *American Indian Children at School, 1850–1930* (Jackson: University Press of Mississippi, 1993); Ward Churchill's *Kill the Indian, Save the Man: The Genocidal Impact of American Indian Residential Schools* (San Francisco: City Lights, 2004); chapter 3 of Robert Warrior's *The People and the Word: Reading Native Nonfiction* (Minneapolis: University of Minnesota Press, 2005).

7. Brace, *The Dangerous Classes of New York*, 97.

8. Shari M. Huhndorf, *Going Native: Indians in the American Cultural Imagination* (Ithaca, NY: Cornell University Press, 2001), 20.

9. Lyman Abbott, "Education for the Indian," in *Americanizing the American Indians: Writings by the "Friends of the Indian," 1880–1900*, ed. Francis Paul Prucha (Cambridge, MA: Harvard University Press, 1973), 208.

10. Elaine Goodale Eastman, *Pratt: The Red Man's Moses* (Norman: University of Oklahoma Press, 1935), 62.

11. H. David Brumble III, *American Indian Autobiography* (Berkeley: University of California Press, 1988), 148–50. This connection is also explored by David Adams in *Education for Extinction* and Amelia V. Katanski in her book *Learning to Write "Indian": The Boarding-School Experience and American Indian Literature* (Norman: University of Oklahoma Press, 2005). For an interesting discussion of how such characterizations were related to boyology and the feral tale, see chapter 3 of Kidd's *Making American Boys*.

12. Board of Indian Commissioners, "Indian Education," in Abbott, *Americanizing the American Indians,* 194.

13. Thomas J. Morgan, "A Plea for the Papoose," in Abbott, *Americanizing the American Indians,* 241.

14. Hall, *Adolescence,* 2:649, 694, 748.

15. Embe, *Stiya: A Carlisle Indian Girl at Home* (Cambridge, MA: Riverside, 1891), ii. For more background information on Stiya and an insightful analysis, see chapter 2 of Katanski's *Learning to Write "Indian."*

16. Embe, *Stiya,* 3–4.

17. Ibid., 12.

18. Ibid., 18, 20, 21, 22.

19. Ibid., 45.

20. Ibid., 60, 67, 71, 87.

21. Ibid., 74, 89, 112.

22. Ibid., 115.

23. "School Days of an Indian Girl," *Red Man,* February 1900, 8.

24. Zitkala-Ša, "Impressions of an Indian Childhood," in *American Indian Stories* (Lincoln: University of Nebraska Press, 1985), 8, 10.

25. Ibid., 23, 24.

26. Zitkala-Ša, "The School Days of an Indian Girl," in *American Indian Stories,* 67.

27. Ibid., 69.

28. Zitkala-Ša, "An Indian Teacher among Indians," in *American Indian Stories,* 95–97.

29. Ibid., 97–98.

30. Katanski, *Learning to Write "Indian,"* 164.

31. Leerom Medovoi, *Rebels: Youth and the Cold War Origins of Identity* (Durham, NC: Duke University Press, 2005), 6.

32. Erikson, *Identity: Youth and Crisis,* 47.

33. Ibid., 128.

34. Medovoi, *Rebels,* 25.

Chapter 4

1. Ernest Thompson Seton, "The Rise of the Woodcraft Indians," in *Ernest Thompson Seton's America: Selections from the Writings of the Artist-Naturalist,* ed. Farida A. Wiley (New York: Devin-Adair, 1954), 345–46, 354.

2. Ernest Thompson Seton, "Ernest Thompson Seton's Boys," *Ladies' Home Journal,* May 1902, 15, 41; June 1902, 15; July 1902, 16; August 1902, 16; September 1902, 15; October 1902, 14; November 1902, 15.

3. Betty Keller, *Blackwolf: The Life of Ernest Thompson Seton* (Vancouver: Douglas & McIntyre, 1984), 165.

4. For a historical overview of Ernest Thompson Seton and the founding of the Woodcraft Indians/Boy Scouts movement, see Keller, *Blackwolf;* H. Allen Anderson, *The Chief: Ernest Thompson Seton and the Changing West* (College Station: Texas A & M University Press, 1986); John Henry Wadland, *Ernest Thompson Seton: Man in Nature and the Progressive Era, 1880–1915* (New York: Arno, 1978). Also of interest in this regard is Brian Morris's article "Ernest Thompson Seton and the Origins of the Woodcraft Movement," *Journal of Contemporary History* 5 (1970): 194.

For a discussion of the Woodcraft Indian youth movement and its relation to American cultural values, see H. Allen Anderson's article "Ernest Thompson Seton and the Woodcraft Indians," *Journal of American Culture* 8, no. 1 (1985): 43–50. Jay Mechling has written a number of articles on youth movements, including Seton's, and their relationships with aspects of American culture, including "Heroism and the Problem of Impulsiveness for Early Twentieth-Century American Youth," which appears in *Generations of Youth: Youth Cultures and History in Twentieth-Century America,* ed. Joe Austin and Michael Nevin Willard (New York: New York University Press, 1998); "The Collecting Self and American Youth Movements," in *Consuming Visions: Accumulation and Display of Goods in America, 1880–1920,* ed. Simon J. Bronner (New York: W. W. Norton, 1989); "The Manliness Paradox in Ernest Thompson Seton's Ideology of Play and Games," in *Meaningful Play, Playful Meaning,* ed. Gary Alan Fine (Champaign, IL: Human Kinetics, 1987); "Playing Indian and the Search for Authenticity in Modern White America," *Prospects* 5 (1980). Philip Deloria devotes a chapter of his 1998 book *Playing Indian* to Seton's Woodcraft Indians and Daniel Beard's youth organization, the Sons of Daniel Boone.

In regard to the Boy Scouts of America youth movement, see Jay Mechling's book *On My Honor: Boy Scouts and the Making of American Youth* (Chicago: University of Chicago Press, 2001). Mark Seltzer devotes a chapter of *Bodies and Machines* (New York: Routledge, 1992) to the Boy Scouts of America. Also of interest is Jeffrey P. Hantover's article, "The Boy Scouts and the Validation of Masculinity," *Journal of Social Issues* 34, no. 1 (1978): 184–95. For a historical account of early twentieth-century American youth movements, see David Macleod's *Building Character.*

For a discussion of the British Boy Scouts movement and its relation to Edwardian culture, see Michael Rosenthal's *The Character Factory: Baden-Powell and the Origins of the Boy Scout Movement* (New York: Pantheon, 1984); Robert H. MacDonald's *Sons of the Empire: The Frontier and the Boy Scout Movement* (Toronto: University of Toronto Press, 1993); John Springhall's *Youth, Empire, and Society: British Youth Movements, 1883–1940* (London: Archon, 1977). For a humorous meditation on the latest edition of *The Official Boy Scout Handbook,* see the opening chapter of Paul Fussell's *The Boy Scout Handbook and Other Observations* (Oxford: Oxford University Press, 1982).

5. "Work in Children's Court: First Annual Report Shows That Frequent Use of the Parole System Was Successful," *New York Times,* January 14, 1904, sec. 5, 1; "Founding a New Arcadia for New York's Street Arabs," *New York Times,* December 17, 1905,

sec. 3, 1+; "Judge Olmsted of Children's Court Criticizes the Board of Education," *New York Times*, April 8, 1906, sec. 4, 8.

6. "Getting at the Boys," *Outlook*, December 2, 1905, 822–26; "The Causes of Juvenile Crime," *Outlook*, August 4, 1906, 796–801; "Delinquent and Wayward Children," *Outlook*, September 22, 1906, 151–53; "The Defective Home and Juvenile Delinquency," *Outlook*, August 28, 1909, 965–66.

7. "Why Boys Go Wrong," *Ladies' Home Journal*, November 1906, 14; "The Bad Boy of the Street," *Ladies' Home Journal*, October 1909, 17, 76.

8. "Delinquent and Wayward Children," 151; "The Causes of Juvenile Crime," 796.

9. Seton, "The Rise of the Woodcraft Indians," 346.

10. Anderson, *The Chief*, 184.

11. "The Bad Boy of the Street," 17; "Why Boys Go Wrong," 14.

12. Macleod, *Building Character*, 97. Other theorists have commented on the connection between Hall's phylogenetic theory of adolescence and Seton's youth movement. For example, in "The Collecting Self and American Youth Movements," Jay Mechling suggests that Hall's "instinct psychology" informed Seton's belief in the instinct for play and collecting in the child (262, 277), and in her essay "From the Turn of the Century to the New Age: Playing Indian, Past and Present," which appears in *As We Are Now: Mixblood Essays on Race and Identity*, ed. William S. Penn (Berkeley: University of California Press, 1997), Shari Huhndorf argues that Seton's use of the Indian was inspired by Hall's assertion that boys were naturally attracted to the habits of feral men. There is an identifiable link between Hall and the Boy Scouts. In both Seton's 1910 *Boy Scouts of America* and Baden-Powell's 1908 *Scouting for Boys*, William Byron Forbush's popular 1901 work *The Boy Problem: A Study in Social Pedagogy* (Chicago: Pilgrim, 1901) is listed in the "Books to Read." Forbush was a disciple of Hall, and Hall wrote the introduction to *The Boy Problem*, in which he states: "The author, who is both a clergyman and a Doctor of Philosophy, has been among boys and done work with them that I consider hardly less than epoch-making in significance. Dr. Forbush understands the natural boy and how to approach and handle him, and has also put himself abreast of the new psycho-genetic and pedagogical literature" (3).

13. Ernest Thompson Seton, "Organized Boyhood: The Boy Scout Movement, Its Purposes and Laws," *Success*, December 13, 1910, 804.

14. Ernest Thompson Seton, *The Birch-bark Roll of the Woodcraft Indians* (New York: Doubleday, Page, 1907), 1.

15. Roderick Nash, *Wilderness and the American Mind* (New Haven, CT: Yale University Press, 1967), 143, 145.

16. Seton, "Ernest Thompson Seton's Boys," June 1902, 15; Seton, *The Birch-bark Roll*, 3.

17. Ernest Thompson Seton and Julia M. Seton, *The Gospel of the Redman: A Way of Life* (Santa Fe, NM: Seton Village, 1966), xvi, 9–14.

18. Ibid., 29, 26.

19. Ibid., 50–66; Seton, *The Birch-bark Roll*, 12–13.

20. Ernest Thompson Seton, *Boy Scouts of America: A Handbook of Woodcraft, Scouting, and Life-Craft* (New York: Doubleday, Page, 1910), 32–33.

21. Deloria, *Playing Indian*, 101.

22. Seton, "The Rise of the Woodcraft Indians," 354.

23. Robert W. Peterson, *The Boy Scouts: An American Adventure* (New York: American Heritage, 1984), 32, 250.

24. Keller, *Blackwolf*, 166.

25. Seton, "Organized Boyhood," 805.

26. Keller, *Blackwolf*, 176.

27. Seton, *Boy Scouts of America*, xi.

28. Robert Baden-Powell, *Scouting for Boys: A Handbook for Instruction in Good Citizenship* (London: C. A. Pearson, 1908), 261–63.

29. MacDonald, *Sons of the Empire*, 5.

30. Ibid., 119.

31. Bederman, *Manliness & Civilization*, 171.

32. Anthony E. Rotundo, *American Manhood: Transformations in Masculinity from the Revolution to the Modern Era* (New York: HarperCollins, 1993), 238, 240. According to Shari Huhndorf, this virile masculinity found a natural ideal in the Indian, because: "While 'civilized' white men were becoming soft and effeminate as a result of the ease of modern life . . . Indians, the stereotype seemed to demonstrate, had always managed to maintain their virility through constant warfare" ("From the Turn of the Century to the New Age," 188). For more on this shift in how masculinity was conceived, see Michael Kimmel's book *Manhood in America: A Cultural History* (New York: Free Press, 1996).

33. This shift to war scouts was not entirely seamless. Many expressed fear that the Boy Scouts would appear to be simply a military training program, and as a result protective parents would not allow their children to join. For more on this issue, see Rosenthal's *The Character Factory*.

34. Anderson, *The Chief*, 188.

35. Rosenthal, *The Character Factory*, 11.

36. Agnes Baden-Powell, *The Handbook for Girl Guides* (London: Thomas Nelson and Sons, 1912), 17.

37. Ibid., 22, 456.

38. For a more detailed discussion of Girl Scouting and American culture, see Sherrie Inness's "Girl Scouts, Camp Fire Girls, and Woodcraft Girls: The Ideology of Girls' Scouting Novels, 1910–1935," in *Nancy Drew and Company: Culture, Gender, and Girls' Series*, ed. Sherrie A. Inness (Bowling Green, OH: Popular, 1997); Laureen Tedesco's "Making a Girl into a Scout: Americanizing Scouting for Girls," in *Delinquents and Debutantes: Twentieth-Century American Girls' Cultures*, ed. Sherrie A. Inness (New York: New York University Press, 1998).

39. Anderson, *The Chief*, 168.

40. *The Book of the Camp Fire Girls*, 5th ed. (New York: National Headquarters, 1914), 21.

41. Helen Buckler, Mary F. Fiedler, and Martha F. Allen, *WO-HE-LO: The Story of Camp Fire Girls, 1910–1960* (New York: Holt, Rinehart & Winston, 1961), 6, 12, 43, 21.

42. Luther Halsey Gulick, "Address Delivered by Dr. Luther H. Gulick before the Connecticut Valley Public Recreation Conference, Springfield, Mass., April 1912," *Journal of the Proceedings and Addresses of the Annual Meeting* [of the National Education Association of the United States] (1912): 10, 11.

43. Macleod, *Building Character*, 51.

Chapter 5

1. See John A. Tebbel, *A History of Book Publishing in the United States*, vol. 2: *The Expansion of an Industry, 1865–1919* (New York: R. R. Bowker, 1975); Hellmut Lehmann-Haupt, *The Book in America: A History of the Making and Selling of Books in the United States* (New York: R. R. Bowker, 1952). For a discussion of literacy rates and their relationship with textbooks, newspapers, and children's literature, see Lee Soltow, *The Rise of Literacy and the Common School in the United States: A Socioeconomic Analysis to 1870* (Chicago: University of Chicago Press, 1981).

2. Madeleine B. Stern, ed., *Publishers for Mass Entertainment in Nineteenth Century America* (Boston: G. K. Hall, 1980), xii. See also Raymond H. Shove, *Cheap Book Production in the United States, 1870–1891* (Urbana: University of Illinois Library, 1937).

3. Vicki Anderson, *The Dime Novel in Children's Literature* (Jefferson, NC: McFarland, 2005), 4; Gail Schmunk Murray, *American Children's Literature and the Construction of Childhood* (New York: Twayne, 1998), 81; Kenneth C. Donelson and Alleen Pace Nilsen, eds., *Literature for Today's Young Adults* (Boston: Pearson, 2004), 54. See also Anne Scott MacLeod, *American Childhood: Essays on Children's Literature of the Nineteenth and Twentieth Centuries* (Athens: University of Georgia Press, 1994).

4. Michael Denning, *Mechanic Accents: Dime Novels and Working-Class Culture in America* (New York: Verso, 1987), 30, 27.

5. Quoted in Jack Salzman, "Literature for the Populace," in *Columbia Literary History of the United States*, ed. Emory Elliott (New York: Columbia University Press, 1988), 552.

6. Denning, *Mechanic Accents*, 51.

7. Beverly Lyon Clark, *Kiddie Lit: The Cultural Construction of Children's Literature in America* (Baltimore: Johns Hopkins University Press, 2003), 74.

8. For a full discussion of Alger's relationship to the dime novel, see Gary Scharnhorst, *Horatio Alger, Jr.* (Boston: Twayne, 1980). Alger is discussed by both Vicki Anderson and Michael Denning in their treatments of the dime novels.

9. Gary Scharnhorst, *The Lost Life of Horatio Alger, Jr.* (Bloomington: Indiana University Press, 1985), 62.

10. The six volumes in the Ragged Dick series are *Ragged Dick; or, Street Life in New York with the Bootblacks* (Boston: Loring, 1868; repr., New York: Macmillan, 1962); *Fame and Fortune; or, The Progress of Richard Hunter* (Boston: Loring, 1868; repr., Phila-

delphia: Pavilion, 2003); *Mark, the Match Boy; or, Richard Hunter's Ward* (Boston: Loring, 1869; repr., New York: Macmillan, 1962); *Rough and Ready; or, Life among the New York Newsboys* (Boston: Loring, 1869; repr., Philadelphia: Pavilion, 2003); *Ben the Luggage Boy; or, Among the Wharves* (Boston: Loring, 1870; repr., Philadelphia: Pavilion, 2003); and *Rufus and Rose; or, The Fortunes of Rough and Ready* (Boston: Loring, 1870; repr., Philadelphia: Pavilion, 2003). Textual references in this chapter are keyed to the reprints, which use the original text published by Loring. Note that Macmillan published *Ragged Dick* and *Mark, the Match Boy* together in a single volume.

11. See, for example, *Ben the Luggage Boy*, 80, and *Rough and Ready*, 59. Actually three dozen of Alger's novels, most of which appeared prior to 1880, refer to the Children's Aid Society, Brace, or the lodge. See Scharnhorst, *Horatio Alger, Jr.,* 105.

12. Stephen O'Connor, *Orphan Trains: The Story of Charles Loring Brace and the Children He Saved and Failed* (Boston: Houghton Mifflin, 2001), 80.

13. Brace, *The Dangerous Classes of New York*, 114.

14. Emma Brace, *The Life of Charles Loring Brace Told Chiefly in His Own Letters* (New York: Charles Scribner's Sons, 1894), 302.

15. Richard Hofstadter, *Social Darwinism in American Thought* (New York: George Braziller, 1959), 31. On Spencer's influence on American thought, see also Ronald E. Martin, *American Literature and the Universe of Force* (Durham, NC: Duke University Press, 1981).

16. Brace, *The Dangerous Classes of New York*, 96.

17. Ibid., 430.

18. The use of economic terminology can be seen in other areas of late nineteenth-century intellectual thought. Cynthia Eagle Russett, for example, has noted the use of such terminology in describing neurasthenic collapse (*Sexual Science*, 116).

19. Carol Nackenoff, *The Fictional Republic: Horatio Alger and American Political Discourse* (New York: Oxford University Press, 1994), 34. For many years, and arguably still today, Alger's work has been viewed in the popular consciousness as a celebration of laissez-faire economics and an apologia for the myth of capitalist success. This mythology has been questioned by many critics, who have demonstrated that rather than promising "riches" to their boy readers, Alger's texts offer the prospect of a middle-class respectability. Similarly, the competition that is said to reward hard work and "pluck" is often complicated by patronage and just plain luck. For some key voices in the revisionary history of Alger, see Nackenoff's book as well as John G. Cawelti's chapter on Alger in his book *Apostles of the Self-Made Man* (Chicago: University of Chicago Press, 1965); Gary Scharnhorst's biography *Horatio Alger, Jr.;* Michael Denning's *Mechanic Accents*.

20. Horatio Alger Jr., "The Newsboys' Lodging-House," *Liberal Christian*, April 20, 1867: 6.

21. Alger, *Fame and Fortune*, xiii.

22. Alger, *Ragged Dick*, 43.

23. Alger, *Ben the Luggage Boy*, 169.

24. Alger, *Mark, the Match Boy,* 256.

25. Michael Moon, "'The Gentle Boy from the Dangerous Classes': Pederasty, Domesticity, and Capitalism in Horatio Alger," *Representations* 19 (Summer 1987): 101.

26. Alger, *Mark, the Match Boy,* 361. The phenomenon of the "Orphan Trains" is turned into an entire novel in *Julius; or, The Street Boy Out West* (1874), where Julius is selected by the Children's Aid Society to be resettled on a farm in Wisconsin.

27. Alger, *Rough and Ready,* 27.

28. Alger, *Ragged Dick,* 133, 167; Alger, *Fame and Fortune,* 101.

29. Alger, *Mark, the Match Boy,* 300.

30. Scharnhorst, *Horatio Alger, Jr.,* 88.

31. Alger, *Ben the Luggage Boy,* 31.

32. Alger, *Ragged Dick,* 55.

33. Ibid., 40, 55, 148; Alger, *Fame and Fortune,* 116. In volume 4, *Rough and Ready,* Rufus is described as "stoutly built, with a clear, fresh complexion, and a resolute, good-humored face" (29). In volume 5, *Ben the Luggage Boy,* Ben is said to have "a pleasant face, and would be considered good-looking" (31). Rufus retains his good looks when he returns in volume 6, *Rufus and Rose,* where he is described as a "stout, well-grown boy of fifteen, with a pleasant face" (23).

34. Alger, *Ragged Dick,* 175, 181.

35. Ibid., 92, 94.

36. Alger, *Mark, the Match Boy,* 245; Alger, *Rough and Ready,* 105; Alger, *Rufus and Rose,* 92.

37. Alger, *Mark, the Match Boy,* 314.

38. Alger, *Fame and Fortune,* 80.

39. Alger, *Ragged Dick,* 122.

40. Carol Nackenoff has made the interesting observation that such access was actually quite at odds with how most youth were employed in the late nineteenth century. She points out: "All [Alger's] boys find employment in the white-collar workforce though less than 20% of all workers are so employed by 1900. Boys are found earning at the high end of the scales for average weekly adult earnings during this period." Nackenoff makes the point that such access was becoming less commonplace in the new, "modern" industrial order—as such, Alger's work demonstrates a kind of nostalgia. See "Of Factories and Failures: Exploring the Invisible Factory Gates of Horatio Alger, Jr.," *Journal of Popular Culture* 25, no. 4 (1992): 63–80.

41. Alger, *Ragged Dick,* 130, 166.

42. Nackenoff, *The Fictional Republic,* 138.

43. Alger, *Fame and Fortune,* 31.

44. Alger, *Ragged Dick,* 89.

45. See, for example, references to Dick's opposition to stealing in ibid., 39, 44, 86, and *Fame and Fortune,* 101; references to Rufus not being tempted to steal in *Rough and Ready,* 77; and Ben's resistance to stealing in *Ben the Luggage Boy,* 63.

46. Alger, *Ragged Dick,* 147.

47. Ibid., 193.

48. See, for example, Aaron Shaheen's interesting discussion of luck in her article "Endless Frontiers and Emancipation from History: Horatio Alger's Reconstruction of Place and Time in Ragged Dick," *Children's Literature* 33 (2005): 20–40.

49. Alger, *Ragged Dick,* 210, 214.

50. Alger, *Fame and Fortune,* 156.

51. Scharnhorst, *The Lost Life of Horatio Alger, Jr.*, 149, 150.

Chapter 6

1. "For It Was Indeed He," *Fortune,* April 1934, 87.

2. Deidre Johnson, *Edward Stratemeyer and the Stratemeyer Syndicate* (New York: Twayne, 1993), ix.

3. Franklin K. Mathiews, "Blowing Out the Boy's Brains," *Outlook,* November 18, 1914, 653.

4. Carol Billman, *The Secret of the Stratemeyer Syndicate: Nancy Drew, the Hardy Boys, and the Million Dollar Fiction Factory* (New York: Ungar, 1986), 17. See also John T. Dizer's *Tom Swift & Company: "Boys Books" by Stratemeyer and Others* (Jefferson, NC: McFarland, 1982) for a similar characterization of Stratemeyer.

5. Dizer, *Tom Swift & Company,* 11–12.

6. Johnson, *Edward Stratemeyer,* ix. According to Deidre Johnson, the syndicate has sold over 200 million copies of its series books (ix). Johnson estimates that, during his lifetime, Stratemeyer wrote approximately 275 stories and outlined over 690 more (ix). In regard to the popularity of the Stratemeyer series books during the early decades of the twentieth century, Johnson notes that "a 1929 study tracking one week's reading by boys in junior high showed that *Tom Swift* books were second only to the Bible as the books most frequently read. When the same boys were asked to list the novels they had read during the school year, the *Tom Swift* series topped the list, with the *Rover Boys* third. . . . Five years later, an article on series books estimated that the top three publishing houses turned out over 5,000,000 series books a year, and that works by Stratemeyer and the Syndicate had already sold 20,000,000 copies, roughly 6,500,000 of which were *Tom Swift* titles and another 5,000,000 *Rover Boys* books" (162).

7. Even though Edward Stratemeyer outlined the syndicate's books and thus had a considerable influence on the plotlines and characters, recent scholarship has revealed much about the ghostwriters of these texts and their unique imprints. See, for example, Marilyn Greenwald, *The Secret of the Hardy Boys: Leslie McFarlane and the Stratemeyer Syndicate* (Athens: Ohio University Press, 2004); Melanie Rehak, *Girl Sleuth: Nancy Drew and the Women Who Created Her* (New York, Harcourt, 2005). After Edward Stratemeyer's death in 1930, the outlines for the series books were composed primarily by his two daughters, Edna Stratemeyer and Harriet Stratemeyer Adams. In this chapter, I will focus primarily on the series books published before his death.

8. Stratemeyer contributed to the eleven-volume series, *Rise in Life,* published between 1901 and 1912. The initial volumes of this series are stories begun by Alger, and the series was published under Alger's name. For more on this, see Scharnhorst, *Horatio Alger, Jr.*

9. Donnarae MacCann, "Nancy Drew and the Myth of White Supremacy," in *Rediscovering Nancy Drew,* ed. Carolyn Stewart Dyer and Nancy Tillman Romalov (Iowa City: University of Iowa Press, 1995), 129; Nancy Tillman Romalov, "Children's Series Books and the Rhetoric of Guidance: A Historical Overview," in Dyer and Romalov, *Rediscovering Nancy Drew,* 113.

10. Billman, *The Secret of the Stratemeyer Syndicate,* 6.

11. D. A. Miller, *The Novel and the Police* (Berkeley: University of California Press, 1988), 34.

12. Victor Appleton, *Tom Swift and His Motor-Boat* (New York: Grosset & Dunlap, 1910), 83.

13. James Cody Ferris, *The X Bar X Boys on the Ranch* (New York: Grosset & Dunlap, 1926), 15, 144.

14. Franklin W. Dixon, *The Tower Treasure* (New York: Grosset & Dunlap, 1927), 22, 174, 24.

15. Carolyn Keene, *The Clue in the Diary* (New York: Grosset & Dunlap, 1932), 37, 201–2.

16. Billman, *The Secret of the Stratemeyer Syndicate,* 26.

17. Victor Appleton, *Tom Swift and His Sky Racer* (New York: Grosset & Dunlap, 1911), 40, 149. A similar example can be found in *Tom Swift and His Motor-Boat.* Tom and his friend Ned are up late working on the boat. The next day, Tom must go back home to check on his father's inventions, as opposed to giving Miss Nestor her motor-boat lesson. Ned suggests that he may give the lessons when Tom is gone. We expect a sign of jealousy to appear, but no real argument ensues and the discussion of Miss Nestor, the expression of Tom's desire, is censored by his concentration on his work: "Never mind, I'm giving you a show. Now let's get to bed early, as I want to get a good start" (91). Tom's invention is also referred to as "she" in this book: "Tom saw it in an instant and knew it for the *Arrow.* 'There she is!' he cried" (151).

18. Ferris, *The X Bar X Boys on the Ranch,* 2, 69, 11, 213.

19. Bobbie Ann Mason, *The Girl Sleuth* (Athens: University of Georgia Press, 1995), 59; Lee Zacharias, "Nancy Drew, Ballbuster," *Journal of Popular Culture* 9 (1976): 1031. On the Nancy Drew series, see also Inness, *Nancy Drew and Company;* Ilana Nash, *American Sweethearts: Teenage Girls in Twentieth-Century Popular Culture* (Bloomington: Indiana University Press, 2006).

20. Roland Barthes, *S/Z* (New York: Hill & Wang, 1974), 76.

21. A similar example can be seen in the second volume of the X Bar X Boys series, *The X Bar X Boys in Thunder Canyon* (New York: Grosset & Dunlap, 1926). In this volume, the love interests we saw (or, perhaps more accurately, didn't see) in the first volume, Ethel and Nell, are held for ransom by the same rustlers who stole the Man-

leys' horses. The second-to-last chapter of the book, ambiguously titled "Retribution," promises someone will get something, but the reader must push forward to find out.

22. Appleton, *Tom Swift and His Motor-Boat,* 7, 212. This internal reference to other works reaches rather absurd proportions as the series continues; in the ninth volume of the Tom Swift series, *Tom Swift and His Sky Racer,* the author devotes two full pages to summarizing the first eight volumes of the series.

23. Victor Appleton, *Tom Swift and His House on Wheels* (New York: Grosset & Dunlap, 1929), 216.

24. Billman, *The Secret of the Stratemeyer Syndicate,* 49.

25. Suzanna Rose, "Is Romance Dysfunctional?" *International Journal of Women's Studies* 8, no. 3 (1985): 250–65.

26. Johnson, *Edward Stratemeyer,* 50.

27. Jean Baudrillard, "Consumer Society," in *Selected Writings,* ed. Mark Poster (Stanford, CA: Stanford University Press, 1988), 50, 42.

28. Dixon, *The Tower Treasure,* 2, 3, 203.

29. Dixon, *The House on the Cliff,* 109.

Selected Bibliography

Anderson, H. Allen. "Ernest Thompson Seton and the Woodcraft Indians." *Journal of American Culture* 8, no. 1 (1985): 43–50.

Ariès, Philippe. *Centuries of Childhood: A Social History of Family Life.* Translated by Robert Baldick. New York: Vintage, 1962.

Aronson, Marc. *Exploding the Myths: The Truth about Teenagers and Reading.* Lanham, MD: Scarecrow, 2001.

Austin, Joe, and Michael Nevin Willard, eds. *Generations of Youth: Youth Cultures and History in Twentieth-Century America.* New York: New York University Press, 1998.

Beales, Ross W., Jr. "In Search of the Historical Child: Miniature Adulthood and Youth in Colonial New England." *American Quarterly* 27, no. 4 (1975): 379–98.

Bostrom, Meg. *Teenhood: Understanding Attitudes toward Those Transitioning from Childhood to Adulthood.* Washington, DC: FrameWorks Institute, 2001.

———. *The 21st Century Teen: Public Perception and Teen Reality.* Washington, DC: FrameWorks Institute, 2001.

Bremner, Robert H., ed. *Children and Youth in America: A Documentary History.* 3 vols. Cambridge, MA: Harvard University Press, 1970–74.

Burt, Stephen. *The Forms of Youth: 20th Century Poetry and Adolescence.* New York: Columbia University Press, 2007.

Capp, Bernard. "English Youth Groups and the Pindar of Wakefield." *Past and Present* 76 (August 1977): 126–33.

Cart, Michael. *From Romance to Realism: 50 Years of Growth and Change in Young Adult Literature.* New York: HarperCollins, 1996.

Clark, Beverly Lyon. *Kiddie Lit: The Cultural Construction of Children's Literature in America.* Baltimore: Johns Hopkins University Press, 2003.

Davis, Natalie Zemon. "The Reasons of Misrule: Youth Groups and Charivaris in Sixteenth-Century France." *Past and Present* 50 (February 1971): 41–75.

Deloria, Philip J. *Playing Indian.* New Haven, CT: Yale University Press, 1998.

Demos, John, and Virginia Demos. "Adolescence in Historical Perspective." *Journal of Marriage and the Family* 31, no. 4 (1969): 632–38.

Erikson, Erik. *Childhood and Society.* New York: W. W. Norton, 1964.

———. *Identity: Youth and Crisis.* New York: W. W. Norton, 1968.

———. *The Life Cycle Completed.* New York: W. W. Norton, 1997.

Esman, Aaron H. *Adolescence and Culture.* New York: Columbia University Press, 1990.

Gillis, John R. *Youth and History: Tradition and Change in European Age Relations, 1770–Present.* New York: Academic, 1974.

Hall, G. Stanley. *Adolescence: Its Psychology and Its Relations to Physiology, Anthropology, Sociology, Sex, Crime, Religion, and Education.* 2 vols. New York: D. Appleton, 1904.

———. *Life and Confessions of a Psychologist.* New York: D. Appleton, 1923.

Hantover, Jeffrey P. "The Boy Scouts and the Validation of Masculinity." *Journal of Social Issues* 34, no. 1 (1978): 184–95.

Hawes, Joseph. *Children in Urban Society: Juvenile Delinquency in Nineteenth-Century America.* New York: Oxford University Press, 1971.

Hine, Thomas. *The Rise and Fall of the American Teenager.* New York: Avon, 1999.

Hiner, N. Ray. "Adolescence in Eighteenth-Century America." *History of Childhood Quarterly* 3 (1975): 253–80.

Holloran, Peter. *Boston's Wayward Children: Social Services for Homeless Children, 1830–1930.* London: Associated University Presses, 1989.

Huhndorf, Shari. "From the Turn of the Century to the New Age: Playing Indian, Past and Present." In *As We Are Now: Mixblood Essays on Race and Identity,* edited by William S. Penn, 181–98. Berkeley: University of California Press, 1997.

Inness, Sherrie A., ed. *Delinquents and Debutantes: Twentieth-Century American Girls' Cultures.* New York: New York University Press, 1998.

———. *Nancy Drew and Company: Culture, Gender, and Girls' Series.* Bowling Green, OH: Popular, 1997.

Jacobson, Marcia. *Being a Boy Again: Autobiography and the American Boy Book.* Tuscaloosa: University of Alabama Press, 1994.

Kett, Joseph F. "Adolescence and Youth in Nineteenth-Century America." In *The Family in History: Interdisciplinary Essays,* edited by Theodore K. Rabb and Robert I. Rotberg, 95–110. New York: Harper & Row, 1971.

———. *Rites of Passage: Adolescence in America, 1790 to the Present.* New York: Basic, 1977.

Kidd, Kenneth B. *Making American Boys: Boyology and the Feral Tale.* Minneapolis: University of Minnesota Press, 2004.

Kincaid, James R. *Child-Loving: The Erotic Child and Victorian Culture.* New York: Routledge, 1992.

———. *Erotic Innocence: The Culture of Child Molesting.* Durham, NC: Duke University Press, 1998.

Kristeva, Julia. "The Adolescent Novel." In *Abjection, Melancholia, and Love: The Works of Julia Kristeva,* edited by John Fletcher and Andrew Benjamin, 8–23. New York: Routledge, 1990.

MacDonald, Robert H. *Sons of the Empire: The Frontier and the Boy Scout Movement.* Toronto: University of Toronto Press, 1993.

Macleod, David I. *The Age of the Child: Children in America, 1890–1920.* New York: Twayne, 1998.

———. *Building Character in the American Boy: The Boy Scouts, YMCA, and Their Forerunners, 1870–1920.* Madison: University of Wisconsin Press, 1983.

Males, Mike A. *Framing Youth: 10 Myths about the Next Generation.* Monroe, ME: Common Courage, 1999.

———. *"Kids and Guns": How Politicians, Experts, and the Press Fabricate Fear of Youth.* Monroe, ME: Common Courage, 2001.

———. *The Scapegoat Generation: America's War on Adolescents.* Monroe, ME: Common Courage, 1999.

Mead, Margaret. *Coming of Age in Samoa.* New York: W. Morrow, 1928.

———. *From the South Seas: Studies of Adolescence and Sex in Primitive Societies.* New York: W. Morrow, 1939.

———. *Growing Up in New Guinea: A Comparative Study of Primitive Education.* New York: W. Morrow, 1975.

———. *Male and Female: A Study of the Sexes in a Changing World.* New York: W. Morrow, 1967.

———. *Sex and Temperament in Three Primitive Societies.* New York: W. Morrow, 1935.

Mechling, Jay. "The Collecting Self and American Youth Movements." In *Consuming Visions: Accumulation and Display of Goods in America, 1880–1920,* edited by Simon J. Bronner, 255–85. New York: W. W. Norton, 1989.

———. "The Manliness Paradox in Ernest Thompson Seton's Ideology of Play and Games." In *Meaningful Play, Playful Meaning,* edited by Gary Alan Fine, 45–59. Champaign, IL: Human Kinetics, 1987.

———. *On My Honor: Boy Scouts and the Making of American Youth.* Chicago: University of Chicago Press, 2001.

———. "Playing Indian and the Search for Authenticity in Modern White America." *Prospects* 5 (1980): 17–33.

Medovoi, Leerom. *Rebels: Youth and the Cold War Origins of Identity.* Durham, NC: Duke University Press, 2005.

Mennel, Robert M. *Thorns & Thistles: Juvenile Delinquents in the United States, 1825–1940.* Hanover, NH: University Press of New England, 1973.

Mintz, Steven. *Huck's Raft: A History of American Childhood.* Cambridge, MA: Belknap, 2004.

Moran, Gerald F., and Maris A. Vinovskis. *Religion, Family, and the Life Course: Explorations in the Social History of Early America.* Ann Arbor: University of Michigan Press, 1992.

Nash, Ilana. *American Sweethearts: Teenage Girls in Twentieth-Century Popular Culture.* Bloomington: Indiana University Press, 2006.

Neubauer, John. *The Fin-de-Siècle Culture of Adolescence.* New Haven, CT.: Yale University Press, 1992.

Platt, Anthony M. *The Child Savers: The Invention of Delinquency.* Chicago: University of Chicago Press, 1969.

Rosenheim, Margaret Keeney, ed. *Justice for the Child: The Juvenile Court in Transition.* New York: Free Press of Glencoe, 1962.

Rosenthal, Michael. *The Character Factory: Baden-Powell and the Origins of the Boy Scout Movement.* New York: Pantheon, 1984.

Sanders, Wiley B., ed. *Juvenile Offenders for a Thousand Years: Selected Readings from Anglo-Saxon Times to 1900.* Chapel Hill: University of North Carolina Press, 1970.

Savage, Jon. *Teenage: The Creation of Youth Culture.* New York: Viking, 2007.

Seltzer, Mark. *Bodies and Machines.* New York: Routledge, 1992.

Shulman, Harry Manuel. *Juvenile Delinquency in American Society.* New York: Harper & Brothers, 1961.

Sizer, Theodore R. *Secondary Schools at the Turn of the Century.* New Haven, CT: Yale University Press, 1964.

Smith, Steven R. "The London Apprentices as Seventeenth-Century Adolescents." *Past and Present* 61 (November 1973): 149–61.

———. "Religion and the Conception of Youth in Seventeenth Century England." *History of Childhood Quarterly* 2 (1974–75): 493–516.

Spacks, Patricia Meyer. *The Adolescent Idea: Myths of Youth and the Adult Imagination.* New York: Basic, 1981.

Springhall, John. *Coming of Age: Adolescence in Britain, 1860–1960.* Dublin: Gill & MacMillan, 1986.

———. *Youth, Empire, and Society: British Youth Movements, 1883–1940.* London: Archon, 1977.

Stone, Lawrence. *The Family, Sex, and Marriage in England, 1500–1800.* New York: Harper & Row, 1977.

Trexler, Richard C. "Ritual in Florence: Adolescence and Salvation in the Renaissance." In *The Pursuit of Holiness in Late Medieval and Renaissance Religion,* edited by Charles Trinkaus and Heiko A. Oberman, 200–264. Leiden, Netherlands: E. J. Brill, 1974.

Vann, Richard T. "The Youth of Centuries of Childhood." *History and Theory* 21, no. 2 (1982): 279–97.

Witham, W. Tasker. *The Adolescent in the American Novel, 1920–1960.* New York: Frederick Ungar, 1964.

Yarbrough, Anne. "Apprentices as Adolescents in Sixteenth Century Bristol." *Journal of Social History* 13, no. 1 (1979): 67–81.

Index

Abbott, Reverend Lyman, 78

adolescence: adulthood and, 19; age as system and, 17–19; appearance in American society, 3–4, 23–24, 40; appearance in British society, 157n5; bifurcation of, 12–13, 14, 156n11; childhood and, 9, 11, 15, 18; class and, 13; compared to America, 16, 124; consumer culture and, 151–52; defined by G. Stanley Hall, 47–53; defined by Margaret Mead, 54–61; education and, 25–29; ending of, 40; Sigmund Freud and, 46–47, 68; gender and, 13, 40–42, 61–62; genealogy of term, 158n9; ideal vs. real, 12–13, 71–72, 111, 114–15; Indian boarding schools and, 5, 73–74; "invention" of, 3, 8, 9, 15, 20, 23–24, 29; juvenile court and, 30–42; Native Americans and, 80; novel of, 11, 155n9; origins of, 21–24; race and, 13; as reaction to savage child, 9; as rehabilitative concept, 5, 8, 15, 24, 37–40, 46, 52, 60–61, 62–64, 81, 84, 119, 126, 137, 149; sexuality and, 68–71; "teenager" and, 13; theories about, 4, 44, 45; as universal experience, 13, 91; urbanization and, 25, 36, 42–43; work and, 152–54; young adult literature and, 14–15; youth and, 22, 42, 45, 157n3. *See also* adolescents

Adolescence (Hall), 4, 16, 44, 48, 50–53, 61, 62–63, 65–66, 69, 80

Adolescence and Culture (Esman), 23

"adolescentlike" spaces in other periods, 22–23, 157n3

adolescent literature. *See* young adult literature

adolescents: appearance in American society, 27, 29; cheap books and, 116–19; controlling, 28–29; education and, 3–4, 26; industrialization and, 25–29; juvenile court and, 4; loitering, 28, 36; misperceptions of, 1–2; myths about, 1–2; negative attitude toward, 27, 42–43; rehabilitation of, 5, 8, 15, 24, 37–40, 46, 52, 60–61, 62–64, 81, 84, 119, 126, 137, 149; urbanization and, 25–29, 36

age, 17–19, 37–40

ageism, 17–18

Aldrich, Thomas Bailey, 10, 49

Alger, Horatio, Jr., 7, 11, 119–21; benefactor figures in works, 127; *Ben the Luggage Boy; or, Among the Wharves*, 126, 127, 130, 134; Charles Loring Brace and, 120–21, 124; cheap books and, 118–19; *Fame and Fortune; or, The Progress of Richard Hunter*, 125, 127, 129, 130, 132, 133–34, 135; *Mark, the Match Boy; or, Richard Hunter's Ward*, 127, 128, 129, 131, 132; *Ragged Dick; or, Street Life in New York with the Bootblacks*, 126, 127, 129, 130, 131, 132, 133, 134, 135; Ragged Dick series, 120,